"Vivid oral history."

*   *   *

"RIVETING...what you get is the smell and feel of combat and waiting for combat—the terror and excitement, the huge bunker rats, the sudden death, the screams and laughter...the pages chronicling PFC. Lawrence Seavy-Cioffi's actions in taking command of his overrun platoon and saving it is the most gripping battle narrative I've ever read."
—*Washington Post Book World*

*   *   *

"A HARROWING, GUT-LEVEL RECORD of the Vietnam War's Khe Sanh Campaign...a vivid, day-by-day log of the ordeals...imparting human-scale significance to the blood sacrifices that were made."
—*Kirkus Reviews*

*   *   *

"A REMARKABLY PERSONAL ACCOUNT of a crucial 77-day battle in this remarkably personal war retold as an oral history by the men who fought in it, which gives the account not only a vividness and immediacy but a human perspective...this eyewitness montage is the ideal way to write history."
—*Playboy*

*   *   *

"It is a mark of Mr. Hammel's skill that he has pieced together often conflicting fragments and yet makes a whole. *KHE SANH* HOLDS YOU IN BATTLE...PRESSING HOME THE HORRIBLE AMBIGUITY OF WAR."
—*New York Times Book Review*

*   *   *

OTHER BOOKS BY ERIC HAMMEL

□

THE ASSAULT ON

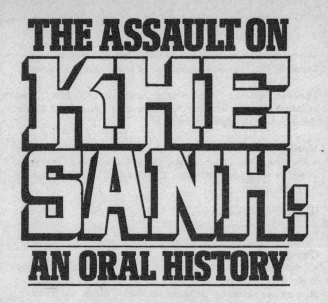

KHE SANH:

AN ORAL HISTORY

ERIC HAMMEL

WARNER BOOKS

A Warner Communications Company

WARNER BOOKS EDITION

This Warner Books Edition is published by arrangement with Crown Publishers, Inc., 225 Park Avenue South, New York, New York 10003

Cover design by Don Puckey
Cover photo by DAVA

Warner Books, Inc.
666 Fifth Avenue
New York, N.Y. 10103

 A Warner Communications Company

Printed in the United States of America

First Warner Books Printing: May, 1990

10 9 8 7 6 5 4 3 2 1

GUIDE TO TERMS AND ABBREVIATIONS

A-1	Douglas Skyraider propeller-driven attack bomber
A-4	Douglas Skyhawk jet attack bomber
A-6	Grumman Intruder jet attack bomber
AK-47	Soviet-pattern 7.62mm assault rifle
AN/TPQ-10	Ground-based aircraft radar guidance system
Arclight	B-52 high-altitude bombing program
ARVN	Army of Republic of Vietnam
ASP	Ammunition Supply Point
ASRT	Air Support Radar Team
B-52	Boeing Stratofortress jet heavy bomber
BGen	Brigadier General
C-123	Fairchild Provider medium cargo transport
C-130	Lockheed Hercules medium cargo transport
C4	Plastic explosive
Capt	Captain
CH-46	Boeing Sea Knight medium cargo helicopter
CH-53	Sikorsky Sea Stallion heavy cargo helicopter
Chicom	Chinese Communist (used for NVA hand grenade)
CIA	Central Intelligence Agency
CIDG	Civilian Irregular Defense Group
Claymore	U.S. directional antipersonnel mine
CN	Teargas
CO	Commanding Officer
COFRAM	Controlled Fragmentation Munitions (Firecracker)

Col	Colonel
Comm	Communications
CP	Command Post
CS	Teargas
DMZ	Demilitarized Zone
Duster	U.S. Army tracked 40mm gun carrier
EC-121	Lockheed Super Constellation electronics warfare aircraft
EOD	Explosive Ordnance Disposal
Exec	Executive Officer
F-4B	McDonnell Phantom jet fighter-bomber
1stLt	First Lieutenant
FOB	Forward Operating Base (Special Forces)
Gravel	Pressure-detonated explosive device
GySgt	Gunnery Sergeant
H-34	Sikorsky Sea Horse medium transport helicopter
H&I	Harassment-and-Interdiction
H&S	Headquarters-and-Service
HM3	Hospital Corpsman 3rd Class
HMC	Chief Hospital Corpsman
HN	Hospitalman
Hooch	Living quarters
HST	Helicopter Support Team
Huey	Bell UH-1E light attack/transport helicopter
KC-130	C-130 fuel tanker variant
KIA	Killed In Action
KSCB	Khe Sanh Combat Base
LAAW	U.S. light antitank assault weapon
LAPES	Low Altitude Proximity Extraction System
LBJ	President Lyndon B. Johnson
LCpl	Lance Corporal
Lt	Lieutenant
LtCol	Lieutenant Colonel
LtGen	Lieutenant General
LZ	Landing Zone
M-16	U.S. 5.56mm rifle
M-60	U.S. 7.62mm machine gun
M-79	U.S. 40mm grenade launcher
MACV	Military Assistance Command, Vietnam

Maj	Major
MCHD	Marine Corps Historical Division
Med	Medical (e.g., 3rd Medical Battalion)
MGen	Major General
MGySgt	Master Gunnery Sergeant
MIA	Missing In Action
NOD	Night Observation Device
NVA	North Vietnamese Army
Ontos	U.S. tracked 106mm recoilless rifle carrier
PAVN	People's Army of Vietnam (NVA)
Pfc	Private First Class
PT-76	Soviet tracked amphibious reconnaissance vehicle
Puff	Minigun-armed C-47 airplane
Pvt	Private
R&R	Rest and Rehabilitation (i.e., leave)
RPG	Soviet-pattern 40mm rocket-propelled grenade
S-3	Operations Officer
2ndLt	Second Lieutenant
SFC	Sergeant First Class
Sgt	Sergeant
SgtMaj	Sergeant Major
SKS	Soviet-pattern 7.62mm bolt-action carbine
SSgt	Staff Sergeant
TOT	Time On Target (artillery technique)
UH-1E	Bell Huey light attack/transport helicopter
USA	U.S. Army
USAF	U.S. Air Force
USAID	U.S. Agency for International Development
USMC	U.S. Marine Corps
USN	U.S. Navy
USS	United States Ship
VC	Viet Cong
VT	Variable Time (artillery airburst fuse)
WIA	Wounded In Action
Willy-Peter	WP (i.e., waterproof)

PHONETIC ALPHABET

Alpha	November
Bravo	Oscar
Charlie	Papa
Delta	Quebec
Echo	Romeo
Foxtrot	Sierra
Golf	Tango
Hotel	Uniform
India	Victor
Juliet	Whiskey
Kilo	X-Ray
Lima	Yankee
Mike	Zulu

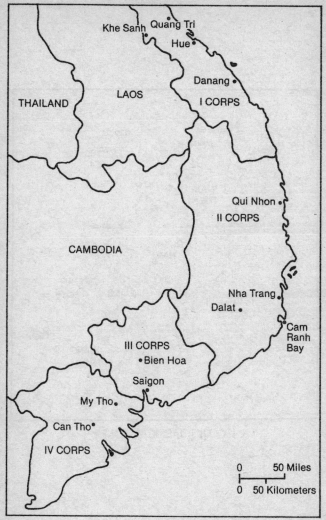

Khe Sanh • • Quang Tri
Hue •

Danang •

THAILAND   LAOS

I CORPS

Qui Nhon •

II CORPS

CAMBODIA

Nha Trang •
Dalat •

Cam
Ranh
Bay

III CORPS

• Bien Hoa

Saigon •

My Tho •

Can Tho •

IV CORPS

0   50 Miles
0   50 Kilometers

© F. F. Parry (used with permission)

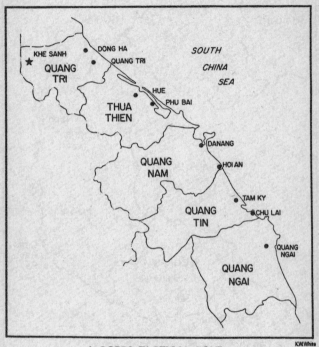

KHE SANH

DONG HA

QUANG TRI

QUANG TRI

SOUTH

CHINA

SEA

HUE

PHU BAI

THUA THIEN

DANANG

QUANG NAM

HOI AN

TAM KY

CHU LAI

QUANG TIN

QUANG NGAI

QUANG NGAI

K.W.White

I CORPS TACTICAL ZONE

NORTHERN QUANG TRI PROVINCE

E.L. WILSON

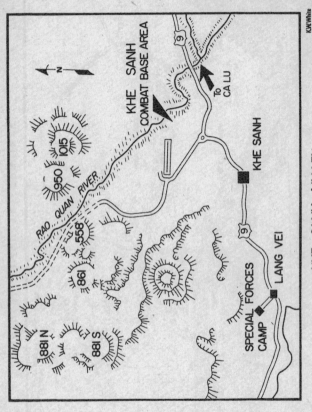

KHE SANH VALLEY

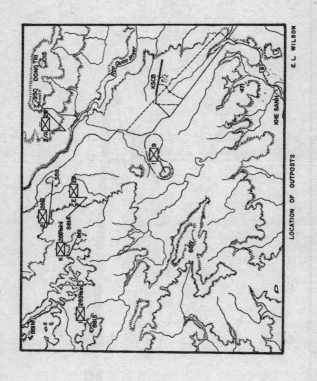

LOCATION OF OUTPOSTS

E. L. WILSON

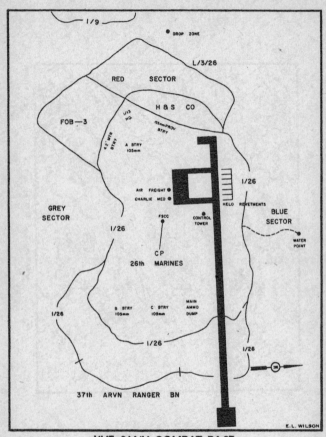

KHE SANH COMBAT BASE

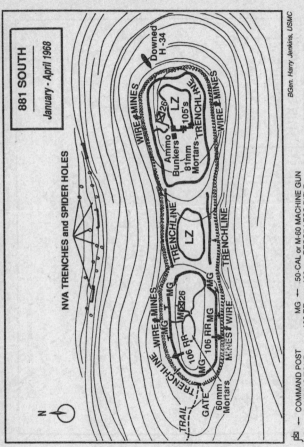

881 SOUTH

January - April 1968

BGen. Harry Jenkins, USMC

NVA TRENCHES and SPIDER HOLES

Downed H-34

WIRE MINES

LZ
105's
26

Ammo Bunkers
81mm Mortars
TRENCHLINE

WIRE MINES

TRENCHLINE

LZ

TRENCHLINE

MG
MG
26
MP
MG
106 RR
MG 106 RR MG
MINES WIRE
WIRE MINES
TRENCHLINE

60mm Mortars

TRAIL

GATE

N

MG — 50-CAL or M-60 MACHINE GUN
106 RR — 106mm RECOILLESS RIFLE
≢ — 105mm HOWITZER

⊠ — COMMAND POST
LZ — LANDING ZONE
T — TRENCH TO BUNKER

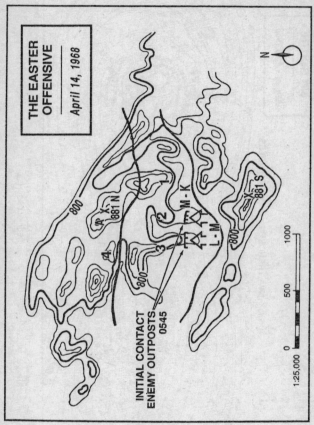

THE EASTER
OFFENSIVE
___
April 14, 1968

N

800

881 N

X

1

2

M - K

3

A

800

800

X
881 S

800

L - M

INITIAL CONTACT
ENEMY OUTPOSTS
0545

1:25,000   0   500   1000

Marine Corps Gazette (used with permission)

"They have us just where we want them."

LtCol Lewis "Chesty" Puller, USMC,
to his men when surrounded by
a superior Japanese force
on Guadalcanal in 1942

PART ONE

BEFORE

January 1–19, 1968

Prologue

It is generally held that the importance of the Khe Sanh Combat Base lay in its position astride a major North Vietnamese infiltration route, via Laos, around the Demilitarized Zone (DMZ). Located in western Quang Tri Province, nearly at the corner of South Vietnam, bordered to the west by Laos and to the north by the DMZ and North Vietnam, the Khe Sanh Plateau is a smuggler's dream of hilly trails obscured from aerial observation by high, dense, triple-canopy foliage and from ground patrols by rugged, piedmont-type hills covered by dense bamboo thickets and sight-obscuring high stands of elephant grass. Americans who served on the Khe Sanh Plateau found it ruggedly beautiful—a Shangri-la for the eye—and pleasantly cool during seasons when the Vietnamese lowlands were virtually too hot to live in. Sparsely settled, the region is vast, high, and impenetrable, and it can suck up many thousands of precious troops if it is to be effectively interdicted.

The United States military became involved in at least patrolling the Khe Sanh Plateau in 1962, when a U.S. Army Special Forces contingent set up a base camp and recruited local Bru montagnard villagers into a Vietnamese Civilian

Irregular Defense Group (CIDG) they established there. In April 1966, fully thirteen months after the first U.S. Marine infantry battalions arrived in coastal northern South Vietnam, a battalion of the 1st Marine Regiment (1st Marines) passed through the Khe Sanh Plateau during a large-scale sweep. Shortly thereafter, U.S. Navy Seabees hard-surfaced the small dirt runway that had been serving the Special Forces encampment since 1962. In October 1966, another Marine infantry battalion, plus an artillery battery, moved into the Special Forces camp, and the Special Forces detachment and its force of Vietnamese irregulars established a new camp at nearby Lang Vei village.

The Marine battalion remained at Khe Sanh until February 1967, when, having made no significant contacts with enemy forces, it was replaced by a single Marine rifle company. That company became involved in a significant fight in March 1967, and a second Marine company was sent to support it. At the conclusion of the fight, one company withdrew and the other remained. Around the same time, a Marine combined action company and a South Vietnamese Regional Forces company took up residence at Khe Sanh village, home of the Huong Hoa District Head-quarters, the local "county seat."

At some undetermined point, at least one of the high hills overlooking the Khe Sanh base was turned into an electronic intelligence listening post devoted to eavesdropping on radio traffic in North Vietnam. The records in this regard, where any are available, are understandably evasive, but the rumors are so persistent that the existence of such an installation—or installations—can be taken as virtual certainty.

Aside from the electronic eavesdroppers, the combined South Vietnamese and American military establishment on the Khe Sanh Plateau was devoted totally to denying the North Vietnamese a strategic invasion route through Laos into the heart of Quang Tri Province. Emphasis was on patrolling. If anything turned up, air and artillery support could be provided from all over the region, and reinforcements could be airlifted into the area aboard helicopters or by means of the hard-surfaced runway at the Marine base atop the plateau.

The North Vietnamese apparently decided to overrun Khe Sanh in early May 1967, but their plans came a cropper when a Marine patrol operating out of the base became heavily engaged with a large North Vietnamese Army (NVA) force on April 24.

In a continuing action since dubbed the Hill Fights, the Marine plan to come to the aid of the Khe Sanh base was put into action. A full infantry battalion of the 3rd Marines was sent up on April 25, and another followed on April 26. On April 27, a second artillery battery was dispatched.

Beginning on April 28, 1967, the two-battalion Marine force drove out of the base and moved to wrest from enemy hands three hill masses—Hill 861 (names of hills are their heights in meters), Hill 881 North (881N), and Hill 881 South (881S)—that dominated the combat base. Support was provided by the howitzers and heavy mortars inside the base, by a U.S. Army 175mm artillery battery located at Camp Carroll, and by Marine tactical aviation units based mainly at Danang.

The two Marine battalions engaged in the Hill Fights ground forward against all three objectives until, on May 3, the North Vietnamese defenders spent themselves in an abortive counterattack and apparently withdrew.

Beginning on May 11, 1967, the 1st Battalion, 27th Marines (1/26) relieved the two battalions of the 3rd Marines, which left the area. Hills 881S and 861 were outposted, each by one company of 1/26. On May 13, the skeleton headquarters of the recently activated 26th Marine Regiment arrived at Khe Sanh to establish a permanent presence.

Within months of the Hill Fights, the major focus of action in the I Corps region of South Vietnam shifted to Con Thien, far to the east of Khe Sanh and directly overlooking the DMZ. The North Vietnamese Army laid siege to the tiny, Marine-held Con Thien Combat Base, and supporting and maintaining the action took virtually all the assets either side was willing to contribute to a formal, protracted, set-piece battle.

Meanwhile, around Khe Sanh, a rather endless spate of small-unit sparring ebbed and flowed well into the summer. In due course, on June 13, the 3rd Battalion, 26th Marines (3/26), was committed to the Khe Sanh Plateau. However, in August, 3/26 was drawn off to help in a distant operation south of Con Thien.

Through the last quarter of 1967, 1/26 took steps to build up the Khe Sanh Combat Base, maintain its hill outposts, and conduct aggressive patrolling throughout the plateau. Also, the U.S. Army Special Forces established its Forward Operating Base 3 (FOB-3) at the Marine combat base and began running deep patrols from there—undoubtedly including forays into Laos—using Bru montagnard tribesmen recruited from local villages and formed into a new CIDG company. During the same period, the hard-surfaced runway was lengthened, to 3,900 feet, and upgraded to all-weather status. To accomplish the mission, the Seabees quarried their own rock from a hill to the west of the base perimeter, laid it over the runway and its extension, and covered it over with aluminum matting to make it absolutely weathertight. Soon, for the first time in the base's history, new building materials, armaments, troops, tracked weapons, and supplies were being lifted in aboard rather large Marine and Air Force C-130 Hercules transports.

Beginning in early December 1967, reconnaissance patrols conducted by a resident Marine recon company—Bravo Company, 3rd Reconnaissance Battalion—picked up increasing signs of escalating North Vietnamese activity in the area. It soon became a matter of faith among intelligence analysts that the NVA was planning a major sweep through the Khe Sanh Plateau and, very likely, on to Dong Ha and Quang Tri city. The number and size of North Vietnamese units spotted by Marine patrols centered on Khe Sanh rose to the point where, on December 13, the entire 3rd Battalion, 26th Marines, was returned to the combat base.

On December 21, Col David Lownds, the 26th Marines commander, sent 3/26 on a sweep starting at Hill 881S, running five kilometers west toward Hill 981, and returning to the combat base from the southwest via Hill 689. The

five-day sweep turned up no hard contacts with the large
North Vietnamese forces identified by recon patrols, but it
did turn up numerous signs of the reported enemy presence—
bunkers, fresh fighting holes, well-used trails, and arms and
supply caches. There was no doubt by Christmas 1967 that
a large—if elusive—NVA force was settling in around the
Khe Sanh Plateau.

Chapter 1

The area of operations, consisting of some 403 square miles, is located in northwestern Quang Tri Province. Bordered on the north by the DMZ and west by the Laotian border, the area of operations generally encompasses all of Huong Hoa District.

The area is thinly populated, rugged, and mountainous. Heights over 500 meters are common throughout the area. Terrain is severely dissected and thickly vegetated with dense undergrowth, broad-leaf evergreen forests, and bamboo thickets. Trail networks are plentiful, but trafficability to vehicles is almost uniformly restricted to National Route 9. Excellent cover and concealment exist throughout most of the area of operations and provide both friendly and enemy forces numerous covered approaches to attack positions and protection from enemy fire.

The heavy vegetation throughout the area of operations consists of a 60-foot-high jungle canopy, elephant grass, and dense areas of bamboo and vine thickets, which, combined with the steep slopes, create an effective natural obstacle to cross-country movement and greatly reduce long-range observation. In general, cross-country movement is restricted to existing trails and streams. Periods of steady heavy rainfall also make many of the streams in the area of operations difficult to impossible to cross.

There are five avenues of approach into the area of operations. Two avenues of approach enter from the northwest. One crosses the Laos/Vietnam border and moves southeast along streams and valley that join the Rivere De Rao Quan and continues southeast until it joins Route 9. The second approach from the northwest crosses the Laos/Vietnam border and continues southeast along the ridgeline to Hills 881S. Route 9 provides a major east-west avenue of approach across the area of operations. The approach from the southeast is the Da Krong Valley, which enters the area of operations and moves northwest until it reaches Route 9. An approach from the northwest enters the area of operations just south of Hill 1123 and runs southwest along the Khe Xa Bai River to a point just north of Hill 558.

Dong Tri Mountain, the highest peak (1,015 meters) in the area of operations dominates the Khe Sanh Valley. Hill 861 controls the approaches from the north and northwest. Hills 881S and 881N and Hill 918 dominate the approaches from the west. The [hill masses] south of Route 9 are important as they dominate the eastern approaches of Route 9 into the area of operations.

The area is lightly populated. The population center of the area is Khe Sanh Village, located on Route 9 approximately 5,000 meters from the combat base, where approximately 1,250 Vietnamese reside. This is also the Huong Hoa District Headquarters. The natives of the area are predominantly from the Bru montagnard tribe of the Mon Khymer ethno-linguistic group. The Bru tribal area extends throughout northeast Laos, southern North Vietnam, and the local area. The Bru, numbering approximately 10,000, primarily reside in a dozen small villages and resettlement areas located within 5 kilometers of Khe Sanh Village. There are also three French families who own coffee plantations, two French Catholic priests, two nuns (one French, one Vietnamese), and one American missionary family in the immediate area.

26th Marines After Action Report _____

The mission of the 26th Marine Regiment was to conduct reconnaissance and combat patrols in the assigned [area] to detect and destroy enemy personnel infiltrating into and through the Khe Sanh Tactical Area of Responsibility; provide security for the airfield and ancillary facilities at Khe Sanh and other vital installations in the area; open and secure lines; maintain active ground surveillance within the tactical area of responsibility; provide artillery support for [the] combined action company [at Khe Sanh village]; and be prepared to conduct operation in relief of or reinforcement of the CIDG Camp at Lang Vei.

The concept of operations [is to]:

a. Establish and maintain defensive positions on prominent terrain features within the area of operations for surveillance and control purposes. Utilize reconnaissance elements in the area of responsibility within artillery range to maintain surveillance over the area, and exploit sightings primarily with artillery and aircraft.

b. Conduct search-and-destroy operations with all available forces throughout the area of operations, taking advantage of intelligence provided and generated.

c. Maintain the defense of the KSCB [Khe Sanh Combat Base] and ancillary facilities.

BOB BREWER
Quang Tri Province Senior Adviser _____

My main emphasis was on the *chieu hoi*—defector—program. I directed that, each morning before the regular 0700 staff meeting, the picture and biographical data of each defector coming in within the last twenty-four hours would be on my desk for review. In early September 1967, there appeared a five-inch-by-eight-inch card on an individual who I felt needed more questioning. His hair was too long for his alleged rank and his listed education, versus age, didn't sound right. I asked our Special Branch (Vietnamese FBI) adviser to zero in on this guy. Within a few days, this defector was unmasked as a Moscow-trained long-range penetration agent. We "doubled" him immediately, and the take was astounding.

For example, he brought us "Resolution 13." The intelligence community had been looking forward to it for years. (Ho Chi Minh had issued Resolution 1 in 1918, and only eleven others had been promulgated in the intervening fifty years). Resolution 13 was the master plan for the Tet Offensive, including the elimination of Khe Sanh.

Our double agent, whom we tabbed "X-1," was not to be totally trusted, but I drew up a long list of indicators which, if they surfaced between September 1967 and January 1968, would validate our double agent's Resolution 13. In November 1967, he brought out an updated version of Resolution 13. It was much more specific as to targets and timetables, and it was not written in the usual Communist argot.

Throughout December 1967 and January 1968, the enemy tripped one indicator after another . . . I called a meeting of the principal American and Government of Vietnam advisers in Quang Tri. I told them that the attack was coming, aimed primarily at the seats of government, and that it would be launched at 0100 hours, January 31. I stressed that our U.S. bases—such as Khe Sanh, Con Thien, and Gio Linh—would be engaged by the enemy so as to diminish U.S. military support to the Government of Vietnam power seats and the civilian population in our prime pacification areas.

Chapter 2

JANUARY 2

Capt DICK CAMP
Lima Company, 3/26 _____

As we did every night, Lima Company got ready for its night defense. In the fifteen or twenty minutes before dusk, we had our usual stand-to. Everyone got all his gear laid out in case we got hit during the night. I had dug my own foxhole, which was where I slept alone. It was four feet wide and about six feet long, a little cramped for me. As was my custom, I spoke briefly with the radio operators and everyone else in the command group before I hit the sack.

Somewhere around 2030, I woke up on sheer intuition just as one of the radio operators crawled over to me and whispered, "Skipper! Skipper! Get up. The 1st Platoon listening post hears something." It was standard operating procedure in Lima Company that when a listening post made contact or heard something, the situation immediately belonged to the company commander.

A listening post was a fire team—four riflemen—which

was sent out by each platoon to monitor a likely avenue of approach on our lines. We usually had three or four listening posts out on any given night, depending on how many avenues of approach we had to cover.

The alert had come in from the 1st Platoon listening post, which was screening the company right flank. One of the members of the fire team had heard something and had immediately alerted the company radio operators, who immediately alerted me.

The radio operators were all in a big hole near my hole. Their hole had a tarpaulin stretched over the top of it in such a way as to make it absolutely lightproof. As I crawled to the radio bunker, I whispered a call for Corporal Brady, my mortar section leader. As soon as Brady crawled up beside me, I whispered, "Brady, get your ammo humpers up and have them stand by." The 60mm ammo party was my reaction force, the group of Marines to which the company commander had immediate access in case something happened. I could use them to stop a breakthrough or reinforce a listening post—whatever—without having to steal men from the rifle platoons.

Next, I rolled beneath the radio bunker tarp and dropped into the hole. As soon as I got there, one of the radiomen gave me a handset and I called up the 1st Platoon listening post, which was "Lima 1-1"—1st Squad of 1st Platoon of Lima Company. My call sign was Lima 6.

"Lima 1-1. Lima 6." I waited, but there was no response. "Lima 1-1. Lima 6." No response again. I tried it two or three more times, but the listening post was not answering—or could not.

I was sorting out options when we heard two clicks from the radio. Someone in the listening post had keyed his own handset twice to tell us he was alive but did not want to talk. I came right back up on the radio and said, "Lima 1-1. Lima 6. If you hear this transmission, key your handset twice."

"*Click. Click.*"

I knew the fire team could not talk but that they were listening to me.

"Lima 1-1. Lima 6. When you can talk, let me know what's going on."

And then we waited. The adrenaline went straight through me. I had four Marines out there who thought they saw or heard something. It was darker than pitch. I had no idea what was coming in on them, and maybe they didn't either. I worked up a lot of empathy for those four Marines, but there was not a thing I could do until I heard from them or until something happened.

I was listening so hard I almost missed the faint whisper coming in over my handset: "We see something. Out."

That was enough for me. I was galvanized to action. "Brady," I yelled, "Brady, get your people up and get them ready to go." At the same time, I called the 1st Platoon commander, 1stLt Nile Buffington: "Lima 1. Lima 6. Are you monitoring this transmission?"

"Lima 6. Lima 1. Roger that."

"Lima 1. Lima 6. Did you personally put them out?"

He replied that he had put them out and that he knew precisely where they were.

There was a small draw that came out of a valley seventy or eighty meters from our main line. There was a tree there we called the Hanging Tree because it had an odd-shaped, bent-up limb. When Buffington told me that the listening post was out near the Hanging Tree, I knew right where it was.

"Lima 1. Lima 6. Stand by. I'm going to send a reaction force down to you. You take it over. We might go out and reinforce the listening post, depending on what they've got out there."

Typically, a listening post was like a grape. If we did not get them in on time, they stood a good chance of being swallowed up as the enemy moved right up to our main line to launch an assault. On the other hand, if we pulled a listening post in too early, we would not know what the hell was going on right in front of our line. Timing was everything.

My solution to this age-old quandary was to try to reinforce a listening post that had detected a movement on its front. Doing so would offset the possibility of its being overrun if it stayed out too long. It also might be given more time to report everything it could hear and see. In the best of all worlds, a reinforced listening post just might provide us with a sizable force in the enemy's path or even in his rear.

This was an extremely delicate operation. We had practiced it several times in the past, but this was the first chance to do it live.

As soon as I made my decision, Corporal Brady sent his ammo humpers—eight Marines in all—down to the 1st Platoon command post.

There was one little flaw in the plan. The eight men in the reaction force were all mortarmen—not riflemen. Moreover, they were all very junior in rank, all privates first class and lance corporals, if that. All of a sudden, they were faced with the very real prospect of having to advance beyond our prepared defenses in the dead of night. Once they were in the open, they would have to locate a well-camouflaged friendly position they had never seen. If they got that far, there was a good chance that they would have to duke it out with who knew how many NVA Regulars. I knew that the ammo humpers were pretty excited about what they faced, but they were all I had. Short of defending a key sector during an all-out attack, there was no way I was going to thin out my platoons manning the main line.

The adrenaline was coursing through everybody at this stage.

After Brady sent out the reaction force, I finally got back in touch with the listening post. During the course of five or ten minutes—time was going fast *and* slow—I spoke with the fire team twice more. During the first transmission, the fire team leader out there was whispering so low that I could not make out what he was saying. But the last transmission was, "We see something. Six of them just walked by us." Then there was a pause and the fire team leader asked, "You want me to tell you what they are armed with?" I knew that he wanted to make sure that I knew that he wasn't bullshitting out there.

"No. Hold your position. We're gonna reinforce you."

Next, Lieutenant Buffington came up on the net to tell me that he was with the reaction force. I said, "Lima 1. Lima 6. Take them out. Be careful."

I now had a four-man Marine listening post standing by near the Hanging Tree. One officer and the eight ammo humpers were going to work their way out to the listening post. I had an unknown number of NVA out there, too—at least six. The situation was extremely dangerous.

LCpl CHARLIE THORNTON
Lima Company, 3/26 _____

As we moved up to and through our concertina wire it was so dark I literally could not see my hand in front of my face.

Capt DICK CAMP
Lima Company, 3/26 _____

While I was waiting to hear back from Buffington, I had the radio operators contact Battalion and let them know what we had. When my radiomen got through, I told them at Battalion, "We have some friendlies out in front of the wire. Alert the line at Khe Sanh so they don't start shooting at our people out there." Battalion verified that they had heard and understood my transmission, which is not the same as assuring me that my Marines would not be endangered by other units if they were heard or seen.

I was tense from waiting, so I told Corporal Brady to break out his 60mm mortar illumination rounds and prepare to fire them immediately on my command. I had no sooner said that than, all of a sudden, Lieutenant Buffington came up on the net: "Lima 6. Lima 1. We made contact with the listening post." So that part was over with. Lima Company now had a dozen Marines and a lieutenant out in front of our lines.

Brady reported back that he had the illume broken out. I told him, "Have them standing by to fire."

We had three 60mm mortars in the company position, all under my direct control. Brady actually had a round "hanging" in each tube—that is, a gunner was holding a round at the mouth of each tube, ready to drop on command. There is no faster way to get the first rounds up.

As soon as I knew Brady's mortars were set, I told Buffington to get all his people in line, that as soon as we started the illumination he was to sweep through the area where the listening post fire team thought they saw the North Vietnamese. We were all set to go. Buffington was then about seventy or eighty meters in front of the 1st Platoon line, about a hundred meters in front of the company command post.

There was another wait. Then Buffington came up on the net: "Lima 6. Lima 1. I'm ready to go."

I turned to my mortar squad leader. "Brady, start the illumination."

LCpl CHARLIE THORNTON
Lima Company, 3/26 _____

From behind the wire, our mortars began popping flares overhead. The night was illuminated in a very strange manner as the flares slowly drifted through the cloud cover, swinging back and forth suspended on their parachutes. There were intervals of darkness and light between the rounds fired.

Capt DICK CAMP
Lima Company, 3/26 _____

I was staring as hard as I could, dead ahead into the harsh white magnesium light of the illume, but I could not see anything. I hopped out of the radio bunker for a better look, and all my radio operators stood up around me. I was waiting for something to happen, but it was dead quiet out there. The only thing I heard was the *thung* of the second illumination round being fired as the first one started to wane.

LCpl CHARLIE THORNTON
Lima Company, 3/26 _____

The lieutenant had us get on line, spread out, and begin moving into the darkness ahead. As we walked on line, hunched over and listening only to the sounds of the night, my heart pounded in my chest with anticipation. I heard the lieutenant, who was just off to my right, shouting at someone to identify himself. He finally said, "Identify yourself or we will fire." Just at that moment, all hell broke loose. There were weapons firing from all around, and tracer sounds from automatic weapons cutting through the darkness. We returned fire in the direction from which the first shots began.

Capt DICK CAMP
Lima Company, 3/26 _____

All of a sudden, there was a burst of fire, ten or fifteen rounds. This was followed a half-beat later by a terrific volume of automatic-weapons fire. It all sounded like one continuous roar, and I do not think it lasted for more than a few seconds. Then there was nothing, absolutely nothing— dead silence. The next thing anyone heard was me yelling into the handset, "What the hell's going on? What the hell's going on out there? Tell me what's happening out there! What's happening, Nile? What's going on?"

Suddenly, I heard Buffington's voice break into my stream of questions. He was yelling at the top of his voice. I heard him on the handset and through the air. We did not need the radio.

"We have contact. We can't figure out what's going on."

I tried to sound calm. "Tell me what the hell's happening!"

Before Buffington could answer, an Army duster [a dual 40mm automatic antiaircraft gun mount on a tracked armored chassis] opened fire from our right flank. I could not hear anything except the 40mm guns and I was afraid that the Army people were blowing away our people. The only thing I could do was call Battalion and scream at them to get the Army to knock off the fire, that we were trying to find out what was going on with Buffington and his crew.

The duster kept putting out rounds, but somehow I managed to hear Buffington's next radio call: "We're down; we can't see anything."

The Army duster was still throwing rounds out there, so I yelled into the handset, "What've you got?" But Buffington said he had no idea. "Well," I asked, "is anybody hurt?"

"No, not that I can tell."

"Okay, then, bring them on in, bring them on in." I was not sure he could hear me over the continuous roar of the Army duster. "I said bring them all in, bring them all in before somebody gets hurt."

I did not get acknowledgment that I could understand, but I passed the word all up and down our line to watch for friendlies trying to reenter the company position.

LCpl CHARLIE THORNTON
Lima Company, 3/26 _____

As the fighting subsided, we again got on line and swept through the area where we thought the firing had originated. It was very dark, and after finding nothing or encountering any additional resistance, we returned to the company perimeter. I was scared, but I also felt the rush of excitement my first fire fight had generated.

Capt DICK CAMP
Lima Company, 3/26 _____

About ten minutes later, someone told me that Lieutenant Buffington was back inside our wire. He had come back in through his own platoon's lines because they knew him and knew where he was. I sent word for him to come straight to the company command post, and he and the ammo humpers and the original fire team got to me all at once within a minute.

I was going to ask what happened, but the whole bunch of them started talking a mile a minute before I opened my mouth. They were all incredibly hyper, and they all wanted to talk. I could see the adrenaline pouring through them. They were all bunched up in front of me, jabbering away, talking with their hands. They looked like a bunch of escapees from the asylum.

There was no way they were going to wind down on their

own anytime soon, so I yelled, "Shut up, goddammit! Sit
down!" That snapped all of them out of their high. They all
sat down—fell down, really—and I said as calmly as I was
able, "Okay, Lieutenant Buffington, tell me what happened."

Buffington told me that he had gotten all twelve Marines
formed up in a single line and started moving them forward
to sweep out in front of the listening post. All of a sudden,
almost as soon as the first illumination round popped overhead, the Marine in the middle of the line, right in front of
Buffington, stopped in his tracks. Instantly, the entire line
stopped with him. Then the kid said, "Who's there?"

Nothing happened and the kid kept staring at something
straight ahead, so Buffington closed up on the kid, looked
ahead over the kid's shoulder, and said, "You fuckers better
say something."

And that is what they did; one of them fired about fifteen
rounds right over Buffington's head. Fortunately, there is a
tendency to fire high at night. Buffington said he felt the
rounds missing his head.

Every one of the Marines had set his weapon on full
automatic, and each man had eighteen rounds in the magazine. That is thirteen Marines with eighteen rounds apiece.
Every one of them instantly opened fire on full automatic.
Naturally, every one of them ran out of ammunition at
exactly the same moment. That was when I heard it get
quiet all of a sudden.

As soon as everyone had emptied his first magazine, all
hands dropped onto the ground to present less of a silhouette. Then everyone started fumbling around on the ground
trying to find a fresh magazine, and trying to put the fresh
magazines into their M-16s. Of course, when they all fell
down, some of them were pointing their weapons one way
and others were pointing their weapons the other way. The
result was that they were as likely to blow away one another
as any North Vietnamese. Buffington was yelling at them,
trying to get them squared away: "Where the hell is everybody?" and calm questions like that. Everyone was crawling
around out there, thoroughly confused, thoroughly scared.

Buffington finished telling the story and I patted everybody on the back while exclaiming, "Way to go, Marines!" and "Well done!" and "Good job! Whatever's out there, I know you just scared the shit out of them. They know you alerted the lines. Well done." I made a special effort to pat the listening post Marines on their backs; they had done good.

Nile Buffington and I trekked down to Battalion to give them a brief. I was stunned to see that no one at the battalion command post appeared particularly interested in our story. Noting all the bored expressions, we gave a quick brief and headed home.

By the time we got back to my command post, it was probably 0400. I told Buffington to send out another listening post, but not in that same vicinity. Then I jumped into my hole and crashed.

After a few hours sleep, I called Buffington and told him that we had to search around the Hanging Tree to try to find out what had happened in the night.

As I was getting set to go down to 1st Platoon, two of the ammo humpers who had been in the fire fight came over and asked if they could help search for bodies. I told them they sure could, and they accompanied me to the 1st Platoon command post. I guess they had become bored with the easy life of the rear echelon.

I was just rubbernecking while Buffington's people and the ammo humpers were kicking around out in front of the lines. I had even less of a sense of what to look for than they did. I doubted we would find anything; it was always extremely difficult to find any results from a fight because the North Vietnamese were always very good about dragging their bodies off. I happened to be watching the two ammo humpers, who were about seventy meters from where I was standing. No sooner did I take my eyes off them than I heard them both yell, "Skipper! Hey, Skipper!" When I lifted my eyes, they were jumping up and down and yelling, "Come out here quick. Come on out here. See what we got!"

I grabbed a bunch of other onlookers and we ran out there at high port. The ammo humpers had found five dead NVA officers, all stretched right out on the ground. All of them had been hit literally from the top of their brain housing groups to their toenails, and it looked like somebody had raked the ground around them. That was the result of all that automatic fire that the listening post fire team and the reaction force had put out. They put out over 230 rounds, and all of them were right on target. My Marines had really hit the mark.

The dead men were all wearing black pajamas and Ho Chi Minh sandals. And all of them were really big men, a lot bigger than most Vietnamese are. One of them had pulled a hand grenade halfway out of his pouch, and another one was gripping a pistol with his arm outstretched. Rigor mortis had set in, so they were all frozen in the positions in which they had died, like wax statues.

After staring at the bodies for a few moments, I noticed that all their shoulder straps had been cut. The listening post had told us early on that there were six of them. That explained the cut shoulder straps. One of them had survived and had apparently had the presence of mind to cut away their dispatch cases before he took off out of the area. That is fantastic discipline, particularly if he had been wounded, which was a good bet.

For once, we had the proof of our success. I turned to Lieutenant Buffington and the others. "Let's bring the whole company out here by squads to see the results."

First, I brought out all the ammo humpers who had been on the reaction force; it was important for them to see what they had accomplished.

While the squads were rubbernecking, I told my exec to contact the 17th ITT—Interrogation-Translation Team—to get them out to view the remains and take whatever they needed for intelligence purposes. The dead North Vietnamese were definitely big fish; every one of them was wearing a gold or silver belt buckle, not the standard aluminum type. Dispatch cases, pistols, expensive belt buckles—it was obvious to me that these people were special.

GySgt MAX FRIEDLANDER
17th Interrogation-Translation Team _____

Early in the morning, I received a call from Regiment asking me to go out and check the bodies that were lying in front of the lines. I did so, and I found that there was very little information—papers, documents, maps—to be gathered from the bodies themselves. There was a bit of evidence, though, that there had been another member of the group. There were five bodies and a sixth had probably been wounded and dragged himself off. It was our guess that he had collected the documents that may have been valuable to us and took them with him.

One of the NVA was still holding a hand grenade. One of the Explosive Ordnance Disposal [EOD] people had to be called to get the hand grenade out of his hand. All of the other weapons, if they were carrying any, were missing.

There were a few things that were rather unusual about these five bodies. One of them was extremely tall for a North Vietnamese. A lieutenant colonel who was out there and I sent word back to Colonel Lownds about this because there was a possibility he was Chinese.

While we were waiting around, I started following what I thought was the route the escaped NVA had taken. I started walking in that direction, which led me toward a wooded area. I didn't see anything and I lost the trail, so I walked a little bit further. By then, I was about sixty yards from the bodies. I saw a large log on the right, where the treeline was, and for some reason I stopped, looked around, and walked back up to where everybody was standing around. I later learned that an NVA company was in the treeline, ready to open fire on me and the Marines around the bodies if I took even one more step.

By the time I got back to the bodies, word had come back from Regiment. Colonel Lownds asked us to take the body down to one of the empty tents in back of Charlie-Med and have him examined by both the medical officer and the dental officer to see if there was any way to determine if he was, in fact, Chinese.

I accompanied the tall NVA soldier to the tent. The doctor was checking him over, and the dental officer came in and tried to make some sort of a determination on his teeth. There was nothing definite that could be determined. They could not come to a definite conclusion that he was Chinese. However, since there was a possibility he was, Colonel Lownds had radioed the news down to 3rd Marine Division headquarters, at Phu Bai. I heard it threw a scare into people. If the Chinese were involved and were sending high-ranking officers, it could have turned into quite a big thing. However, it was all forgotten shortly thereafter.

I did get information off several of the NVA bodies—a pay card from one, one or two watches, some photos of a family. We were able to determine their units and ranks.

Capt DICK CAMP
Lima Company, 3/26 ⎯⎯⎯⎯⎯⎯⎯⎯⎯⎯⎯⎯⎯⎯⎯⎯⎯⎯⎯

What it all added up to is that we had killed the commander of an NVA regiment and his staff. This was incredibly lucky for Lima Company. The only thing officers as senior as that could have been doing out there was reconnoitering our lines in preparation for a major ground assault.

The only casualty we suffered came to my attention when one of the kids in the listening post fire team showed me an ugly bruise over the orbit bone of his right eye, which, he told me, had been inflicted when a bullet glanced off his face. I had the first sergeant write him up for a Purple Heart, and I made sure everyone in the fire team and all the ammo humpers got souvenirs, the gold and silver belt buckles, the officers' pistols, whatever.

1stLt NICK ROMANETZ
Charlie Company, 1/26 ⎯⎯⎯⎯⎯⎯⎯⎯⎯⎯⎯⎯⎯⎯⎯⎯⎯⎯⎯

The bodies of the NVA officers were the first dead bad guys any of us had seen in a long time. They drew a lot of attention.

Chapter 3

JANUARY 5

At 0655, Charlie Company, 1/26 (reinforced), departed the Khe Sanh Combat Base with the assigned mission of conducting a two-day combat patrol/search-and-destroy operation northwest of the combat base, and with the additional mission of inserting a reconnaissance team. At 1615, while the reconnaissance team was being inserted, it observed three NVA. Small arms were exchanged and the reconnaissance team withdrew to the Charlie Company position. Charlie Company continued its assigned mission without incident, returning to the Khe Sanh Combat Base on January 6 at 1215.

At 0730, Alpha Company, 1/26 (minus) (reinforced), departed the Khe Sanh Combat Base to conduct a two-day combat patrol/search-and-destroy operation southeast of the combat base. The patrol proceeded without incident and Alpha Company returned to the Khe Sanh Combat Base on January 6 at 1530.

26th Marines Command Chronology ―――――――

At 1600, Recon team 2B1 made contact with three NVA.
The team received automatic weapons fire and observed
10 NVA wearing green utility uniforms and carrying
AK-47s trying to outflank them from the northeast. The
team broke contact.

At 2031, Recon team 3B3 observed 7 red lights. An
artillery mission was fired and the lights went out.

1/26 Command Chronology ―――――――――

At 2245, Alpha Company, 1/26, listening posts heard
movement and received one incoming grenade resulting
in one friendly WIA (non-serious).

JANUARY 6

26th Marines Command Chronology ―――――――

At 1055, Recon Team 1B3 exchanged small-arms fire with
a small enemy unit resulting in 1 NVA KIA (confirmed).

JANUARY 8

1/26 Command Chronology ―――――――――

At 0230, Bravo Company, 1/26, listening posts observed
two lights near the trash dump. The area was searched at
first light, revealing three sets of footprints heading in a
southwesterly direction. Patrol unable to follow due to
thick vegetation.

At 0700, 1/26 (minus) commenced a battalion search-
and-destroy operation for a period of six days. The
assigned mission was to interdict likely enemy routes of
infiltration southwest of the Khe Sanh Combat Base.
There were no enemy contacts during this operation.

At 1010, the Alpha Company, 1/26, platoon on Hill 950
found fresh footprints. The footprints headed in a westerly direction for approximately 100 meters and disappeared.

At 1245, Bravo Company, 1/26, found a 10–15-man harbor site approximately a week old. Conducted search of trails leading from the area with negative results.

JANUARY 10

Lt. RAY STUBBE
1/26 Battalion Chaplain _____

[DIARY ENTRY] At the regimental briefing, Colonel Lownds said the enemy has completed their recon and he expects an attack in the next ten days. "They're going to attack, and we're going to inflict a heavy loss on them."

JANUARY 11

26th Marines Command Chronology _____

At 1315, an aerial observer observed 12 NVA on a trail. The [helicopter] gunships on station took them under attack, resulting in 6 NVA KIA (confirmed).

JANUARY 12

26th Marines Command Chronology _____

At 1417, two Special Forces patrols observed NVA in their general vicinity. Artillery and small-arms fire resulted in 12 NVA KIA (confirmed). Special Forces had one friendly WIA and one friendly KIA.

JANUARY 13

Capt KEN PIPES
Bravo Company, 1/26 _____

During our sweep into the hills west of the combat base, one of my platoons ambushed an NVA recon unit that had been tracing all the avenues of approach into the combat base. Apparently, in the gear they left behind were maps showing the approach routes into the base and the hill outposts. The routes provided that long columns of troops could move off the trails if they were discovered and bombed by aircraft, so the troops wouldn't be exposed to the aircraft in long, easy-to-hit columns.

LtCol JIM WILKINSON
1/26 Commanding Officer _____

Bravo Company killed one member of the NVA recon team. Regiment was in such a state because we had killed an NVA that they ordered us to bring in the body. In fact, Colonel Lownds personally flew out in a helicopter to check the NVA. We were quite impressed. He was taller than the average NVA, well clothed, and well armed.

One of the maps we captured showed indications of where the major thrust was going to take place at Khe Sanh.

Capt KEN PIPES
Bravo Company, 1/26 _____

As soon as the information we sent in—along with one of the NVA bodies—had been checked by higher headquarters, the sweep operation was cut short and we were all ordered back to the combat base to assume defensive positions.

1stLt NICK ROMANETZ
Charlie Company, 1/26 _____

As we were coming into Khe Sanh following our battalion sweep, we could see the base from a couple of miles off. I was astounded at how many C-130s the Air Force and Marines were landing. Almost like cars going through a tollbooth, these things were coming down with material, ammo, food, and troops. Helicopters were coming in, too. Up until this time, we had not received much indication of hostile activity, so I was really astounded. I began thinking that something was really going to happen.

Lt RAY STUBBE
1/26 Battalion Chaplain ————————————

[DIARY ENTRY] Colonel Lownds announced the following at the regimental meeting:

1. All personnel will have fighting holes where they work and where they live.
2. These holes will be built so one can fight from them, and they will be covered with runway matting to be brought up from the south.
3. The holes will be supplied with rations. All water cans will be always filled since the water point will probably be hit.
4. Beginning Monday [January 15], all personnel will wear flak jackets and carry a weapon.
5. Wire will be laid for internal security all about the base.

Leaving the meeting, I asked [the 26th Marines regimental intelligence officer] if it was really as bad as all that. He said, "All indications are that we're going to be hit. How bad, I can't say."

1stLt NICK ROMANETZ
Charlie Company, 1/26 ————————————————

An order came down that every Marine was always to wear his helmet and flak jacket and carry his weapon and gas mask. Until this point, the only time we wore a flak jacket or helmet was when we went on patrols or work parties outside the wire, or when we were standing to or standing down. When this word came down, it really had a lot of guys chuckling. Everybody was saying, "Hey, who are these guys kidding? This is Khe Sanh. It's the quietest place." It really took a lot of getting used to to carry a weapon at all times and keep that flak jacket on. A lot of guys thought it was a real joke.

LCpl CHARLIE THORNTON
Lima Company, 3/26 _____

We began to dig in deeper and prepare for the worst. We
were told that we were surrounded and heavily outnumbered
by thousands of NVA regulars.

JANUARY 14

Capt BILL DABNEY
India Company, 3/26 (Hill 881S) _____

The intelligence that filtered down to my level was minimal,
virtually nonexistent. India Company had been on 881S
since about December 20. Since I was not able to sit in on
regiment or battalion briefings, I was not informed in
specific detail of the probability of attack. . . . However, the
potential was obvious to myself and my officers and I
therefore patrolled actively as far as four kilometers from
the hill to the north, south, and west. Hill 861 was to the
east, so there wasn't any patrolling in that direction.

Until about January 13, the patrols turned up no evidence
of recent NVA activity. On the fourteenth, I sent 2ndLt Tom
Brindley's 3rd Platoon to patrol Hill 881N. Accompanying
it was an eight-man reconnaissance patrol which was to
drop off clandestinely along the route of march on 881N.
There was no contact and the recon patrol remained on
881N after the platoon left to patrol. The platoon set up a
patrol base with one squad plus two 60mm mortars along
the ridgeline west from 881N and the other along the fingers
extending southwest. There were no contacts or sightings.
Then, on January 14, 2ndLt Mike Thomas's 2nd Platoon
patrolled to the ridge about one kilometer or so south, then
along the ridge, and then returned via the valley between the
ridge and 881S. Again, there were no sightings, no contacts. However, at about 1400 on January 14, Battalion
informed us that the recon team inserted by 3rd Platoon on
the thirteenth had made contact with NVA on the north slope
of 881N, had wounded, and required assistance. I said we'd

provide same. Lieutenant Brindley volunteered to take his platoon to assist. Time was critical, both because the recon team could not carry its own casualties and because the platoon (Brindley's) would have about four kilometers to cover—two up and two back—to the north side of 881N. Since there were NVA in the area, the platoon had to be back on Hill 881S by dark since India Company's mission was to hold that hill; we couldn't leave large units out overnight.

Simultaneously, while I sent the 3rd Platoon north to recover the recon team, I ordered 2nd Platoon to return expeditiously from the southern patrol, which it did. Brindley's 3rd Platoon shucked its packs, flak jackets, and all except weapons, ammo, and water, and literally double-timed to 881N in three squad columns. We planned but did not register fires because, one, we didn't have time, and, two, we didn't know exactly where the recon team was. In that country it was risky tactics, but justified, Tom and I felt, by the situation and by the fact that the platoon knew the terrain intimately, having patrolled there several times before, both day and night, in the past month. In less than two hours, about 1600, the platoon found the recon team, set up a landing zone to evac the wounded, and returned to 881S, arriving about 1900 with the six uninjured recon team members in tow. There was no contact. Upon debriefing the recon team, we discovered that during the contact they had abandoned a radio and some [code] sheets. We so reported to Battalion.[1]

26th Marines Command Chronology _____

Enemy sightings and contacts increased slightly during the first two weeks of January, and emphasis was shifted from harassing and reconnaissance activities to probes. Reconnaissance teams consistently made sightings or saw indications of heavy enemy activity, and contact was made frequently. Each contact and sighting added to an evolving pattern which indicated that the enemy was increasingly interested in the defensive posture of Hills 950, 881S, 861, the Combined Action Company at Khe Sanh village, and the combat base itself.

During January 9–13, patrols from the CIDG camp at Lang Vei made five contacts. Similarly, a rash of sightings along the perimeter of the combat base culminated in the slaying of five of a party of six NVA near the wire on the night of January 2–3. Later in the month, the wire was reported cut and replaced by the NVA in such a manner as to escape detection.

1/26 Command Chronology ⎯⎯⎯⎯⎯⎯⎯⎯⎯⎯

On January 14, increased emphasis was placed on the defense of the Khe Sanh Combat Base as a result of an overall intelligence build-up in the 26th Marines area of operations. An additional company was placed in the perimeter to meet the increased enemy threat.

JANUARY 15

26th Marines Command Chronology ⎯⎯⎯⎯⎯⎯⎯

At 1120, a patrol from India Company, 3/26 [near Hill 881S] found 50 old fighting holes which had been cleaned out and showed recent use. Also found were three canisters of 82mm ammunition with Chinese writing.

During the afternoon, a Special Forces patrol observed 30–35 NVA bathing in a stream and called in artillery fire from the Khe Sanh Combat Base. Artillery resulted in 10 NVA KIA (confirmed).

MGen TOMMY TOMPKINS
3rd Marine Division Commanding General ⎯⎯⎯⎯⎯⎯

On January 15, I decided that Colonel Lownds didn't have enough people at Khe Sanh—he had a regiment less a battalion—so I sent a UNODIR—"Unless Otherwise Directed" —to LtGen Robert Cushman [III Marine Amphibious Force commander]. I told him I was going to send another battalion in. I waited sixty minutes, didn't hear from him, and so began loading [2/26] in.[2]

2/26 Command Chronology

The 2nd Battalion, 26th Marines, was relieved of the Phu Bai Tactical Area of Responsibility on January 15 by the 5th Marines. An advance party [had] departed on January 14 to establish facilities in the Dong Ha Combat Base to receive the remainder of the battalion, which was to depart Phu Bai on January 16 and 18. However, on the afternoon of January 15, the destination of the battalion was changed from Dong Ha to Khe Sanh.

The arrival of 2/26 at Khe Sanh marked the first time since World War II that the 26th Marine Regiment was whole.

HM3 DAVID STEINBERG
3/26 Battalion Aid Station

January 15, 1968

My Dearest Sharon,
   I was sitting on the airstrip at Dong Ha awaiting a flight to Khe Sanh. Would you believe I sat there twelve days, and slept there also? Back at the airstrip this morning, I was still sitting there on my thirteenth day, and it looked bad for me as far as getting out. Suddenly, out of the sky came, not a bird or a transport plane, as planned, but a lousy helicopter. Well, I drove my ambulance full of needed supplies aboard, and off we flew for Khe Sanh, elevation 1,500 feet in the mountains. I started to say a prayer as we lifted off because, the day before,

one of these copters crashed, killing 40 Marines.

Needless to say, I made it safely, as did my ambulance. I had a heck of a time backing it off the copter with a trailer on it, but I made it and am now joined again with my unit.

Khe Sanh is at the top of South Vietnam, on the Laotian border. It is in a jungle region where, unlike the rest of Nam, we have no rice paddies. Here, we have Montagnard Indians of the mountain tribes. Elephants are plentiful and have been sighted. I keep my weapon close at hand to shoot elephants with gym shoes out of trees. You can tell they're there by the peanuts on their breath.

Presently, it is 0115, January 15, and I am on watch. Actually, I am to lay awake in my rack for two hours and listen for sirens or incoming attacks. My watch ends in fifteen minutes and I can wake my relief and go off to sleepville. This candlelight may be romantic, but it sure makes letter writing hard.

JANUARY 16

2/26 Command Chronology _____

Commencing at 0800, 2/26 was flown by fixed-wing aircraft to the Khe Sanh Combat Base. Upon arrival at Khe Sanh, the battalion established an assembly area west of the combat base. All four companies closed the assembly area before darkness. Foxtrot Company moved from the assembly area to the northwest to occupy Hill 558 at 1400.

Capt EARLE BREEDING
Echo Company, 2/26 _____

I went to a meeting down in what looked to me like an underground dungeon—Colonel Lownds's command post. I had worked for Colonel Lownds years before, when he was a regimental intelligence officer and I was a slick-sleeve private acting as his chief scout. I didn't even know he was the 26th Marines regimental commander until I saw him in his command post bunker because 2/26 had never once worked directly for Regiment since it had been in-country. I didn't think he remembered me, but he did.

I was standing in the back, minding my own business, while he delivered his pep talk. At one point he said, "We're going to hold," and, looking at me, "Aren't we, Captain Breeding?"

I was stunned, but, never being at a loss for words, I said, "Colonel, as long as Echo Company is here, Khe Sanh will hold."

You can imagine the look the brass gave me, but, in a way, that's how it worked out.

JANUARY 17

2/26 Command Chronology _____

On January 17, the remainder of 2/26 conducted a tactical march to Hill 558 to form a battalion defensive position to block enemy movement through the Rao Quan Valley. After a reconnaissance of the area, the companies were deployed as follows: three companies formed a perimeter defense encompassing Hill 558 and one company [Echo] was chopped to 3/26 and occupied high ground west of Hill 558. Reinforced platoon-size patrols were conducted from the battalion's position to determine the enemy's location and disposition.

HM3 DAVID STEINBERG
3/26 Battalion Aid Station _____

January 17, 1968

My Dearest Darlin',
    It is 0400 in the morning and I am on watch. I just sit here and think about you. What else can

take my mind off war and put me into the future at a time very near, yet far, when I'll be home again. We have so much to look forward to and many memories to cultivate. I miss you so much, but thanks to all your pictures I can stare at you as though you were right before me.

I guess that Khe Sanh is getting to be an important place nowadays, and I even heard that the Stateside newspapers call it the hotspot of Nam. Things are quiet, although we have spent a week filling sandbags and building bunkers. Hanoi Hannah (the Tokyo Rose of this war) has told us on the radio that they would take this place. I thought it was all talk, but General Westmoreland was here today, and enemy troops are a day away.

We have to set up a clearing station for casualties, and I have been working with the battalion surgeon, getting a treatment facility and a medevac landing zone set up here. While nothing may ever take place, we will be ready in case something breaks.

It is funny to walk in Khe Sanh because, being at 1,500 feet on top of a mountain, the clouds roll along the ground. It's like a fog except it rolls in small white patches. When there is a thick cloud cover, it's like being in heaven, and you're lucky to see two feet in front of you.

Well, I have to hold reveille on the troops, so I'll close. Sharon, you know that I truly love you and always have you on my mind. Well, Smokey Robinson is on the radio, so excuse me while I do the boogaloo.

JANUARY 18

26th Marines Command Chronology _____

There was a sudden increase in enemy sightings, and heavy activity was noted on the extensive trail networks to the north and northwest of the combat base.

JANUARY 19

Cpl WILLIAM ROBERTSON
Logistics Support Unit _____

Until mid-January, whenever we went to the trash dump, there would be at least a hundred montagnards out there. We didn't ever have to unload anything. We just backed the truck up and they would unload everything, going through and getting wood or anything else they felt they could use. Starting in mid-January, the number of montagnards at the trash dump started dwindling down. When I went to the dump on January 19, there probably weren't fifteen montagnards there. That was enough right there to let me know that things were bad. These people knew what was going on. They had their intelligence sources. They were clearing the area, moving out.

Pfc ELWIN BACON
Kilo Company, 3/26 (Hill 861) _____

My first time as point was when we took off on a routine patrol on January 19. We took a route that had been taken many times before by our platoon as well as others. We headed northwest up a little smaller ridge between us and Hill 881S. When we got to the summit of the hill, the area was pretty well open except for the tall elephant grass that is typical of the region. However, the trail was well walked on in the past so there was no reason at first to see fresh footprints on it. But it didn't take but a few steps to realize they were a lot different than the prints our boots would make.

I stopped and motioned to the guy behind me, who I think was one of the snipers. I didn't like the look in his eyes when he looked back at me. The squad leader was called up immediately and a discussion took place, but I was completely left out.

About this time we could hear the clanging of heavy

metal in the valley just below us. This was accompanied by
the distinct voices of Vietnamese, and they weren't trying to
talk that loud either. The squad leader went back and talked
on our radio. The word came down to be alert. We had
support fire from our 4.2-inch mortars coming into the
valley.

As pointman, I was looking down the trail, not knowing
what I would do if something moved up the trail toward me,
but I stayed in a crouched position until the 200 mortar
rounds were delivered into the valley below.

Smoke and the sounds of screaming people were all that
came out of that hollow. At this same time we could hear
small-arms fire coming from the direction of Hill 881S. We
stayed there for a few minutes, then my squad leader came
up and told us that we had orders to go down into the valley
and report on the results.

I was told to lead out at a slow pace, and that was just
what I did. The bridal step is about the speed we were
going, knowing from the sound that there were many mad
bastards still making noise down there. I knew that they
knew someone was watching them and that they would be
looking for us also.

God was with us. Well, at least the battalion commander
was, because we only got about fifty or so feet when I was
told to stop. We had direct orders from the Khe Sanh base
to get back to our hill. I guess it took us about an hour and a
half to get to that position, but it took us only about ten
minutes to get back to our base on Hill 861.

1stLt JOHN KAHENY
1/26 Combat Operations Center _____

The commander of the battalion 106mm Recoilless Rifle
Platoon, 1stLt Paul McGrath, came in to tell me about a
"neat stunt" he had pulled. He told me that he and his
platoon sergeant had taken a starlight scope—a piece of

highly classified equipment—and had gone out and tracked "a platoon of Charlie Company" as it was making a night patrol. Since I worked in the operations center, I knew that the Charlie Company patrol was not operating anywhere near the position Paul described. It must have been a reinforced platoon of NVA. I did not want to ruin Paul's career by telling the story, but I did have to do something. I went to the battalion commander, LtCol James Wilkinson, and told him the story, but added that I could not reveal the source. Lieutenant Colonel Wilkinson did not press me to tell him.

HM3 DAVID STEINBERG
3/26 Battalion Aid Station _____

January 19, 1968

My Dearest Sharon,

Well, they're at it again with no mail for a week. Bullets, bandages, and bombs have priority over mail, so we have plenty of everything except mail.

We have been on alert for three days now and the tension is easing up because the NVA said they would attack yesterday, and they didn't. I even slept in a six-foot-deep foxhole last night.

The month of January is about over, and time is really moving now. I can hardly wait to get home so we can be together. I can't tell you how much I miss you, Sharon. I'll just have to be content with your picture and, of course, your letters and cards, which are great, just like you.

Nothing too much new because the Nam is the same from day to day. Your letters are all that make a difference, and thoughts of you make me feel closer to home.

On January 18, India Company, 3/26, on Hill 881S, was directed to dispatch a patrol to recover a radio and codes that had been left behind in the wake of the January 14 ambush of a recon team on Hill 881N.

Capt BILL DABNEY
India Company, 3/26 (Hill 881S) _____

2ndLt Richard Fromme's 1st Platoon—reinforced with a section of M-60 machine guns, a section of 60mm mortars, and the 81mm forward observer—jumped off about dawn on January 19. Since there were no friendlies to the north, we both preplanned and registered 81s along the route. First Platoon maneuvered carefully, and, about noon and about 500 meters short of the crest of 881—that's the south side of the hill—made point-to-point contact with an NVA unit which Fromme estimated to be about platoon size. It was maneuvering south along the same finger. There was brief fire fighting, during which 1st Platoon's pointman killed the NVA pointman. In accordance with my instructions, Lieutenant Fromme immediately withdrew 300 meters and called in 81s to his front. There was no further contact and the radio and [code] sheets were not recovered. We never got to where we thought they might be.

I also sent squad-sized patrols around 881S to check out the valleys on either side while Fromme was going north. No contacts, no sighting, but it was obvious to me that something was about to happen.[3]

Lt RAY STUBBE
1/26 Battalion Chaplain _____

[DIARY ENTRY] It's almost hard to keep track of the casualties. Lieutenant Yeary and Corporal Healy, from Recon, [killed] on Sunday [January 14]. One was one of the worst casualties here; he received an RPG round, and his whole body from the diaphragm down was missing. Then Wednesday [January 17], the Air Force plane [crashed] with the pilot and FOB [Forward Operating Base] man killed. Both were charred. In fact, the bodies were still simmering. Then more casualties the same day—two dead, four wounded.

Now the men from India Company, 3/26, at Triage. One was the 3/26 chaplain's clerk who wanted to go back to the field. He was hit in the groin. Then a man with a back wound; they put a tube in his chest to drain off the internal bleeding. Then two heat-exhaustion cases.

Then a dead [India Company] Marine, hit in the right eye socket. I helped carry him to Graves Registration. The others left. All there was was myself and an empty tent, a stretcher over the corpse. The sun was shining on the toes of two combat jungle boots.

Now, six more casualties. Then two Bru *children* were brought in with shrapnel wounds. One girl had her femur broken, crying in almost a chant, and had to go to the hospital in Danang. The other, a boy, had minor wounds.

26th Marines Command Chronology _____

Intelligence reports . . . [are] showing a tremendous movement south from the DMZ and east from Laos, of large numbers of personnel and several trucks. On one occasion, tanks were reported just across the Laotian border on National Route 9. As a result of this information, the regiment began conducting heavy H&I [harassment-and-interdiction] fires on known and suspected enemy locations. . . . Planning commenced for the interdiction of enemy avenues of approach by CS [tear gas] chemicals and special [delay-fuse and cluster] bombs to be placed in position in early February.

BOB BREWER
Quang Tri Province Senior Adviser _____

The enemy we faced was quite human. They had the same physical discomforts, bad habits, morale problems, etc., etc., as we did. It was important, then, to read each piece of intelligence in that light. They made mistakes, and often repeated them. In looking for those indicators of the coming attack, I constantly encountered these little human foibles that helped sort things out. For instance, I knew that getting food to the assembly areas would be an enemy problem. Solution: Look for Communist midnight requisitions in the nearby pacified areas. When not much happened in that vein, I suspected that the hostiles might try a forced march from the DMZ around Cam Lo District timed to arrive just before the battle. In comes the Marine intelligence officer from Khe Sanh with a question, "Why are the villagers around Ca Lu being ordered to make hundreds of paper cones?" Elementary! So the NVA can put them on their flashlights as diffusers when they go for their forced march!

Capt HARRY BAIG
26th Marines Target Information Officer _____

When Khe Sanh was invested by the 304th and 325C Divisions of the People's Army of Vietnam (PAVN), a 3rd Marine Division Intelligence augmentation team was flown to the combat base for the purpose of assisting in the development of intelligence and target information. It consisted of myself and Maj Robert Coolidge. A third member, Maj Jerry Hudson, had arrived earlier and had been appointed intelligence officer of the regiment. Major Coolidge became the 3rd Marine Division intelligence representative and Special Intelligence Officer and I became the regimental Target Intelligence and Information Officer. Together we developed the intelligence and target information, which helped deny the ambitions of General Giap and destroy the best part of two enemy divisions.

I went to Khe Sanh with four assumptions in mind:

a. That the enemy would conduct the investment of the base in accordance with a master plan, prepared and promulgated by a headquarters other than that of the field force conducting a siege.

b. That, because of this, the North Vietnamese commander in the field could not and would not alter the battle plan to any significant degree, regardless of facts bearing on the subsequent situation on account of doctrinal requirements—other than to retire from the field.

c. That the modus operandi was predictable and the general concept determinable once the opening moves had occurred (or were revealed—as in fact happened).

d. That the plan encompassed classic siege tactics as practiced and studied by General Giap during and after the siege of Dienbienphu and as modified by experiences at Con Thien in September 1967.[4]

Maj JIM STANTON
26th Marines Fire Support Coordination Center _____

The activities reported around to the north, west, and south were very heavy. As an artillery aerial observer, I flew mission after mission and saw literally hundreds of North Vietnamese soldiers in their bright green, easy-to-see uniforms. They were in large numbers, they were bivouacking in the open, they were doing things that made it very difficult for Marines to patrol. I could go out and recon areas by fire and *always* get North Vietnamese to scatter. I knew where to shoot artillery and get immediate reaction by their troops on the ground and in the open.

Capt DICK CAMP
Lima Company, 3/26 _____

I could smell them.

PART TWO

ASSAULT

January 20–21, 1968

Chapter 4

JANUARY 20
ATTACK ON HILL 88IN

Capt BILL DABNEY
India Company 3/26 _____

[Following the patrol contact on Hill 881N on January 19], I
requested from Battalion permission to have a reconnaissance-
in-force to 881N with India Company, reinforced, the next
day and to man the perimeter of 881S, with Charlie Battery,
1/13, Radio Relay, our 106mm recoilless rifle section, and
other noninfantry personnel. I asked them to send up a
platoon from Mike Company, 3/26, which was then at the
Khe Sanh Combat Base perimeter, to help man the 881S
line while we were gone.[1]

HM3 MIKE RAY
India Company, 3/26 _____

The morning of January 20 started early. First call went out
at 0530, with 1stSgt Willis Happlo, affectionately known as
"Happy," sticking his head into each bunker to wake us.

Little did we know that this day would take us into a fiery hell and back. Many would never receive another first call.

When I emerged from my bunker a few minutes later, the sun was up. The day was clear from our vantage point on Hill 881S. But, as I looked over the valleys and mountain slopes around the outpost, I could see that all but it and the highest peaks were enveloped in fog.

There was small talk among some of the boys in the 3rd Platoon, mostly about how short a time each had and how good it would be to get home. Some had only a couple of months, others a little longer. Me? Well, I had only been in-country a little over two months, so I didn't get too excited with the conversation.

When I finished my meal, I headed for my bunker to inventory my aid bag. I wanted to make sure I had the necessary items—battle dressings, tourniquets, and morphine. I didn't want to be caught short in case the shit hit the fan. I then took a few minutes to write a short note to my wife and son. I left it with my personal gear so it would be found and delivered if I didn't return. This was a ritual before each patrol into the bush. I feared that I would get blown away and my family would have no last word from me. I didn't dwell on death, but I thought endlessly about the sadness I would bring into the lives of those I loved in the event of my death. This made me fear my death.

The word was finally passed around at 0800 to saddle up and get into platoon formation. The order of march would be the 3rd Platoon, then the 1st Platoon. The 2nd Platoon was to be held in reserve. By 0830, the 3rd Platoon departed the outpost. This patrol was to be a company-size move, but not in mass. Each platoon was to act independently. Once we left the hill, we didn't see the rest of the company again.

We moved silently away from the hill, keeping our intervals as we slipped through the waist-to-head-high elephant grass. We followed the trail down from our vantage point into the valleys and sloughs and then edged along the ridges of the lower hills. We came down through the fog cover. As we went deeper, the bright sun turned into a faint glow. Then, in time, we were in a gray, overcast world. The fog must have been at least several hundred feet thick! Moving as slowly and cautiously as we did, it took quite some time to get completely through that fog.

The morning grew long, but eventually we reached the base of what I later found was our objective, Hill 881N. The platoon paused there for a short time and then started our long climb to the top, entering the fog a short time later. Time seemed endless while we moved only short distances at a time without being able to see the sun.

The fog was still pretty thick, even though the platoon had started through. The word came down the line to take a short break. The word was usually to take fifteen minutes, but we expected ten, and most of the time we only got five. This time, though, it seemed like we got the entire fifteen minutes. I sat on that well-worn trail in the fog, in silence and alone with my thoughts. I don't remember all that went through my mind, but I do remember wondering why we had stopped. Our intelligence had been telling us that the enemy's presence was here in force. This was hard to believe because there had been very little contact, and none of it had been by our battalion. We had gone out a couple of times to rescue some recon elements that had gotten into trouble, but both times all we found were dead bodies.

My thoughts rambled through that and the two small fire fights I had been involved in since I had been in-country. I did not want to be involved in any more, but found that desire unlikely since I had been in-country only a short time. I drifted in and out of reality, looking into the long, sober faces of those men closest to me, both in front and behind me. I could see in their faces the fear of the unknown that I felt inside. I wondered if my eyes revealed the same about me. I felt a sense of responsibility to them for two reasons. First, I was older than the average trooper in the platoon. Second, they called me "Doc." They expected me to be there if they went down. I represented to them the link to life, the small thread to which they could cling when there was no hope left. They expected me to save them from death, and at the age of twenty-two, that was a heavy

burden to bear. I had already found that it didn't always
work that way.

Soon the signal to move came silently down the trail. As
each man passed the signal to another, he rose to his feet
almost instantaneously. The column started to move as
slowly as ever, but it was with the hope that we could reach
our objective and return without incident.

The platoon had only moved a few meters when that
gut-wrenching sound rang across the silence of my mind.
The first shot was fired. The sudden rush of adrenaline
made me want to instantly vomit. Before I could blink an
eye, there were more shots fired. These had the distinctive
pop of an AK-47, and I knew that I would be dead before
long. From then on, events took place so rapidly that they
are difficult to remember. The whine of bullets could be
heard all around. The fire fight intensified. The platoon
finally recovered from the shock of being taken by surprise
and started returning fire. The initial sickness remained even
though we were minutes into the fire fight. It seemed the
enemy was on both sides. They were so close that their
grenades rained in on us from everywhere.

Capt BILL DABNEY
India Company, 3/26 _____

The right platoon [1st], under 2ndLt Richard Fromme, held
fast on good ground. . . . Lieutenant Thomas Brindley's [3rd]
platoon, on the left, found itself pinned down on exposed
ground about two hundred meters short of a commanding
knoll from which the North Vietnamese were firing with
telling effect.[2]

Capt DICK CAMP
Lima Company, 3/26 _____

I was in my rack, resting and sort of listening in on the
chatter over the battalion tactical radio net, when the India
Company platoon commander announced that he was under
attack. Shit, I thought, this is it. I was so sure the whole
battalion would counterattack that I ordered Lima Company

to saddle up and get ready to fly to Hill 881S. But the call never came.

HM3 MIKE RAY
India Company, 3/26 _____

The cry "Doc, up!" rang above the noise of the fire fight. I wanted this to end. My God, what was I doing here? I had been in fire fights before, but nothing like this. I tried to move forward in response to the call for "Doc." The fire was so intense that I felt I couldn't move, but I did, slowly, holding the earth close to my breast. Fear gripped every fiber of my being. As I moved forward, I began finding the wounded. My squad leader was a sergeant from Kentucky, a hill boy. He would play his guitar and sing at night when the situation permitted. He wouldn't sing again for a long time. His chin had been shot off from the corners of his mouth to about three-fourths of the way back to his throat. He asked me, "Doc, how bad is it?" I didn't have the heart to tell him. He asked me for morphine, but I refused, telling him I didn't want him to be a litter case while he could still walk. I gave him a large battle dressing and told him to hold it to the area where his mouth would have been. I sent him back down the trail, promising him, when things quieted and when it came time for his evacuation, that I would give him the coveted morphine.

There was another call, "Doc, up!" This boy had gotten a piece of sharp metal from a grenade. It had entered to the right and below his left eye, gone through the roof of his mouth, and exited under his chin. This left a small but gaping hole that bled profusely. I administered first aid and sent him back.

I moved forward, for the first time looking at my hands. They were caked with mud, but the liquid agent, I realized, was blood. What a putrid smell! I will never forget that smell; it was an indescribable smell. I rolled from my belly to my back and tried to wipe my hands off on my utility pants. Some of the debris crumbled from my hands, but it was under my fingernails too. I realized that I was too busy to worry about something like that. As I resumed my prone position, I saw a grenade bounce onto the trail not more than twelve feet in front of me. It was like staring a rattlesnake in the eye, on his level. I hollered, "Grenade!" and buried my face in the dirt and waited for it to go off. It never did, thank God. Who knows what damage it would have done.

I moved forward. By the time I reached the point where the grenade had been, it had been disposed of. Someone had thrown it back from where it came. By this time, relief had come. We had gotten our pointmen out and we were to fall back. There are no words available to describe this scene. It was panic—pure bedlam. The retreat was anything but orderly. Men got up and ran in a low crouch, dropping magazines full of ammunition and grenades. They kicked these items as they ran. I'm surprised they didn't leave their weapons where they stood. The platoon leader, 2ndLt Thomas Brindley, was screaming for people to pick these items up as they went. Few listened. As the lead men in the platoon came by me, I could see the terror in their faces. This was the first time I had looked into their faces. I followed, finding myself at a plateau about halfway between the top and bottom of the hill. The pointman was delivered to me seconds later. The other platoon corpsman was beside me. We looked into the face of the dead trooper at our knees. We looked at each other and a nonverbal message transmitted between us: there was no doubt in either of our minds that he was dead. We made the attempt to save his life—CPR, mouth-to-mouth, and starting an IV solution of serum albumin, a blood-volume expander. The IV could not be started because there was no blood pressure to expand his veins. There was no pulse and no breathing, but still we tried. His flesh was cold to the touch, his lips were blue, and his eyes were half open and lifeless. There was no one in there. He was dead.

This was the man for whom the first call "Doc, up!" had gone out. Could I have saved him? I don't know; he was shot bad. If I had taken more of a chance with my own life—the ultimate gift of risking my life for his—would he be at home with a family now? How could I have altered time and history? Someday I may know, but for now I can only wonder. I suffered with the burden of that man's death for years. I considered myself cowardly and tried desperately to block it out of my mind. I will never forget. I can see his face as clearly now as I did that day. I was responsible; maybe I even let him down when he depended on me for life. He was dead. Not the first I had seen, but each time the horror of the violence sends every sense reeling. The touch, smell, sight, and taste of war leaves its mark on those who remain. Sometimes I think those who died were the lucky ones.

For the first time in over an hour and a half I had the opportunity to sense what was going on around me. Now that I wasn't so busy trying to stay alive and care for the wounded, I had a wider perspective of what was going on around me. I realized the fog was gone. The sun was shining brightly and the cool, muggy morning had turned into a sweltering furnace.

Capt BILL DABNEY
India Company, 3/26 _____

A squad of the 2nd Platoon was assigned to provide security for a medevac landing zone immediately behind the heavily engaged 1st Platoon. As the medevac aircraft [a CH-46 helicopter] approached the zone, it was hit by a burst from an antiaircraft weapon and immediately caught fire. The pilot, apparently realizing the consequences of crash-landing a burning aircraft in a landing zone where several severely wounded men were staged, sheered off into a gully and made a controlled crash about 200 meters west of the zone, close to where the antiaircraft fire had come from. The members of the landing-zone security force immediately and spontaneously, without waiting for orders, rose from their positions and charged down the side of the hill at high port toward the burning aircraft. The suddenness and speed of their rush probably ensured its success and the quick extrication of all Marines from the aircraft before it was engulfed in flame. About five NVA soldiers, who, unknown to the Marines, were between them and the crash site were so surprised by the mad dash that they turned tail and ran off to the west.[3]

HM3 MIKE RAY
India Company, 3/26 _____

We had pulled what the Marines called a retrograde. I called it a retreat. Whatever. We were no longer engaging the enemy. We medevacked our wounded and dead. The platoon leader called for fire support and we got 106mm recoilless fire from our outpost on 881S. The fire continued for fifteen or twenty minutes. During that time, we talked about what had just happened—more like joked, trying to cover the fear we all felt. We believed, with all the fire being leveled on the top of the hill, that there could be nothing left. The fire subsided and we all wondered what was going to happen. We didn't have long to wait before the word came down: "Take the hill and hold it."

Capt BILL DABNEY
India Company, 3/26 _____

[Lieutenant] Brindley, a man who was by nature not inclined to retreat, realized he could not hold his present position without support, and so he directed several barrages of artillery on the [NVA-held] knoll. Moving his Marines into position under cover of the shell fire, he then launched a classic infantry assault and stormed the hill.[4]

HM3 MIKE RAY
India Company, 3/26 _____

My gut turned flip-flops and I became instantly sick. Who was the nut who gave that order? Didn't he know we could be killed?

   That was an insane order. Our platoon suffered ten casualties—nine wounded and one dead—from our first contact with the enemy. One of our two M-60 machine guns was out of action, and the remaining one only had 500 rounds of ammunition left. For an M-60, that's nothing. The troops had divided their grenades and ammunition equally. Then the clincher came. Not only were we to capture the hill from the entrenched enemy, we were to do it in a certain manner. We were to form skirmish lines, fix bayonets, and take the hill.

At that very moment the rush of adrenaline was sufficient to make me feel as if hot lead had been poured through my veins. My heart started pounding in my ears, my mouth became dry, and I again became sick to my stomach. I took a drink from my canteen and realized I didn't have a choice; someone else had made the decision for me. The line formed as the troops affixed their bayonets to their weapons. I thought it was stupid enough to go back up there, but to expect hand-to-hand combat—I couldn't imagine it. To get into a fire fight when taken by surprise or ambushed is one thing, but to go in knowing the enemy is probably going to be there to greet you is another.

Nonetheless, the 3rd Platoon moved forward with me to the rear of the skirmish line. I found myself hoping the enemy had gone, had run away, but it was not to be. As we climbed closer to the summit, we started drawing fire. I found myself on a trail, which I left quickly for the cover of the elephant grass. I looked around and quickly found I was alone. My God, what would I do? I was lost! I feared two things the most. One was being killed by a sniper and the second being taken prisoner. That's exactly what ran through my mind at the time—"I'm going to be taken prisoner."

The fight had intensified in its fury, and I could hear the bullets ripple through the elephant grass above my head. For the first time, I drew my weapon and cocked it. I wished my head could turn 360 degrees continuously. I shook with fear, still trying to decide what to do. Finally, with gun in hand, I jumped back to the trail, hoping that from there I would be able to at least see other troopers. Just as I landed firmly on the trail so did a young Marine. He had been in the elephant grass only a few feet in front of me. We were both relieved to see each other. I reholstered my weapon as we talked about what we should do.

I never carried a bigger weapon than my .45-caliber automatic pistol. I always felt that if the situation dictated that I become offensive there would be plenty of other weapons lying around. I found that a long weapon was too cumbersome and only got in my way while I was doing my job.

The fire fight was very intense by this time. We could hear the wounded screaming for help, and it seemed as though one lay only a short distance in front of us. The Marine said, "Let's go help him, Doc." I replied, "Lead the way. I'll follow." We crawled forward, following the call for help. We had gone about half the distance when, out of nowhere, the Marine in front of me was shot. The bullet entered his upper thigh just below his hip, traveled along the bone, and exited just above his knee. It whizzed past my left ear. This stopped us short in our quest, and we decided that we should remain where we were. I ripped his pants leg open and checked his wound. It was a neat entrance and exit wound with little bleeding, so there was not much I could do for him at the time.

Lost, with no help, battle raging around us, and now a wounded trooper for me to take care of. The rest of the platoon must be close, but where? Which way to go? I thought east, then west. Then I thought the worst thought of all: *Prisoner of war.* A vision flashed across my mind of what I thought being a prisoner would be like. I didn't like it, so for lack of direction, we stayed where we were. Where was the sucker who shot the Marine? Was he toying with us? Were we in his sight now? Was he squeezing the trigger this instant? Yet we stayed there, not knowing what to do. For fear of doing something wrong, we did nothing.

Suddenly, my senses returned to reality and I could hear the screaming of the wounded. The cry for help rang above the intensity of the battle. I saw the elephant grass to my left move, and all my fears were once again manifest in my head. I drew my weapon and nudged the Marine, pointing in that direction. We both turned to face the oncoming doom. Once again, my heart beat like a drum in my ears. My whole body shook. We readied ourselves, I with the thought of now dying. We raised our weapons. I took the slack out of the trigger and waited. We didn't have to wait long. A gun barrel appeared. Then a head. Thank God, it was a friendly face! He smiled and said, "I came to get you guys. The platoon is right over here." The tension left my body, and if I could have, I would have collapsed. I was sick again. My "savior" turned, and I followed without question. I didn't care how he knew we were there. Maybe it was just luck, but I didn't want to know. I just followed. With the wounded Marine between us, we moved off through the elephant grass. Just a stone's throw from where we had been, we joined what was left of the platoon. They were in a tight 360-degree defensive position, firing just enough to keep the enemy from pouring over us. We were hurt; we had no momentum left. I only hoped the enemy could not make an offensive move. We would have been eliminated in the twinkling of an eye.

Capt BILL DABNEY
India Company, 3/26 _____

[Lieutenant Brindley] was killed as he reached the crest [of the NVA-held knoll], and with numerous other casualties, the [3rd] platoon found itself holding the piece of high ground with depleted ammunition stocks and . . . a lance corporal in command.

An enemy skirmish line then charged up the rear slope to retake the hill but was annihilated by a napalm drop so close to the Marines that several had their eyebrows singed.[5]

HM3 MIKE RAY
India Company, 3/26 _____

We finally got close air support. I was impressed. Never before had I been in such a position that it was needed. Jets started coming in. They were so close, they almost gave me the impression I could reach out and touch them. I watched plane after plane come in. One pilot turned his head our way, and if his visor hadn't been down, I believe I could have seen his face. Those big bombs came slipping from underneath the planes. They looked like they drifted effortlessly to the ground. Once they made contact, the results would lift us off the ground. The napalm was neat. I enjoyed watching it tumble end over end and then seeing a huge fireball rise high into the air.

Capt BILL DABNEY
India Company, 3/26 _____

The situation, however, was still desperate, and, with Fromme [1st Platoon] holding on the right, I took [2ndLt Michael] Thomas's reserve [2nd] platoon across the intervening gully to relieve the Marines on the knoll and move the wounded back for medevac.[6]

HM3 MIKE RAY
India Company, 3/26

The 2nd Platoon moved up to enlarge our perimeter. The 2nd Platoon leader brought his platoon forward, distributing his men to the north of us. He laid down about six feet in front of me. The cries of our wounded still rang out. The lieutenant turned and said, "I want four volunteers and you, Doc. We're going to get our boys." I thought, "Why me? I didn't volunteer." The lieutenant got up in a low crouch in preparation to move forward, but instantly got back down into a prone position. Then he said, "Okay. We're ready to go." He got up, but fell to the ground. This time he had a bullet wound to the gut and another to the head. He was dead by the time he hit the ground. The clincher is that the bullet that ripped through his guts also sliced through my shoulder and lodged in another Marine's ankle. Three with one shot! Not bad! One dead and two wounded.

I had been lying down with my head across my left shoulder, because the weight of my helmet had been difficult to bear. When the lieutenant had said, "Let's move," I had looked up. The bullet that had gone through his guts whipped past my face. I saw the bullet; not many wounded can boast of that. When it exited his canteen, my perception was that a solid stream of water connected me to the lieutenant. The water spiraled, and so did the bullet. The water spread out as the bullet moved along. It sounded like the first drops of an impending rainstorm. The bullet came so close to my face, I first thought it had smashed through my chin. I heard a loud slap—much like hitting a bare butt with an open hand—as the bullet violated my flesh. I moved back a foot or two in an attempt to get away from what had already happened.

The bullet carried water from the canteen the lieutenant was carrying in the small of his back. The bullet was so close that the water it brought with it from the canteen stung my face. I thought the water was blood. I grabbed my face in terror. I rubbed the liquid between my fingers and looked at it. No blood! I quickly repeated the action. Only this time, the wetness had dried. Still no blood! Even though my face still stung, there was no blood. By then, however, the pain in my face had been replaced by a larger one, the one in my shoulder. As I realized I was not hit in the face, I grabbed my shoulder. Luckily—if you could say anything of that nature is lucky—the wound was minor. The bullet missed my shoulder socket and left my bones intact.

The other platoon corpsman had worked his way around the platoon and found me. He dressed my wound and gave me some words of encouragement, then he moved on to tend other wounded men. Next, the company senior corpsman [HM3 Robert Wickliffe] appeared and told me to gather the wounded and prepare them for evacuation. He also said he would need my help taking them down to the medevac point. We got a couple of Marines to help us with litter patients. There were five of us wounded, plus two other Marines and the company corpsman. We moved down and away from the battle. The company corpsman took the lead and I took the rear. We moved quickly. I had my .45 in hand to protect our rear.

We reached the evac point and a chopper came in. We loaded all the wounded and then the company corpsman turned to me. Yelling to make himself heard above the chopper, he said as he slapped me on the back, "You can go or you can stay. The choice is up to you." I couldn't believe it! I hesitated. I didn't want to run out on my friends. The pilot of the chopper motioned for clearance to leave; he wanted to get out of there. I turned and hopped into the doorway of the chopper, sitting down with my feet and lower legs hanging out the door. The company corpsman smiled at me, gave the pilot the "clear" sign, and, as the chopper lifted off, waved good-bye. That was the last time I saw him. He was killed on 881S. He was a good man; he impressed me with the way he lived and with his ideas. He would have contributed so much to life. I miss him.

Capt BILL DABNEY
India Company, 3/26

Contact began about noon, and by 1500 it was obvious that whatever we found was more than we could handle. The rest of the afternoon was spent evacuating the wounded and dead, recovering the helicopter crew, and breaking contact. The Mike Company headquarters, plus a second Mike Company platoon, was sent to 881S, and the new platoon moved forward to cover our withdrawal.[7]

Sgt FRANK JONES
26th Marines Scout-Sniper Platoon _____

I spent two days down at the airstrip because we could see the fight in the hills from there. I kept trying to get on a chopper and go out there so I could be with my snipers, but I ended up carrying wounded Marines off the medevac choppers. I couldn't believe the wounds those guys had. They were missing big chunks of their skin, their faces, their legs, their private parts. They were crying and screaming.

26th Marines Command Chronology _____

It is estimated that India Company had made contact with an NVA battalion. Results of this day's action were four friendly KIA, 39 WIA (medevacked), and 1 WIA (minor) with 103 NVA KIA (confirmed).

Capt BILL DABNEY
India Company, 3/26

The mission was still to hold 881S, so withdrawal was essential—not that there was much notice, since the prospects of success if we continued north were dim. There were a bunch of those guys up there, and they had come prepared to fight. During and after this scrape, we hosed down 881N and the ground between it and 881S until dark with air, 81mm mortars, 60mm mortars, and all the artillery we could get. For once, we knew where they were. We were not assaulted that night.[8]

Chapter 5

CHIEU HOI

Capt KEN PIPES
Bravo Company, 1/26 _____

Early in the afternoon of January 20, Bravo Company's 2nd Platoon reported the presence of a possible NVA waving a white flag on the northeastern side of the runway. At the same time, an Ontos with a Marine lieutenant acting as safety officer was at that location, preparing to fire on the "range" out toward Hill 1015. I happened to be in the area with my radio operator, walking the lines. With the Ontos on the range covering us, a fire team from the 2nd Platoon, the Ontos officer, and I moved some 500 meters outside the wire. The NVA soldier initially disappeared, so I shouted "Marine *dai-uy* [captain]" several times as we proceeded. The NVA soldier reappeared and surrendered. He was a lieutenant.

GySgt MAX FRIEDLANDER
17th Interrogation-Translation Team

We got a call on the radio in my bunker for me to go down to the east end of the runway to pick up a North Vietnamese lieutenant who had just surrendered. I got in my jeep and zoomed down there. I found several Marines holding the man, and they turned him over to me. When I first met him, he seemed very complacent, not a bit scared. It didn't appear to me that I had to worry about him running away. I put him in my jeep and drove him back to the bunker.

When we got to the bunker, the first thing I did was offer him a cigarette and ask him if he was hungry. He said he definitely was, so I got him something to eat. He devoured it very quickly.

He identified himself as Lt La Thanh Tonc, and he seemed to be kind of anxious to start telling me why he had surrendered and a lot of other information. While he was eating, he talked about his family. He was married and had several children. He was very disillusioned, especially with politics. For example, his superiors were telling him things he knew were not true. He obviously didn't believe in the cause he had been fighting for anymore. He had seen too many of his own people being slaughtered. He didn't like the way many officers had treated him. He was disgruntled because he had been passed over for promotion.

I liked the guy. I was sorry for what his family had been going through and what they were going to go through. He had not even been able to get a letter off to them for two years, which was not unusual for the NVA. Before he finished eating, he asked me if I could get a radio music channel from up north. I did, and he thoroughly enjoyed it. It was the first time he had heard music in a long, long time.

After a while, we got into the actual interrogation. At this point, without my having to goad him or lead him, he started telling me what was going to take place that night. My interrogation notes read as follows:

Hill 881N is presently surrounded. There is a company of sappers presently deployed in general area of 881N. This sapper company will be the company used against Hill 861.

Once Hill 861 has fallen, the general attack against the

Khe Sanh Combat Base will begin. This will consist of a
reinforced regimental-size force from direction of Lang
Hoan Tap by way of Hill 861, where they will link up
with the occupying force there. Once linked up, Khe
Sanh Combat Base will begin receiving heavy artillery
fire and rockets from unknown positions, but from north-
westerly direction. When this occurs, the first regiment
will move to assault positions under cover of fire. One
mortar platoon on northeast side of Hill 1015 will cover
the Marine heavy weapons on Hill 950. One mortar
platoon will begin 82mm mortar barrage on parked helicopters and airstrip. Each of the mortar platoons has one
12.7mm antiaircraft gun platoon in their adjacent areas to
cover them from counter air attack. If the first and second
regiments are forced to withdraw, they will link up with
the third regiment (position unknown) and commence
another attack on Khe Sanh Combat Base. This will occur
before Tet.

At this point, I broke the interrogation off. The other ITT
man who was in on the interrogation stayed with him while
I literally ran down to the regimental combat operations
center with this information. Colonel Lownds sent me straight
down to Lang Vei by chopper to tell them what the lieutenant had said. Then I came right back. All the other information was sent down to 3rd Marine Division headquarters, at
Phu Bai, and General Westmoreland's headquarters, in
Saigon. Also, at the same time, alerts were put out to all the
units in and around the combat base, out along Highway 9,
and in the town of Khe Sanh.

I continued the interrogation when I got back to the ITT
bunker. The lieutenant was at ease. Once he saw how it was
going to go—once I explained that he was going to be sent
to a prisoner-of-war camp and how he would be treated
there—he opened up even more. I got a lot of detail about
various units that were going to be involved in the attacks
on the hills and the base. I also got a lot of information on
routes they were using, types and numbers of vehicles—the
information I got was just endless.

MGen TOMMY TOMPKINS
3rd Marine Division Commander _____

Lieutenant Tonc revealed to our interrogator not only the dispositions of the two assault regiments of the 325C Division (the 95th and 101st Regiments), but also the general plan of attack, which was to take place very early the next morning. I decided that we would accept Tonc's information as valid since we had nothing to lose and much to gain.

Capt HARRY BAIG
26th Marines Target Information Officer _____

The battle plan for Khe Sanh, as revealed by Lieutenant Tonc, had a complementary plan, which was to take effect in the Eastern DMZ, Cua Viet, Dong Ha, and Quang Tri at the same time and on the same night as the commencement of the overture to Hills 881S and 861. Until that time, I was the 3rd Marine Division Intelligence coordinator for military intelligence agencies in the division tactical area of responsibility. The 15th Marine Counter-intelligence Team and U.S. Army intelligence units had established collection nets far across the Ben Hai River [in North Vietnam]. These nets had penetrated several NVA headquarters and other organizations. One of the tasks of the net was to report movements of the 4th Battalion, Van An Rocket Artillery Regiment, and of the Vinh Linh Rocket Battery, together with those of their escorting infantry. These units had caused much damage to the Dong Ha and Cua Viet bases earlier, during the summer and autumn of 1967. On the night of January 19–20, 1968, the rocket units moved south once more. Reported and traced along their route by the agents of the 15th Counterintelligence Team, the batteries and their escort were caught and trapped against a bend in the Cua Viet River. Prisoners taken reported that their mission was to rocket the airstrips at Dong Ha and Quang Tri on the early morning of January 21 to prevent helicopters from flying in support of Hills 881S and 861.[1]

1stLt NICK ROMANETZ
Charlie Company, 1/26 _____

Right away, word went out for everyone to wear helmets and flak jackets. Not only that, we were ordered to sleep in our fighting positions and stay at 50-percent alert on the lines.

□

ATTACK ON HILL 861

Cpl DENNIS MANNION
Charlie Battery, 1/13 _____

On the morning of January 20, I was sitting in my bunker, on the north side of Hill 861, next to a 2,000-pound-bomb crater. We were listening to the artillery requests and jumping the radio frequencies, listening to India Company's fight on Hill 881N. We weren't in any position to help.

Sometime around noontime, someone on the western side of the hill spotted five or six North Vietnamese soldiers on the top of the ridge 500 yards away from us. They weren't visible for more than a couple of seconds, but Capt Norman Jasper, the Kilo Company commander, asked me if I could fire some artillery at that spot. We fired thirty or forty 105mm rounds from the combat base. We had registered targets over the two previous days, so most of them impacted pretty well right up on that hill.

Captain Jasper wanted to send out a platoon to see if it could find anything as a result of the shelling. As the only artillery forward observer attached to Kilo Company since we had arrived on Hill 861 in very late December, I had been on every single patrol off the hill. I volunteered to go with the Kilo platoon on January 20. I didn't have to go on this one because it was only going 500 yards and would be within sight of the hill the whole way. I was so casual about it that I wore my low black Converse sneakers.

We went out the north gate, crossed over through a deep, wooded ravine, and on up to the ridgeline west of Hill 861.

Just as we got up into the area where we could see the impact of the rounds and smell the cordite, we got a call on the radio to come back in. The patrol leader replied that we were right at the spot where the shells had landed and asked permission to drop down over the western side of the ridge, just to see if there were any blood trails or bodies. Captain Jasper personally came up on the radio and told us to come back—immediately, without even taking another look around. So we did. We were back on Hill 861 by 1700 at the latest.

As soon as the patrol was back, I was called with all the platoon commanders and platoon sergeants to a command meeting at Captain Jasper's command-post bunker. The captain told us that we were supposedly going to get attacked that night by a fair-sized number of North Vietnamese soldiers. He told us we would be on 100 percent alert. His concern was with the platoons, but he spoke with me about the targets we had pre-registered with the 105s at Khe Sanh.

During the late afternoon, we registered 175mm guns located nineteen miles away at Camp Carroll. They were programmed and targeted to strike into the area just north of the hill, which is a hell of a shot from nineteen miles out. We had to clear people out of the trenches on the north side of the hill while we were firing the 175s to mark the target.

We settled in to wait. Everybody cleaned their weapons and we ate our C-rations for dinner. Eventually, it got dark. It wasn't a real clear night, but it wasn't the worst fog we had seen up there. It was very dark.

Pfc ELWIN BACON
Kilo Company, 3/26 ⎯⎯⎯⎯⎯⎯⎯⎯⎯⎯⎯⎯⎯⎯⎯⎯⎯⎯⎯

January 20 was just another normal day—routine military life on a godforsaken hill. Nothing unusual was happening, but there were lots of rumors going around the hill that there was an NVA buildup in the area and that we could expect trouble. Everyone took it for granted that the CO would keep us on our toes.

It got extremely foggy that night. There was no visibility. I couldn't see outside my foxhole. I had to focus my ears for the perimeter watch, not my eyes. Hopefully, if anyone was out there, he would set off a tripflare.

Cpl DENNIS MANNION
Charlie Battery, 1/13 _____

At about 2030, after it got really dark, word came up from one of the platoons that they could hear the North Vietnamese outside the wire, down in the ravine off the northwest corner of the hilltop. That was the only place we couldn't put artillery. It was obviously the place they were going to attack from.

I made four or five trips with my radioman, from my bunker through the trenchline, to the 3rd Platoon command post. From there I could hear the NVA outside the wire. They were talking and giving commands. I could hear the wire being cut, could hear the tinny sound when the wire sprang back in both directions. We threw grenades and popped flares, but we never fired a shot. Captain Jasper had specifically ordered us not to because he didn't want us giving away our positions. The North Vietnamese took it—with laughter and an occasional scream. They kept right on cutting. It was almost as if they were out there on a high school field day.

Sgt MIKE STAHL
4.2-inch Mortar Battery, 1/13 _____

We had been running 100-percent alerts for quite a while. We'd all get out of our hooches, man the lines, wait until it was called off, and go back to our hooches. The night of January 20 was just like that. We had received a 100-percent-alert order from Regiment that, unknown to me at that time, was based largely on the information obtained from the North Vietnamese lieutenant who had surrendered that afternoon.

We went down and got into the trenches. Then, around 2300, the alert was secured and we went back to our hooches.

Pfc ELWIN BACON
Kilo Company, 3/26 _____

We—the 2nd Platoon—started hearing noises on a ridge to
the west of us. We had patrolled it on January 19. Now it
was swarming with gooks, and they were not being all that
quiet about it. Between us and the ridge was a steep-sided
ravine. We didn't understand what was going on.

It started by sounding like a party. They were making
noises with pans and blowing horns. They were also calling
at us with warnings of "Death tonight." Some of them had
had an English lesson or two in the Bronx, I think. We were
right in among the clouds, so the visibility was bad and I
was about ready to shit my trousers.

Cpl DENNIS MANNION
Charlie Battery, 1/13 _____

I was back in my bunker a little before midnight when
Captain Jasper called on the land line to tell me that
someone at the southern end of the hill had spotted some
North Vietnamese near the landing zone. He wanted me to
go down there in case artillery was needed. I grabbed my
rifle on the way out the door, but my radioman, Pfc Dave
Kron, took only his .45-caliber pistol and our radio.

Dave and I crossed over the top of the hill, heading south,
and made our way across the landing zone to find the
platoon commander in charge of that sector of the hill. He
told us that whoever had been out there had not been seen
since the original sighting, that they had been seen only
momentarily in the light of a flare when the fog lifted.

We were about to use the platoon radio to call back up to
the company command-post bunker, to see what they wanted
us to do, when, at that very moment, everything started up.

HM3 Malcolmb Mole was an all-around decent guy. He
wasn't the biggest guy around, but he did his job on all the
patrols I was ever on with him. He wanted to be a radio
deejay when he got out of the Navy. He was always going
around practicing his deejay voice and using radio sayings.

Just before Dave and I were ordered south to the landing

zone, Malcolmb had come up from the 3rd Platoon trenchline
to use the fairly elaborate shitter that was just to the right of
our bunker. Dave and I had seen him come out of the mist,
and we had tensed. But he had identified himself with that
radio deejay voice, and we had laughed out loud at that. We
spoke for a few minutes, and then Captain Jasper called.

Apparently the NVA opened up as Malcolmb was walking
back down to the northern trenchline after using the shitter.
He was caught out in the clear. There wasn't much left to
identify him.

Sgt MIKE STAHL
4.2-inch Mortar Battery, 1/13 _____

At about 2300, word came around to go on 100-percent
alert again. I woke up again, put on my gear, and went back
down to the trenchline held by Kilo Company's 2nd Platoon. This was the trenchline nearest the 4.2-inch mortars. I
went there because, as the 4.2-inch platoon sergeant, I was
useless when the crews were running their guns. When I got
there, one of the new guys asked me, "Gee, Sarge, do you
think we're really going to get it tonight?" Months earlier, I
had worked with the Special Forces out around Lang Vei and
I knew what we had out there; I knew it would be impossible to mass a meaningful assault on Khe Sanh without
someone in Saigon knowing all about it. So, being the sage
war veteran I had become, I told him, "There isn't a North
Vietnamese within a hundred miles of here." Just as I said
that, the first RPG slammed into the hill.

Pfc ELWIN BACON
Kilo Company, 3/26 _____

As the assault started, the first thing I knew was that the top
of the hill was being completely saturated with mortars and
RPGs. I could hear rounds from the NVA .51-caliber machine guns on the next ridge pounding into the hill. They
had at least three .51-calibers over there.

Sgt MIKE STAHL
4.2-inch Mortar Battery, 1/13 _____

I went down the trenchline to find the 2nd Platoon commander, 2ndLt Benjamin Fordham. By the time I found
him, 2nd Platoon had already begun taking casualties from
the incoming. Almost immediately, I saw green tracer and
heard the distinctive sound of AK-47s. We fought back, but
it wasn't easy. The rolling fog was extremely thick, which
obscured the North Vietnamese attacking up the slope toward us. Also, there was a lot of growth in front of us, and
we had not effectively covered the dead space with indirect-
fire weapons. We couldn't see them until they got to within
fifteen or twenty meters of the trenchline. We fired into the
fog, mainly at muzzle flashes and the sources of the green
tracer.

Pfc ELWIN BACON
Kilo Company, 3/26 _____

The NVA were coming through their own storm of fire. I'm
sure that better than half the casualties they were sustaining
were due to their own supporting fire. It was obvious to me
that they were drugged up. Some were not fully equipped
with weapons; they were picking them up from the dead.
They were coming through the wire and running around
from one hole to another, trying to find places to hide, to
jump out of. There was a tremendous amount of noise, a
tremendous amount of firepower being directed against the
hill.

Sgt MIKE STAHL
4.2-inch Mortar Battery, 1/13 _____

They penetrated several concertina barriers and evaded fougasse
traps, neither of which was very effective. They had apparently
reconned the hill very effectively, leaving behind bamboo
stakes they later set their RPGs and other weapons on so
they could hit our key positions and crew-served weapons.
Fairly quickly, they took out the company command post,

both of the 106mm recoilless rifles, and, eventually, the 81mm mortar positions at the top of the hill.

Cpl DENNIS MANNION
Charlie Battery, 1/13 _____

As soon as the RPGs and mortars started hitting the hill, my radioman, Pfc Dave Kron, and I headed back over the top of the hill, on our way from the landing zone to the northwest corner, where the attack was coming in. When we reached the Kilo Company command post, we found GySgt Melvin Rimel dead on the ground right outside. It was too dangerous to look for Captain Jasper or the first sergeant; rounds were hitting and bullets were going by overhead. Dave and I went right back down the hill, heading south, and then veered off toward the west side of the hill, toward the 2nd Platoon area.

When we got to the trenchline, without checking in with anybody, I started calling in target numbers for the ridgeline 500 yards to the west, the one we had hit with artillery and briefly scouted during the day. I pulled the rounds as close as I could get them to the northwest corner.

Communication by radio was extremely difficult because someone out there in the jungle was keying a radio handset, breaking up our voice transmissions and causing background noise over the open mike to interfere with conversation. For all that, the guns in the combat base were extremely good about putting in rounds. I couldn't necessarily see where they were going in, but I could hear them.

Sgt MIKE STAHL
4.2-inch Mortar Battery, 1/13 _____

Within ten or fifteen minutes, word began to spread from our right, from the 3rd Platoon area, that North Vietnamese were in the wire. Their sappers had gone up close by using the dead space in front of the 3rd Platoon trenchline.

Cpl DENNIS MANNION
Charlie Battery, 1/13 _____

As I called artillery fire from the combat base, Pfc Dave Kron and I moved up the trenchline, northward, toward the northwest corner. Then, suddenly, there wasn't anybody there. The last Marine we encountered told us, "I don't think there's anybody to my right. I haven't heard anybody up there in a long time, and nobody's come down from that direction." Dave and I continued up the trench until we got to a machine-gun bunker. There was only one guy in the bunker, and he was firing periodically. As we approached the bunker—the entrance was in the back, right in from the trenchline—we yelled that we were coming. The gunner knew my name. As we got inside the bunker entrance, I said to the gunner, "Where's your team?" He said, "They're gone. I don't know where they are." I asked, "What happened to them?" and he said, "I think they ran."

I asked him if he was firing at people he could see, but he said, "No, I'm just reconning by fire." He told me that there were plenty of North Vietnamese around. I asked him how he knew, and he told me there were grenade holes right by the entrance. I shined my red-lensed flashlight to see them. Sure enough! He told me that the North Vietnamese who had thrown one of the grenades was out in the trenchline, that he had been hit by his own blast. As Dave helped the gunner break out a fresh can of ammunition, I shined my light out real quick and saw a North Vietnamese soldier lying on the ground in the trenchline. I could hear him groaning.

The North Vietnamese soldier in the trenchline presented a problem. We had to get farther up the trenchline if we were to gain any real sense of where our rounds were landing. I took Dave's .45, knelt in the doorway, and reached out with my left hand until I touched the man's head. As soon as my hand made contact with the top of his head, he raised his head up. I put the .45 underneath my left hand, took my left hand away, and pulled the trigger four or five times. When Dave and I moved out from the bunker, we had to step right on the dead North Vietnamese to get by him.

We only went another fifteen or twenty feet before we had to stop. There was small-arms fire back down the trench. There were no Marines, dead or alive, in the trenchline between the machine-gun bunker and where we stopped. Dave and I hugged the inside wall of the trench, but we couldn't go any farther because of the gunfire. We continued talking with the fire direction center down at the combat base—we had been in constant communication from the very start of the action.

Our position was tenuous. The lead wasn't flying in every direction, but we couldn't go any farther. As I continued to direct the artillery fire, an RPG struck the front of the machine-gun bunker and killed the gunner whose teammates had run out on him. Dave and I pulled back most of the way to the bunker and climbed into two fighting holes we found dug into the side of the trench. We directed fire missions from there for the rest of the night.

Sgt MIKE STAHL
4.2-inch Mortar Battery, 1/13

All of a sudden, the 2nd Platoon began taking fire from the rear, so I maneuvered up to a .50-caliber machine-gun position which was just above the 4.2-inch mortar position. The NVA had already wiped that position out, killing the gunner and his assistant. I moved another Marine in there to man the gun and went back down to tell Lieutenant Fordham that they were in behind us, that he should shift some of his people to protect the rear.

While I had been up the hill, at the .50-cal position, I had noticed that I had not heard a lot of firing coming from the 3rd Platoon position. I brought that to the lieutenant's attention, and he said, "Well, we're going to have to send someone over there to check on the 3rd Platoon." I said, "Yeah, that's a good idea. I recommend that you do that." And he said, "Sergeant, I don't have anyone to spare. Guess what!" And I said, "Okay, no problem. I'll do it."

As I started maneuvering up the trenchline, a couple of guys asked me where I was going, and then they followed along. The only one I knew was LCpl Dennis Mutz.

As we maneuvered up, there was a tremendous volume of fire from our front, from four or five North Vietnamese who were in the trenchline, advancing toward us from the 3rd Platoon sector. The fog was very thick there, and they didn't see us until about the time we saw them. There was a furious fight. I emptied one magazine, popped it, threw another magazine in, and went through that, too. I killed the first guy. The second guy killed the Marine right behind me. I took a round in back of my left hand as I was dropping the next NVA. The next NVA hit Mutz, but not badly, and Mutz killed him. It was just a frenzy of firing from very close range.

Next thing I knew, I was face-to-face with a North Vietnamese. I had run through my second magazine. I had no bullets left in my M-16. He had me. He fired, but nothing happened. In that instant, I cringed and tightened up. Quicker than I could react, he bayoneted me in the right chest. Then Mutz shot him. The point of the bayonet punctured me and ripped downward. It didn't penetrate very far, but it broke a rib and left a gash. Not bad. The bayonet damaged my M-16, so I grabbed one of the dead NVAs' AK-47s and a magazine pouch.

Mutz and I continued up the trenchline. The volume of firing around us was incredible. At one point, Mutz said, "Fuck this. I'm not going any farther." It was not the sort of thing you ordered someone to do, so I left him there and continued to work up the trenchline alone. I didn't blame Mutz at all.

I eventually ran into the first 3rd Platoon bunker, which was firing at me. We had built the bunkers across the trenchline. They had apertures on both sides and the front, but none in the back. To get into a bunker from the trenchline, you had to duck your head, get on all fours, and crawl inside.

I tried to throw a grenade in through the aperture on my side of the bunker, but it didn't go in. It rolled back and blew up, and I caught some shrapnel. The explosion knocked back the NVA inside the bunker, and they quit firing. I managed to roll up next to the bunker and drop another grenade in. That killed several NVA.

About this time, there was a big explosion on top of the hill, to my right front. It was either the 106mm or 81mm ammunition. A lot of AK-47s were firing to my right, well inside our perimeter. It wasn't impacting around me, so I tried to continue up the trenchline toward the next 3rd Platoon bunker. I was looking for 3rd Platoon Marines to link up with, but I couldn't find any. In the next bunker were more North Vietnamese. I took it out with a hand grenade and then sprayed it through the aperture with my AK-47.

As I moved on the third bunker, firing into it from a distance, I heard someone yell something that sounded like *"Chieu hoi!"* I stopped firing and yelled back, "Come on out, motherfucker!" And they did; the three North Vietnamese in there surrendered. I guess they must have seen me take out the second bunker, and I'm sure they thought there were more of us than me. When they came out, two had their hands up, but the third was an arrogant, defiant type of guy. When I motioned them back down the trenchline with my AK-47, the last one tried to grab my weapon. I broke his jaw with the AK's butt, which took the fight out of him. I herded the three down to where I had left Lance Corporal Mutz, and I told Mutz to take them back to Lieutenant Fordham.

I went back up the trenchline because I still hadn't made contact with anyone from the 3rd Platoon. While I was gone, no one had occupied the three bunkers I had retaken, and the fourth bunker was empty. I found Marines in the fifth bunker. The gap in the line had to be seventy-five meters, so I went back to tell Lieutenant Fordham that he needed to shift troops into the gap. I led them back up, placed them in the bunkers, and left them.

Pfc ELWIN BACON
Kilo Company, 3/26 ―――――――――――――――

The word got passed down the line that every other man was to go over and support the other side of the hill, where the main assault was getting through. The hill was just a mess of people. I couldn't tell who was next to me, who was friend, who was foe. There was no way to count off every other man. It was mass hysteria.

I got the feeling that we were by ourselves, that there weren't going to be any supporting elements coming to help us out. We couldn't get any direct fire support from Khe Sanh that night. I think it was because we were so close to the enemy. They must have thought they would blow us up, too. The only thing we got was some illumination, which, mixed in with the NVA illumination, gave us some shadowy indication as to who was coming up the hill or down the hill. The hill was just a mass of people fighting, some hand-to-hand. Total chaos and fear filled everyone who was on that hill. Because of the heavy fog that mixed with the darkness, we had little chance to focus on who or what was coming toward us.

Capt BILL DABNEY
India Company, 3/26 (Hill 881S) ――――――――――

When Hill 861 was assaulted from the northwest on the night of January 20–21, the NVA attacked up a slope that was not within high-angle range of the Khe Sanh Combat Base artillery, and was masked by the hill itself from any other Khe Sanh supporting fires. Our two 81mm mortars fired several hundred rounds on that slope, well-controlled by the Kilo Company command post on 861.[2]

LCpl WALT WHITESIDES
3/26 Tactical Air Control Party (Hill 881S) ―――――

All the troops on Hill 881S were put on alert, and we went out to the trenchline. The 81mm and 60mm mortars were firing in support of Kilo Company, on Hill 861. The mortar tubes became so hot that the gunners poured water and fruit juice on them to cool them off. When the NVA fired illumination rounds to guide the attack, we also fired some. This was intended as a deceptive measure in case they were using the illume rounds to orient themselves. This probably just provided them with additional light, since they probably knew their attack positions very well. Everyone was apprehensive as to what was going on, and we were all wondering when *we* were going to be attacked.

Pfc ELWIN BACON
Kilo Company, 3/26 _____

I was scared shitless, totally in fear. I wasn't quite paralyzed—I did what I was told to do—but I had no idea what to expect, what was going to come down the ridge at me. My mind was blank; I was totally caught up in trying to survive. The hill was totally out of control. Sometime during the night, teargas was set off. On the 3rd Platoon side of the hill, we had a box type arrangement that was full of CS canisters that could be shot out in all directions. I assume it was tripped. Maybe the NVA set it off. I don't remember anybody wearing a gas mask. I was so psyched up in the fight that the gas didn't affect me at all.

Sgt MIKE STAHL
4.2-inch Mortar Battery, 1/13 _____

After dropping off the 2nd Platoon Marines in the four unoccupied 3rd Platoon bunkers, I went up the side of the hill to a silent .50-caliber machine-gun position. The Marines in the position were dead, so I started firing the machine gun in front of the 3rd Platoon bunkers that I had retaken. That was where most of the North Vietnamese were. As soon as I opened fire, they threw every goddamned weapon they could in against me. I got a shitload of RPGs and .51-cal, and I think I was even taking some mortar fire. It

was a real pain in the butt because I didn't know how to fire
a .50-cal real well; no one had ever explained the nuances
of headspace and timing to me. I expected to be really
working out with the machine gun, but I'd get off only two
or three rounds before I had to recock it. I was taking so
much fire myself that the position caved in around me and I
had to keep repositioning the gun, lower and lower. I got hit
a few more times with pieces of shrapnel, but nothing really
major. It went on like that until the firing let up, hours later.

*Sgt Mike Stahl was awarded a Navy Cross for his role in
stopping the NVA attack on Hill 861.*

Cpl DENNIS MANNION
Charlie Battery, 1/13 _____

I fired as many rounds as the 105s at the combat base could
give us. At the same time, the 175mm guns at Camp Carroll
were dropping some seriously big stuff down into the ravine,
as close as they could get it. But the way the guns were
lined up with the hill, there was no way they could get
rounds right down into the dead space the North Vietnamese
were using to get in up through our wire. They tried, but
they couldn't do it. I know that there were at least five or
six 105mm rounds that hit the southeast side of Hill 861.
They were fired by the guns in the base, which were trying
to skim the rounds right over the top of the hill.

Pfc ELWIN BACON
Kilo Company, 3/26 _____

The first sign of it letting up was daylight. We were able to
make out silhouettes, but the fog was still so thick that we
couldn't really see much. The NVA withdrew, but some of
them got caught and were unable to get outside the wire.

We found NVA bodies all the way up to the command-
post area. It was just saturated with bodies. There were dead
bodies everywhere I looked. Many of them had towels over
their faces or plastic bags over their heads—instead of gas
masks.

Sgt MIKE STAHL
4.2-inch Mortar Battery, 1/13 _____

When the sun came up, we began to police the hill. We took their dead down to a flat place and burned them to keep the rats off them. We got our badly wounded down to the landing zone and called in medevacs, but they couldn't get in because of the thick fog, which just didn't burn off.

We were hurt very badly, and about out of ammunition. If they had tried one last assault, they'd have had us. I was down to a .45-caliber magazine for my pistol, less than a magazine for my AK-47, just about bingo on my last can of .50-cal, and I had two grenades left. No one could have been much better off.

We had a lot of wounded, and our leadership was gone; the company gunny had been killed early in the battle, the first sergeant was holding the ends of his severed carotid artery together to keep from bleeding to death, the company commander had been very badly wounded, maybe more than once, and the company radioman, who remained at his post, had been blinded by powder burns from a bursting grenade. The Marine survivors were physically and mentally drained. Fortunately, so were the NVA survivors. We wound up punching ineffectually at one another, like punch-drunk fighters who were unable to muster a last blow or give up. Anytime they wanted to get back on line and take us, they could have.

Pfc ELWIN BACON
Kilo Company, 3/26 _____

I was asked to guard one of the prisoners, of which there were only two. They did have three, but one tried to crawl away and was dispensed with. My prisoner was covered with a poncho, and the only thing that was showing was his wounded leg. Someone told me that he was only thirteen years of age while the other one, who they had on the landing zone, was sixteen years old. I was told that the older was an officer and the younger was some sort of noncommissioned officer.

Even though I was very emotional after the night's activities, I offered this guy a cigarette, but he motioned refusal by spitting at me. Boy, did I go through cigarettes that day!

Sgt MIKE STAHL
4.2-inch Mortar Battery, 1/13 _____

There were still NVA between the two outermost wire barriers. The Marines didn't have the strength to go out and get them, and they didn't have the strength to come in and get us—or, apparently, withdraw. It was a stalemate.

Kilo Company eventually received some replacements and was reinforced by a platoon from Alpha Company, 1/26. More important, the adjacent hill, dubbed 861A, was occupied on January 23 by Echo Company, 2/26, which was transferred to the operational control of 3/26.

Chapter 6

JANUARY 21
ARTILLERY ATTACK

2ndLt SKIP WELLS
Charlie Company, 1/26 _____

On January 20, Charlie Company had been moved from the
battalion reserve and assigned the northern part of the
perimeter, north of the airstrip and opposite the water point.
My 3rd Platoon had the center, 1st Platoon was on the left
(west), and 2nd Platoon was on the right (east). We had
responsibility for the east end of the airstrip; 2nd Platoon's
lines extended just south of it and tied in with Bravo
Company.

When we got to the position, all the bunkers were entirely
above ground, there was no continuous trenchline, and in
places the existing trenchline was only about waist-deep.
There was one line of triple concertina, and the elephant
grass came right to the trenchline in spots. I think the main
reason our position was so poor was because it was on the
north side and was not a very likely spot for the NVA to

attack; there wasn't enough room—800 meters—between the gorge and the perimeter. That's a poor reason for being unprepared, but I think that's what happened.

Once we were assigned our sector, I further assigned the squads. We did it by the book: I put out the listening post (the company command post monitored it), set up both M-60s, and began digging the trench. But it was much too late, so my platoon began the night mostly aboveground. We did no work on the bunkers. We worked until about midnight, and then went to 50-percent alert until about 0300. We were still working when the first rounds came in.

Cpl WILLIAM HUBBARD
Echo Company, 2/26 _____

January 20 was the day I was supposed to go home, but I didn't make it out. A whole planeload of boots showed up and they sent me and six or seven other short-timers down to the runway to pick them up. We got them all unloaded and then had to get them to set up tents. There were all kinds of Marines there—gunnery sergeants, lieutenants, guys just out of boot camp—and none of them knew up from down about being in Vietnam. We always said if they didn't have any time in-country, they didn't count, so we put a bunch to work digging trenches, burning shitters, setting up tents, carrying seabags in. It didn't matter if they were privates or officers, we ordered them around. It was up to the short-timers to help the new guys learn the ropes. *We* had the only rank that mattered—experience.

About ten of us—the guys who had been there a long time and a few new gunnery sergeants—slept in the company first sergeant's tent that night. We knew we were going down to the helo pad the next morning to catch a chopper out to Phu Bai and Danang so we could head back to The World. We knew there was a lot of activity around the base; we could see it in the hills that evening. But, mostly, our minds were on going back to the States.

About 0400, I bummed a cigarette off a friend of mine, Corporal Houska, from Hotel Company. He asked me if I knew what that morning was, and I said, "I sure do. We're next."

At just about the crack of dawn, all the guys in the first sergeant's tent got up. I started feeling sorry for the new guys in the next tent. I had been through it all, was getting out in one piece, but they had it all ahead of them. Lots of them were going to get hurt or killed.

I was thinking about that when I heard a rocket. It sounded just like a roman candle going off. Everybody in my tent reacted. I threw the tent flap back and yelled for all the boots to get their asses out. "Get in them holes!" At about the time I finished yelling, I remembered I had left my rifle on the deck in the tent. Cardinal sin. As I turned around, about seventy-five of those boots ran right up over me and right into the trench. I got up cussin' and heard more rockets. Scared me! Half the Marines in the trench were out there without their rifles, and most of them didn't have their boots on. We had some boys there that were pretty salty, and they took care of the boots pretty quick; sent them back in to get their rifles, helmets, flak jackets, and boots.

Sgt FRANK JONES
26th Marines Scout-Sniper Platoon _____

The Sniper Platoon was assigned to provide security for the North Vietnamese lieutenant. I was given the swing shift, 1600 to 2400. After the assignments were made, a bunch of us were drinking some home brew with dehydrated orange juice when Sgt Terence Smith came up and asked me if I would trade shifts with him. He had been assigned the graveyard shift, from midnight to 0800, but he wasn't feeling well. I told him I'd be more than happy to do that for him.

Nothing happened during my original shift. I got up at midnight and went down to relieve Sergeant Smith. All I took was my .357 handgun—no cartridge belt, no rifle. The lieutenant was at the communications center, in an eight-foot-thick concrete bunker. To get in, I had to go through an eight-foot tunnel almost on my hands and knees. I told Sergeant Smith to go on and sleep in my rack. I had some ammo boxes laid out, a rubber air mattress blown up, and my poncho liner and mosquito net hung up.

The lieutenant was young—twenty-five or twenty-six years old—about five-nine or five-ten, and weighed about 150. He had on a khaki uniform. I heard he had advised us that we were being surrounded by several North Vietnamese divisions, and that they were well supplied with mortars, artillery, and rockets—that they could hit us with several hundred rounds of artillery and rocket fire a day until summer came. He had said they were going to overrun us and annihilate us, the way they did the French at Dienbienphu. I thought about how stupid it sounded. I had no opinion. I had been drinking, and I didn't really want to hear it at that time.

Sometime after 0500, January 21, he had to go to the bathroom. He was handcuffed to my partner and me, and we escorted him outside the bunker to one of the piss tubes. We thought nothing of it. As we were walking back, he stopped. The next thing I saw was what appeared to be gigantic orange beach balls—five or six of them—bounce in front of me, about fifty or sixty yards away. It was incoming rockets or artillery rounds exploding. I hadn't even heard them coming in.

They started getting closer. I was terrified. The rounds were hitting all around us. It seemed like the whole Earth had exploded. I wasn't hit, and neither was my partner, but we were so scared that we lay down next to the bunker with the NVA lieutenant handcuffed to us. There was an empty cardboard box that a case of Cokes had come in. I took the box and covered up with it. Finally, I scrambled to my feet, got my partner and the lieutenant, and scrambled back inside the bunker.

LtCol JIM WILKINSON
1/26 Commanding Officer

I was ready for it. As soon as the first rounds landed, I jumped off my cot, got on my helmet and flak vest, and

raced from my living bunker over to the command post. By
then, the mortars were really starting to fall in. I took a dive
and slid in down the staircase.

Lt RAY STUBBE
1/26 Battalion Chaplain _____

[DIARY ENTRY] Woke up to the sounds of rockets whizzing
and loud blasts! We were under rocket and mortar attack.
Rockets and mortars were going off all over. Got dressed
slowly, stunned, cautiously. I knew my bunker would
protect me from flying shrapnel and perhaps a direct hit
by a 60mm or 82mm mortar, but not by a 122mm rocket.
I was all alone, so I knew I had to run to the Charlie-Med
bunker. The whole area was lit up. The [supply dump]
was on fire to the east, with the smell of burning sandbags and the tar drums, and gasoline from the [fuel] area
was on fire to the west. Red flares lit up the sky all over,
and there was a lot of whizzing, cracking, and exploding.
They came in quite rapidly; there were brief pauses, a
couple of seconds. I cautiously went to the door, wondering if I dared run the seventy or so feet to the
Charlie-Med bunker. A round would come whizzing in
and explode nearby. This went on for about fifteen
minutes. I knew that one must never run in an attack, but
that it is much safer just to lie flat on the ground. Finally,
I just ran the short distance to the trench bunker of
Charlie-Med.

Cpl WILLIAM ROBERTSON
Logistics Support Unit _____

When I got to Khe Sanh in July 1967, the base Ammunition
Supply Point [ASP] was sitting on top of the ground. We
were on the edge of the perimeter. On two sides of us there
was nothing, on one side was a 105mm artillery battery, and
back on the other side was where the motor pool people
stayed. We went through a long quiet period, but we more
or less knew it was only a matter of time before we were
going to get hit. The ammo dump was volatile. Through

pestering Colonel Lownds, we were finally able to come up with a bulldozer. During the process of digging berms, we got down deep enough and built up some protection around what we had to leave on top of the ground. But the berms were still only about fifty feet apart. This was not very safe due to the amount of ammo we had there. We were trying to get another location so we could spread the ammo out. When our staff sergeant left in December, I was in charge.

When the rockets or artillery—whatever it was, came in, one struck within probably thirty feet of my bunker. It hit one of the motor pool sandbag bunkers, right at the edge. It knocked the sandbags out. A rather large tree was in the center of the bunker, holding up the steel stakes that were holding the sandbags and the roof. The end of the tree fell down and crushed one of the men who was sleeping in a cot. There was enough concussion to shake me out of my cot.

We grabbed our clothes and headed out. By this time, quite a few rounds had come in. The ASP was on fire. There was very little we could even attempt to do. The only things we had to fight fire with were two shovels and about twenty 55-gallon metal drums full of water that were sitting around through the dump. We had buckets sitting beside those. Once an illumination magazine caught, buckets of water and shovels of dirt couldn't do anything. We just had to make everybody get out and get back to the bunker.

LCpl DAN ANSLINGER
3rd Marine Division Air Section _____

I had been dumped at Khe Sanh on January 20 while "playing hooky" from my unit, which was at Dong Ha. I was aboard a helicopter that landed at the combat base as all hell was breaking loose in the hills. The chopper crew kicked the load off—including me—and left to fly some emergency mission. I was technically absent without leave.

I found my way to the fire support coordination center

because I knew some guys working there. It was also one of the few decent-looking bunkers in the combat base.

On the morning of January 21, the fire support coordination center was crowded with people coming and going. Everyone seemed tense, calm, and cocky at the same time.

Right after the heavy incoming started, the dump blew up with the most godawful explosion I had ever experienced (including when the Dong Ha dump blew the previous September). The concussion knocked me around inside the bunker, and I thought that no one near the dump could have survived. I was surprised when I later learned how few people were killed.

1stLt NICK ROMANETZ
Charlie Company, 1/26 _____

We were on Red Alert because the NVA lieutenant had indicated that something was going to happen. We were sleeping with our helmets and gear. Unfortunately, some of the early rounds hit the ammo dump, which we were close to. The ammo dump started blowing up and it was just raining mortar rounds, artillery rounds, smoke grenades, and gas grenades all over our sector. We were really concerned that some of those rounds, which were hot, could have been very sensitive. We tried to locate them and get them out of our trench or wait until the Explosive Ordnance Disposal people came to remove them. Suddenly, a lot of people were thinking, Geez, this is what it's all about.

There was a lot of C4 plastic explosive stored near us. It took a round and started to burn. It sounded like a lightning bolt that cracks through the air and strikes the ground close to you.

2ndLt DONALD McGUIRE˙
Explosive Ordnance Disposal _____

Several rounds landed in Ammunition Supply Point No. 1, initiating secondary fires and detonations that continued for approximately forty-eight hours and resulted in total destruction of the ASP. Unexploded and hazardous ordnance was thrown to an approximate 2,000-foot radius in all directions from the ASP, contaminating the airstrip, the 26th Marines regimental command post, living areas and quarters, artillery and mortar positions, and the eastern defense perimeter.

LtCol JIM WILKINSON
1/26 Commanding Officer _____

The shock wave from the ammo-dump explosion cracked the timbers holding up the roof of the 1/26 command post. As the roof settled, several members of my staff were knocked to the floor. The battalion adjutant was injured but continued to function effectively. For a moment, I thought that the entire roof of my command post was going to collapse, but after it settled about a foot, the cracked timbers held. We quickly made jury-rig repairs and the command post was not affected.[1]

MGySgt JOHN DRIVER
Explosive Ordnance Disposal _____

The dump held about a dozen 55-gallon drums of CS teargas crystals. These were broken open and their contents were scattered throughout the dump.

LtCol JIM WILKINSON
1/26 Commanding Officer _____

We had been alerted to the possible use of gas, so I had ordered all the troops in 1/26 to be carrying gas masks. We were ready.

Cpl WILLIAM ROBERTSON
Logistics Support Unit _____

We had one person in the bunker who didn't have a gas mask, and we didn't have any for anyone except for the guys who lived there. We had to sit on him and hold him so

we could put towels and water on his face. He wanted to go
back out and attempt to find a gas mask. This would have
been certain death, as close as we were to the ammo dump
and as much stuff as there was flying around.

Lt RAY STUBBE
1/26 Battalion Chaplain ⸻

[DIARY ENTRY] All of a sudden, someone yelled, "Gas!" It
was CS. Not everyone [in Charlie-Med] had a mask, so they
used wet blankets over their faces. I put on my mask and
immediately felt claustrophobic, but I knew I had to have it
on, so I fought a tremendous battle in my mind and kept it
on.

Cpl DENNIS SMITH
Bravo Company, 1/26 ⸻

Teargas was being blown back and forth around the base by
the breeze. I would say that about half the people at Khe
Sanh had gas masks, and that only about half of them were
serviceable. But that was all inconvenience. Rockets were
another matter.

1stLt NICK ROMANETZ
Charlie Company, 1/26 ⸻

We had to don our gas masks and man the lines. We kept
looking out into the fog to see what was going on.

Lt RAY STUBBE
1/26 Battalion Chaplain ⸻

[DIARY ENTRY] Practically everyone [in Charlie-Med] had to
piss very badly, but no one would go out. We just held it in.
Rounds kept falling and exploding. Flashes of light. A
round landed near the triage tent.

  They started bringing in casualties. One man, conscious
and eyes and head moving about, had all his abdominal guts

hanging out. The doctor later told me that the man would die. I was numb; I didn't even go over to comfort him.

HMC FRANK LILES
Base Preventive Medicine Chief _____

So there we were, getting shelled from outside and inside. During this time, several people were wounded and needed to be brought to the medical station, Charlie-Med. Marines and medical personnel alike were busy getting the wounded into the aid station to administer emergency treatment. There were several wounded Marines on stretchers and under treatment when an explosion rocked the top of the aid station and a shell came flying through and into the medical supplies. It was spewing dangerous white-phosphorus smoke. Here's where I got to be a John Wayne hero. I have no idea why I chose to get that shell out of the way. I mixed copper sulfate with intravenous solution in a couple of old towels, wrapped it around the shell, and ran it outside. On the way, the fire was still spewing and was burning my face and arms, and the smoke and fumes were searing the inside of my chest. I couldn't wait to get rid of that hot prick of a shell. Just as I got down into the mud ditch alongside the sickbay, the damned thing went haywire and began getting hotter and spewing more. I couldn't do anything more with it because they were bringing a wounded Marine through the bunker door at the same time, so I climbed that sucker with a flak jacket and field jacket until they got that young man by. This was just a matter of five or ten seconds, but it was enough to burn my face and cause a hell of a lot of respiratory distress.

I made it back into the aid station and went back to my room. To really make my day, those little fuckers had scored a direct hit on my room, getting my new tape deck. I was pissed, pissed, pissed. Next thing I remember was waking up in Danang hospital.

1stLt JOHN KAHENY
1/26 Combat Operations Center _____

I went to the battalion commander's living bunker—which
served at the time as our alternate command post—with the
operations chief, the battalion sergeant major, and a few
other Marines. As we sat out the initial volleys, we had a
young lance corporal out front guarding the door. Every
once in a while, one of us went outside to see if he was
okay since he had just a small hole with no overhead cover
for protection. My turn to check the lance corporal's welfare
finally arrived. As I got up and reached for the door of the
bunker, a round hit right outside and blew the whole bunker
door in, throwing all of us against the wall and covering us
with a lot of dirt, debris, and shrapnel.

I received a long, thin piece of wood in my thumb. I
pulled it out, turned to SgtMaj James Gaynor, and said,
"Sergeant Major! Look! I've been wounded!"

"Well, Lieutenant," he replied, "you better run as fast
as you can to the aid station to get your Purple Heart,
because that thing's liable to heal before you get there."

Sgt FRANK JONES
26th Marines Scout-Sniper Platoon _____

All we could hear on the radios was word about the
incoming rounds. The only thing we could hear was that
there was heavy artillery coming in, that rounds were
exploding, that the combined action company in Khe Sanh
village was being overrun by the North Vietnamese.

There was no way to see out of the bunker, but I could
hear all the explosions outside. I thought I was having a
heart attack. I was hyperventilating and had chest pains. I
was very scared. I was twenty-three years old, and I was
scared almost to death. I thought we were being overrun,
that they were in the wire, because I heard it on the radio
from the combined action company, which was calling in

fire and air strikes on his own position. I didn't know then that he was at Khe Sanh village, and not at the combat base.

They just kept pounding us. The dust and dirt was falling in. It seemed like everything became very pronounced—I could really smell the odor of the sandbags and the dust, the sounds were magnified, the colors were brighter. I sat with my back to a pillar, looking at the entryway tunnel into the bunker. I had my six-shot revolver and was thinking I would stack up anyone who came through the tunnel in front of me. We kept hearing the lieutenant in Khe Sanh village calling for artillery to be fired on top of his own position. It was like listening to a movie. I couldn't believe it was happening, that they were overruning us, that they were going to take us down. I started thinking that we were all going to be killed. I kept having chest pains. I kept talking and laughing, trying to keep my partner calm and not let the NVA lieutenant know that we were scared.

LtCol JIM WILKINSON
1/26 Commanding Officer _____

I was mentally prepared to be hit by rockets; it took nothing for a few guys to hump in and set up a rocket, warhead, and launcher. But the artillery was something else. It was completely unexpected; we didn't have a clue it was out there. I was not prepared for it, and the implications of its being there worried me.

HN ROD DeMOSS
26th Marines Regimental Aid Station _____

We all made it to the bunker, but the regimental aid station was pretty much destroyed. Quite a bit of the damage was from our own ammo dump. We took care of the wounded the best we could, but the bunker wasn't big enough for the wounded who kept coming in. This was my first taste of treating combat wounds, but one guy really stood out in my mind. One of the Marines came in with a completely blue face. A blue smoke canister had gone off in his face and the pigment was pretty well embedded in his skin. It wasn't a funny situation for him, but the sight of it was comical to me.

Sgt FRANK JONES
26th Marines Scout-Sniper Platoon _____

It seemed like it went on all day. The artillery really only came in from about 0530 until 0800. Then it just got quiet. We heard people on the radio asking for casualty reports. I was too scared to go outside the communications bunker. I was afraid of what I'd see or what I'd find. I had to have been thinking that we were the only people left alive on the base. I crawled outside the bunker, laid flat, and looked around the corner. It looked like the moon. There were craters everywhere. There were bodies. There was no noise. There was a lot of dust settling. The smell of gunpowder— the smell of war—was in the air.

I was sure we were the only ones left, that they had overrun us, that everyone else was dead. I didn't see anybody moving, and nobody was around. I crawled out a little farther and heard a lot of small-arms fire, and a lot of what sounded like hand grenades going off, or mortars. I didn't know at the time that it was our ammo dump cooking off.

I got up on my feet and headed down for the sniper hooch. All the tents I could see were burning and leveled. There were vehicles blown up, and the runway had big holes in it. Nobody was moving. I crawled and ran to the sniper hooch, but it was empty. The whole east end of the combat base around the ammo dump—including what used to be my hooch—was leveled. There was no tent.

The first person I saw was Sergeant Dooley, another sniper. I asked him where everybody was. He said some of them were wounded, a couple were dead. He told me that Sgt Terence Smith was dead; the sergeant I had traded shifts with—the man who had been sleeping in my rack—was dead. I couldn't believe it. I went down into the bunker next to the tent and called for him to find out where he was. I felt around in the dark and grabbed an arm that was up in the air. When I pulled on the arm, the top half of a body came down. When I looked, I saw that it was Sergeant Smith. It scared me and I got out of the bunker. As I did, a close buddy who had been wounded came up to me. I just hugged him. I was relieved to know that anyone was alive after all that.

They took me over to a position on the perimeter. There was some whiskey there, and we drank it. We tried to get a damage assessment and a body count, tried to figure out who we had and who we had lost. It was chaotic, but we got the count. Then we were assigned out to different sections of the perimeter. I was sent to the south side of the base. All my gear, including my sniper rifle, had burned up in my tent. I picked up an M-16 I found lying around and started digging in. I talked with the Marines around me, about home and what we would do if they hit us again. At this point, we had a determined attitude. We knew that they had waxed our ass, that if they had hit us right then they'd have had us. But they didn't.

There were a lot of air strikes going on that afternoon, a lot of close air support from Navy and Marine Corps fighters. It looked like a war movie.

Maj JIM STANTON
26th Marines Fire Support Coordination Center _____

On the next aerial-observer mission I flew off the Khe Sanh airstrip after the shelling, I found what I suspected to be an NVA regiment in the open. We stacked up about eight flights of airplanes. I had Air Force, Marines, and Navy. Everybody wanted to get in on the act. Unfortunately, these were all aircraft that had been out in the Khe Sanh area planting time-delay bombs along the NVA routes of approach. These were acetone-fused bombs that were simply planted in the ground to go off hours and hours later. So I had aircraft making runs on this NVA unit that had no live ordnance at all on them! Hopefully, those NVA thought the

bombs were duds and stuck around four or five hours until
they went off.

Capt KEN PIPES
Bravo Company, 1/26 _____

Bravo Company was in a very exposed position, covering
the northeast, east, and southeast perimeter line around the
combat base.

One of the first casualties resulting from the ammo-dump
explosion was my company radio operator. He had forgotten
his gas mask when the incoming started. There were several
55-gallon drums of CS blown right into our company area,
so we immediately got gas into our low-lying command-post
bunker. As we were trying to get organized, he ran back to
his living bunker to get his mask. A 122mm rocket explosion caught him as he was scrambling back down into the
command-post bunker. When we missed him, I went up to
look for him. I found him lying inside the entrance to the
bunker, just outside the canvas tarp we used for a door. He
was very badly hurt.

A steady stream of unexploded 105mm rounds were
hurled through our command-post bunker's entrance by the
continuous explosions in the adjacent ammo dump. Many of
them were smoking when they landed. One of my Marines,
a corporal, cradled each one in his arms and ran outside
with it. Many of those rounds exploded after he left them in
the open. We soon had to move south, away from the main
dump. The new position eventually caved in, and we finally
moved into an unoccupied French concrete bunker.

This was the day the combat base was at its most
vulnerable. If the NVA forces in the area had attacked down
the long axis of the runway, from east to west, they
probably could have punched through. Doctrine told us to
keep our heads up, looking and watching, because that was
the best time for them to hit us. That was true, but when
you're getting hit like that—by the incoming and from the

dump—you just don't get up and mess around in the open a whole lot.

The incoming eventually stopped, but we were plagued by the secondary detonations for many hours after that. The dump blowing up caused us an awful lot of problems. Wire communications to the mortar pits—to everywhere—were out. I had to move my company command post several times during the five or six hours that things were really hot, and that disrupted my control over the company. In the 2nd Platoon area, the trenches were almost filled. Bunkers, which were supported with the flimsy, rotten local wood, were caving in. Flechettes from blown-up beehive artillery rounds were on the ground and in the trenches, all over the place. Some of the troops emerged with the flechettes stuck in their flak jackets and clothing. The 2nd Platoon trenches were filled with exploded and unexploded ordnance. Throughout the ordeal, men were hit in the legs, body, and head with unexploded 155mm, 105mm, 106mm, 81mm, and 3.5-inch rounds. There was so much CS gas that gas masks were only marginally effective. It was just a complete mess and chaos. The troops continued to man the positions, but, with the bunkers caved in and trenches filled, it was a prime time for the NVA to attack.

As soon as it was halfway safe, the platoon commanders and I moved out into the trenches. We had to see the troops, talk with them, let them know we were still organized.

Cpl DENNIS SMITH
Bravo Company, 1/26 _____

I hate to think what might have happened if General Giap had sent an infantry attack against us right after the first rockets came in.

2ndLt SKIP WELLS
Charlie Company, 1/26 _____

We did not suffer many casualties, as most of the rounds seemed to be directed at the airstrip and center of the perimeter, around the artillery battery. However, we were pretty well confused and shocked, and any serious ground attack would have really made our lives difficult. We did not do much except take whatever cover was available until things quieted down. Then we really got to work. There's nothing like a little motivation!

LtCol JIM WILKINSON
1/26 Commanding Officer _____

That was our weakest moment. The ammo dump was still blowing up and I'm not sure we had complete command and control over the units manning the perimeter. Worst-case scenario: If the NVA had rounded up all the local civilians, put them in front of them, and launched an all-out attack with rockets, mortars, and artillery, they might have been able to penetrate the perimeter that morning. We would have been able to contain it, but it would have been a very costly fight. They could not have controlled the base. They could *not* have. There would have been pockets of Marines all over the place, fighting them every step of the way. We had a tremendous amount of firepower in the trenches—automatic weapons, 106s, Claymores, LAAWs, fougasse traps, tanks, Ontos, Army dusters, air. . . . At no time did I feel worried about losing the perimeter.

Sgt MIKE STAHL
4.2-inch Mortar Battery, 1/13 (Hill 861) _____

I took the wounded Kilo Company commander and first sergeant aboard the first chopper that got to Hill 861, at about 1400. I also took one other wounded Marine and the three NVA I had captured during the night. When the chopper set down, I was sure it would be full of reinforcements, but none—not one fresh Marine—was sent to Hill 861 that day.

When we landed at Khe Sanh, I told the regimental intelligence officer everything I knew as I was being carried on a stretcher to a medical bunker. I got my many wounds treated and stitched up. When they were done, I was put in a wooden hooch, above the ground. Khe Sanh was just getting blown to shit, so I just left. I wanted to get back to Hill 861, so I went down to the Ammunition Supply Point to get some ammo for Kilo Company, but the ASP was gone. Since I had been on Hill 861 for about six months, I knew a lot of the infantry officers and noncoms whose companies had cycled through there. I scrounged a case of bullets here and a case of grenades there, until I had a fair amount. I got it all out to the helo pad and commandeered a chopper to get it and me back to 861.

Lt RAY STUBBE
1/26 Battalion Chaplain ————————————————

[DIARY ENTRY] Returned to my hooch [from Charlie-Med]. There was a large part of an 82mm mortar round just by the entrance. Inside, everything was knocked down.

Rounds kept exploding on the east side of the base, where the ASP is located. I walked in that direction, stunned, carrying a brass cross and a metal ammo box with a large wine bottle for communion. It was Sunday, time for church services—that couldn't be held.

The [dump] continued to smolder. Unexploded rounds, dozens of them, were all over. The regimental mess was all burned out. The post office and post exchange were collapsed. Rounds kept exploding nearby, but I wanted to check to see that all the men were okay, so I kept walking. I just kept going, as though in a trance. Our 1/26 command-post mess was smoking; it had been hit by three direct hits.

After that, I continued over the whole base. Got a whiff of teargas. I didn't bother to put on my gas mask, but just let the tears come out until I could no longer see as I aimlessly walked up the road toward Regiment. I finally put the mask on and stopped briefly at the regimental bunker, where I got some water and washed out my eyes.

Returned to the Charlie-Med area and talked with all the newly brought-in casualties. We were all congregated around the triage when a round exploded just by the air terminal on the road. Everyone scrambled. My helmet fell off. Casualties were on stretchers all over, in the open, and couldn't help themselves. I was blown down by a round!

Eight wounded men were brought into my bunker. One was the CO of Kilo Company, 3/26, from Hill 861. One man had white-phosphorus wounds, and his whole face was covered with copper sulfate. His hands were all bandaged, but I helped him eat. I gave them the chocolate cookies I had received from home, and a can of cashews. One man had a leg wound and almost passed out. The captain lay down on the floor; he had shrapnel in his leg.

2ndLt SKIP WELLS
Charlie Company, 1/26 _____

The worst part of the whole time at Khe Sanh for me was that afternoon from 1700 to 1800. At 1700, the NVA hit us with one hour of nonstop rockets and mortars. I don't have any idea how many, but there weren't any lulls. It caught me by surprise, checking the positions that we had been digging nonstop since first light. For the first ten or fifteen minutes I was more scared than I ever had been—or ever would be during two tours in Vietnam. Then it stopped at 1800—with no ground attack, probe, or anything else.

MGySgt JOHN DRIVER
Explosive Ordnance Disposal _____

The ammo dump was a mess. Only a small part of the ammo was destroyed in the explosion. Ammunition involved in an explosion, if it is not destroyed, becomes sensitized. Safety devices are often removed and sensitive detonators exposed. White phosphorus is a special hazard. It

would burn and then crust over. The burning might cause
the fuse and burster to detonate, or it might cause a fire in
other ammunition. If one moved the round and broke the
crust, it would spontaneously ignite upon exposure to air.
Added to all this was the enemy fire, which slowed things up
and caused new fires. Clearance operations disturbed the
dust and caused the CS teargas crystals to float in the air,
where it irritated skin, eyes, and respiratory systems.

PART THREE

THE RING CLOSES

January 22—February 8, 1968

Chapter 7

JANUARY 22

LCpl DAN ANSLINGER
3rd Marine Division Air Section _____

Almost everyone walking around the combat base had little scabs all over their faces and hands from being peppered with tiny bits of shrapnel from the ammo-dump explosion.

HN ROD DeMOSS
26th Marines Regimental Aid Station _____

On morning of January 22, it seemed like everybody was out walking around, assessing the damage and picking up supplies, or whatever. All of a sudden, in the background, I could hear *boomp . . . boomp . . . boomp*. Then someone cried out, "Incoming! Incoming!" I was scared shitless. I frantically searched for cover and dived into a foxhole with another guy. Rounds hit pretty close—close enough. From then on, this became a daily routine. If I was outside, I listened for the *boomp*. This meant that a mortar or rocket or artillery round was about halfway there. I took cover and

waited for the round to hit, praying that it didn't have my
name on it.

Lt RAY STUBBE
1/26 Battalion Chaplain _____

[DIARY ENTRY] In the middle of our 1/26 briefing, an incoming
mortar round exploded and everyone dispersed throughout
the old French bunker. The battalion CO, LtCol James
Wilkinson, continued the briefing just where everyone was—
all scattered. He said he wanted no groupings of more than
ten. Therefore, no regular worship services. 1stLt Andy
Sibley, our battalion intelligence officer, reported that we are
encircled by two NVA divisions.

1stLt NICK ROMANETZ
Charlie Company, 1/26 _____

January 22 was my twenty-third birthday.

At this time, the combat base in my sector was in quite a
bit of confusion. The messhall had been blown up, the
ammo dump had been blown up, we didn't know the status
of our ammunition. My sector was very, very vulnerable to
ground attack. We did not have real good defensive positions; we did not have good, deep trenchlines; we did not
have enough barbed wire or minefields or interlocking fields
of fire; we did not have covered fighting positions for all of
our men. If the enemy had decided to attack the combat
base in force with a ground attack during those first few
days, there is no doubt in my mind that they would have
penetrated our defenses and caused quite a bit of havoc. I
think they missed a good opportunity to get their feet in the
front door.

Around 1100, there was suddenly a lot of commotion at
the water point. A lot of guys were standing there—we
always had someone down there checking on the pumps or
drawing water, so it was not unusual to have a bunch of
guys walking up and down that road. An NVA soldier had

surrendered to 2ndLt Skip Wells's platoon, which covered the road that led to the water point.

NEW ARRIVALS

1stLt ERNIE SPENCER
Delta Company, 1/26 _____

Khe Sanh is hit on my last day of R&R. I felt like a chickenshit for not being there with my company. That's how I return—pissed at myself for not being there.

A CH-46 helicopter takes me back to the base. No trouble getting connections to Khe Sanh now. All hell has broken loose. Khe Sanh is now the hottest show in Nam. Tents are still up, I notice during the approach, but everything has changed since I left. There is an ominousness, a harshness everywhere. Next to the landing pad, full fuel bladders lie scattered like large pillows. Almost like a Charlie Chaplin movie, people are moving in a quick, jerky fashion. . . . Incoming rockets and artillery had changed things.

We take incoming within fifteen minutes of when I land. I come in wearing a soft cap, and it feels good to put my piss pot on again. I'd missed my piss pot when I was on R&R. The thing fit real comfortable; it rode me just right. After wearing one for a while, you rock your head differently when you walk. I also put on my flak jacket, which I never wore before. Flak jacket would not stop a rifle shot, just shrapnel. But life is about adjusting. Khe Sanh meant rockets and artillery, and rockets and artillery are all about shrapnel. Everyone looks fat in a flak jacket. They have square nylon plates sewn in individual packets and overlaid on each other. Like scales, they form another layer of skin for you. You begin to understand other beings when you wear a flak jacket for any length of time. Like turtles. Flak jackets aren't comfortable, but any fool knows they are more comfortable than the alternatives.[1]

Capt JIM LESLIE
26th Marines Assistant Communicator _____

On January 22, my commanding officer called me into his office. The good news was I had been promoted to captain. The bad news was I was going to a place called Khe Sanh, which needed a captain communications officer. I packed my seabag and caught a chopper to Khe Sanh.

We tried to land at the airstrip at Khe Sanh, but each time we tried to touch down the airstrip got mortared. On the fourth attempt, we touched down for a few seconds. My seabag and I went tumbling out the door and the chopper took off.

I didn't see anyone around, and for good reasons. Khe Sanh was in the midst of a barrage of artillery and mortar fire. "Welcome to the Big Leagues," I thought. I found a ditch between the runway and a red dusty road. I saw a few cruddy-looking Marines in there, so I jumped in. I lay there for twenty or thirty minutes as the incoming continued. Eventually the noise stopped and the other Marines got up and casually started walking on their way. I asked one of them how to find the communications bunker. He directed me to a pile of sandbags about halfway down the runway and about fifty meters to the right.

Like a lost sheep, I moseyed down the dusty trail, seabag on my back and .45-caliber automatic on my belt.

I found the comm bunker, opened the plywood door, and said in typical Marine Corps fashion, "I'm Captain Leslie reporting to the 26th Marine Comm Section."

MGen TOMMY TOMPKINS
3rd Marine Division Commanding General _____

On January 21, Colonel Lownds sent me a dispatch and asked for another battalion. I had given him three, and at that point the division reserve was the 1st Battalion, 1st Marines, at Quang Tri. I notified General Cushman [III Marine Amphibious Force commander] that I was commit-

ting the division reserve, 1/1, from Quang Tri and sending
them to Khe Sanh, and that I would reconstitute a division
reserve from cooks and bakers, or some bloody thing.

Cushman sent me a dispatch and said that instead of
sending 1/1, which was to chop back to 1st Marine Division, to send 1/9 from Camp Evans, that he would cover
Camp Evans with 2/4, which was the afloat battalion landing team.[2]

LtCol JOHN MITCHELL
1/9 Commanding Officer _____

At this time (1100, January 22), no mission [order] was
given to [me] by higher authority other than "Destination
Khe Sanh." In view of the lack of further information on
the current situation at Khe Sanh, and not knowing whether
this would be a tactical or administrative assault, I directed
all company commanders to prepare for helo assault, with
only two days ration of food and ammo to be taken, and
only the barest personal necessities.[3]

Cpl BERT MULLINS
H&S Company, 1/9 _____

We were notified shortly after noon that we would be going
to a place called Khe Sanh. None of us had ever heard of
the place. It didn't mean anything much to us. We were told
we would be there about three days and not to take much
gear with us, that we were all going to travel light.

I was assigned that day to be the battalion commander's
radioman, so I got my radio gear together. But this was
going to be my first time in the field, so I didn't know what
to take with me. I was bright enough to take my poncho
because I had noticed it was monsoon season, but I didn't
take much else.

HM3 BILL GESSNER
Delta Company, 1/9 _____

Delta Company was in a fire fight with a small group of
Viet Cong when Battalion told us to break contact and move

to a pickup zone. We were picked up by CH-53s and brought back to Camp Evans.

The entire battalion—including the headquarters—was staging on the airfield. Ammunition and C-rations were being distributed. Medical supplies were available in great quantities, so I gave each man in my platoon two battle dressings, and each squad leader got a bottle of plasma to carry. The chaplain was holding religious services, and we had our choice of steak or chicken for a hot meal. It was easy to see that we were going to be going somewhere terrible. The officers were at a briefing, and rumors flashed through the unit every few minutes. What amazes me is how accurate a picture we had if we knew what rumors to hold on to. I don't remember the bad rumors, but I remember "Khe Sanh," "helicopters not trucks" (a real novelty for moving a battalion at that time), "big attack by the NVA," and "we're getting screwed again." All the rumors scared us. The chow, church, and medical supplies made it worse.

Cpl BERT MULLINS
H&S Company, 1/9 _____

They told us we were going to go right away. Then they told us we wouldn't be leaving soon. Then choppers started coming in waves to the landing zone at Camp Evans. As they offloaded what looked to me like Vietnamese civilians, our troops loaded on and the choppers took off. As soon as the CO, LtCol John Mitchell, was ready to go, the command group went over to the landing zone and we took off in a CH-46. By then, it was fairly late in the afternoon.

As we flew into Khe Sanh, the weather changed on us. It had been clear and sunny at Camp Evans—a break in the monsoon—but it was overcast when we got to Khe Sanh. As we approached the base, the door gunners opened fire with their machine guns. I turned around and looked out the porthole at the ground and I saw muzzle flashes. They were NVA 12.7mm machine guns firing at us. That was my first experience getting shot from the ground. My father had been a B-17 tail gunner in World War II, and he had told me about the flak and how you could fool yourself that the metal skin was going to protect you. All I could think of was a round coming through the floor of the chopper and hitting me.

HM3 BILL GESSNER
Delta Company, 1/9 _____

The entire 2nd Platoon loaded onto one CH-53. The lieutenant got into the helicopter just before it took off and briefed the squad leaders. About the only thing I found out was that the landing zone probably was not hot. The helicopter ride lasted a long time, and our anxiety built during the ride. People were convinced we were going into Laos or North Vietnam. We could see the hills as we prepared to land. I was freezing. We had flown very high to avoid small-arms fire.

The helicopter landed on the airfield, which was strewn with artillery ammunition. At first, we didn't know why— were these duds?—but later we realized the ammunition dump had been hit. I was very nervous about all of those rounds lying around.

We hesitated only long enough to organize for movement, and then we moved through the base. It was in pretty good shape then. The hooches were still up, and we were envious of the relative comfort the Marines on Khe Sanh base seemed to have.

Cpl BERT MULLINS
H&S Company, 1/9 _____

We landed without getting hit and the battalion command group immediately proceeded to the regimental command post, which was easily identified by all the radio antenna masts. The colonel and other officers went in, but I stayed outside with the other radiomen. After a while it got dark. Someone came outside and told us we didn't have to wait around any longer. He told us they had been taking incoming all day and that the ammo dump had been hit. Somebody took us to one of the old French bunkers that was

being used as the artillery battalion fire-direction center.
They gave us a place to sleep that night, on a concrete floor.
We spent a rather uneasy night listening to the stories these
guys had to tell about the massive amounts of incoming
they'd been taking.

LCpl PHIL MINEER
Bravo Battery, 1/13 _____

Bravo Battery [a six-gun 105mm howitzer unit] got a
close-station march order on January 22. We were packed
and out of Dong Ha, just like that. They brought in CH-46
helicopters which set down two at a time near the battery
area. Gun-3 was ready to go; all it needed was the hook.
The gun section got on the CH-46, the CH-46 hovered over
the top of the gun, hooked it up, pulled it up in the air, and
flew the section right into Khe Sanh.

LCpl RAY NICOL
Bravo Battery, 1/13 _____

Our particular gun, Gun-6, fell after the cables broke. It had
to be returned to our former position for test firing.

LCpl PHIL MINEER
Bravo Battery, 1/13 _____

Coming into Khe Sanh, everyone was looking for ground
fire. I was so damned scared, I don't know if we took fire or
not. We came in very low and set down on the runway.
That's when I knew it was serious. There were pieces of
choppers lying all over the runway, and craters in the
runway. I looked over the compound, where guys used to
live aboveground. There wasn't much left of any tents.
Parapets were blown to hell. I had never seen anything like
it.

   Shortly after we set down, a few mortars started coming
in on the runway. We beat it off there. When we got over to

what I believe was the regimental headquarters, they told us where we were going to billet.

LCpl RAY NICOL
Bravo Battery, 1/13 _____

From the air on the way into Khe Sanh, we could see an increasing number of shell holes and bomb craters. We knew from that and the increasing amount of ground fire on the way it was going to be hot when we landed. We had to hover over the landing pad to enable the ground crew to unhook the cable from the howitzer our CH-46 was carrying. As we hovered there, we could see the damage done by the preceding day's incoming artillery and mortars. The base ammo dump had been hit and was still burning. Very little stood aboveground that hadn't been hit. When the chopper touched down and the ramp opened, we were told to haul ass to the bunkers along the edge of the landing pad. Rounds began impacting all over the base, so we had to wait for a break in the incoming to get to our position.

LCpl PHIL MINEER
Bravo Battery, 1/13 _____

Charlie Battery, 1/13, had been there for a little while, and Alpha Battery was up at the other end of the compound. Because of Charlie Battery being short—they had three guns out on 881S—they put Bravo and Charlie together. As a joke, we called it "Barley Battery." We had six guns and Charlie had three—nine guns altogether.

Our position inside Khe Sanh Combat Base was down at the end of the runway, where the planes lifted off. They nestled us right in beside the ammo dump, which was brilliant. (The whole thing was brilliant. Everything they did was against the principles I had been taught.) We moved into the battery position, laid the guns, got all the aiming stakes out, started breaking out rounds—had to lay them right on the parapet—and then fired.

Cpl WILLIAM ROBERTSON
Logistics Support Unit _____

Everything in ASP-1 was gone, except for about 1,500
rounds of 155mm ammunition. I also had a large supply of
40mm antiaircraft rounds for the Army dusters. Also, by
this time, Colonel Lownds had given us a small place
toward the other end of the base, which we called ASP-2. I
had about 800 pounds of 105mm ammunition there, and
about 600 powder charges for the 155s.

That was all we had left.

LCpl RAY NICOL
Bravo Battery, 1/13 _____

Since our gun would not be in until the next morning,
Private Aguilar and I were sent on ammo detail. We dodged
incoming half the night, bringing ammo from a temporary
dump in a truck. We were very nervous loading ammo into
the truck with several thousand tons of explosives piled
around us. About 0200, we finally had enough ammo for
the battery. We went back to our gun position, so tired we
never bothered to dig a hole to sleep in. We just flopped on
the ground and were asleep in seconds.

Capt BILL DABNEY
India Company, 3/26 (Hill 881S) _____

The hill had been socked in for about three days or so.
Heavy fog—really clouds, because 881S was pretty close to
3,000 feet. We hadn't been able to see a damned thing,
couldn't see two feet in the daytime, this stuff was so thick.
So we had been on 100-percent alert for a while and were
getting pretty tired. Finally it was starting to lighten up a
little bit. We were standing down to 50 percent and some
kids were getting some sleep. One kid from Charlie Battery
took the opportunity to go into the gun parapet and swab out
the bore on one of the 105s, which was sitting up there

without its sight aboard. (We always dismounted the sights
when we didn't have fire missions because there were so
many mortar rounds. The guns were pretty tough; mortars
didn't hurt them much, except for the tires, but the sights
were always getting hit. We couldn't fire a gun very well
without the sight, so we always dismounted the sights and
took them down into the bunker hole when we finished our
fire mission.) The gun happened to be oriented toward the
southeast, toward Hill 784, a ridge a thousand or so meters
toward the south. About the time the gunner finished swab-
bing the bore out, this valley opened in the clouds and he
looked down this rift, as it were, and going up the face of
the opposite ridge a thousand meters or so toward our south
was what he described as about twenty guys with what
looked like a couple of tubes of some sort on their shoulders, two or three tubes. It was obviously the enemy. We
had a free-fire zone all around us. Without direction from
anybody, he just hollered out, "Hey, got some NVA on that
goddamned hill down there." He went to the tube and
sighted right through the bore, and then ran over to the
ready box and grabbed a round, fused it for point detonation—
left every damned charge in it—and fired direct fire with
that 105, without sights. According to the machine gunner
up front with him—he was immediately awakened by the
muzzle blast going off 50 feet behind him—the first round
hit right amongst them. This guy fired off four or five more
rounds. By this time, the rest of the artillerymen were
scuttling out of the bunker, wondering what the hell was
going on. About the time everybody else got out there, the
machine gunner opened up—that hill was directly in front of
him. What he could see was more or less the same thing
that the artillery gunner had described. The clouds then
closed up, and that was it. Dead silence; we couldn't see a
damned thing anymore for another day or so.

We reported it just the way it happened. The rest of the
evening and well into the night, we kept getting calls,
"Give us some sort of feel for how many you got . . . any
idea." We couldn't see *anything*. By the time we got our
stuff together enough so that we could even look, there

wasn't anything to see. It was just clouds. But they kept
bugging and bugging. Finally my exec, 1stLt Rich Foley,
got on the radio and said, "Look, if it's any help to you,
from what the gunner described, it sounded like it could
conceivably have been an 82mm mortar section. Our Order
of Battle book says that the NVA 82mm mortar section has
21 men in it," and he hung up. Rich said that just to get
them off our backs.[4]

26th Marines Command Chronology _____

   21 NVA KIA (confirmed).

Capt BILL DABNEY
India Company, 3/26 (Hill 881S) _____

Now, we didn't say that.[5]

Pfc JIM PAYNE
Charlie Battery, 1/13 (Hill 881S) _____

Around midmorning, NVA 120mm mortar fire was hitting
the hill. Up next to the landing zone, LCpl Ronald Pierce
and myself were flattened out in the Gun-1 parapet floor
with our arms wrapped octopus-like, up, over, and around
our helmeted heads. Our comm wires to the artillery exec
pit were out of action and in between incoming rounds,
Pierce and I were both yelling, "Wireman on One! Wireman
on One!"
   During the incoming, approaching medevac choppers
could be heard in the distance. Marine stretcher bearers
were running back and forth across the landing zone. At that
point, another round detonated near the trenchline just
beyond Captain Dabney's bunker. I heard shouts of
"Corpsman, up! Corpsman, up!"
   As Pierce and I looked over a sandbagged wall, an officer
with forward-observer glasses rounded the corner of Dabney's
bunker and ran toward us shouting, "Arty up! Arty up!"

Snarling and pointing toward 881N, he jammed the forward-observer glasses in my face, screaming, "Look down my fuckin' arm! That's a fuckin' good mortar tube out there in that fuckin' crater! Git the motherfuckers!"

While this officer was screaming directions at me and pointing toward 881N, I looked through the glasses, scanning the bomb craters on the southeast slope of 881N, about a thousand yards distant. At the edge of one crater, I saw several dark figures moving around right on the lip facing us. I repeated back to the officer what I was seeing and he yanked the glasses from me, took a quick look through them, and said, "That's them! Git the motherfuckers!" Then he headed back down toward the trench, taking the glasses with him. Now that I knew where to look, I could see those figures out there with my naked eye.

Our 105 was already laid close to the action, so Pierce and I only had to shift the trails a couple of feet. Pierce ran to the ready bunker and assembled a projectile while I opened the breech block and cranked the handwheels. The tube came down and I looked right down the lands and grooves to center the figures in the crater just low of center bore. Pierce ran to the gun with a white-phosphorus round and rammed it home. I closed the breech block and fired.

Our round hit the far end of the bomb crater and the grunts in the north trench started hollering, "Ya-hoo! Git 'em, arty!" and stuff like that. After the shot, our 105 jumped back slightly off the action, but the trails were digging in. Pierce loaded up the second time with a point-detonating, high-explosive round, and we just kept firing straight into the white smoke billowing out of that crater.

After Pierce and I ceased fire, we just sort of stood there, staring at that smoking crater out there on 881N. The officer with the glasses trotted back into our parapet and shortly thereafter, so did 1stLt Tom Biondo, the 1/13 arty officer.

Pierce and I sat down on the ground next to each other with our backs to the parapet wall. We just sat there staring at the ground, puffing on C-ration cigarettes, with all our hands shaking.

HM3 DAVID STEINBERG
3/26 Battalion Aid Station _____

They told me to go up to some hill I had never heard of, so I caught a chopper, a Huey gunship. I had never flown on one of them before. I was half in and half out the same door some fanatical predator was shouting out of. I was hugging the guy next to me as tight as I could; if it hadn't been for him, I would have fallen out. Next thing I knew, the chopper went into a hot landing zone and I was shoved to the ground. There was mass confusion. The incoming had been hitting the top of Hill 881S all day.

I no sooner got out of the chopper than someone dragged me to the ground and the incoming hit. It was just chaos. People were running all over the place.

I had been a corpsman for a year, but the first time I ever got to really use the skills I had developed was right then, as soon as I landed on 881S. The first patient I ever treated in a combat situation, all by myself, far from any doctors, was a sucking chest wound. Sure enough, I pulled out my pack of cigarettes, pulled off the cellophane wrapper, slapped it over the wound, put on a battle dressing, and restored his breathing. We got him medevacked, but my life turned to chaos. It was "Corpsman, up! Corpsman, up! Corpsman, up!" without letup. I finally asked, "Where are the other corpsmen?" They told me that, out of eight corpsmen who had originally been on the hill a few days earlier, there were just two of us. They told us that replacements would be sent, but it never happened.

Chapter 8

KHE SANH VILLAGE OVERRUN

BOB BREWER
Quang Tri Province Senior Adviser _____

Political victories were the prime objective of the enemy's offensive. To capture the KSCB and all the troops there would have been a big political victory, but the capture of the Huong Hoa District Headquarters in Khe Sanh City was to them a bigger prize, and none of our brass have realized it to this day.

I had a detachment of advisers there. The team consisted of U.S. Army Capt Bruce Clarke and his staff of four, a Marine combined action company headquarters of about twelve working with the Bru militia, and a couple of U.S. Special Forces noncommissioned officers. The total strength, including the Bru militia, must have been about 175 men. The district chief was the pride and joy of the Vietnamese military because he was the first montagnard to graduate from the Vietnamese military academy at Dalat. The compound was not good from a defensive point of view. I had an agreement with Colonel Lownds that, should our advisory team at Huong Hoa District Headquarters wind up in extremis, a Marine relief force would come to their aid.

Bruce Clarke had done a lot of scrounging and digging, and his people had their confidence sky-high. I was never convinced, however. On my 1968 New Year's visit, I told Bruce that I would try to reinforce him, if the time ever came, by way of the coffee plantation just south of his perimeter. The trees there were only six or seven feet tall, and I felt they could easily be leveled in advance by fighter-bombers so we could put in one heliborne air assault.

Things happened just as I feared they might. Bruce reported on the night of January 19–20 that he was being invested by a well-armed force of North Vietnamese, estimated to be a reinforced battalion in strength. (Later estimates, based on the number of heavy weapons captured, placed the strength of the attack in the regimental class.)

Bruce and I both called for the promised assistance from the Khe Sanh Combat Base. A marine company sallied forth on January 20, but, only a few kilometers out, they found their going too rough and they turned back.

Maj JERRY HUDSON
26th Marines Intelligence Officer _____

A highlight of the battle for Khe Sanh village was the calling in of VT [variable-time] fire on the friendly positions and surrounding defensive wire. The district chief approved and called for more and more such fires. Well over 1,000 rounds of VT were expended in this effort and were probably a [great] factor in breaking up the attack on the village. . . . Bru villagers and other returnees frequently spoke of large groups of enemy dead in the area surrounding the Khe Sanh village during the days following the battle there.[1]

BOB BREWER
Quang Tri Province Senior Adviser _____

The District Headquarters did get good supporting artillery fire from the combat base, but by then some miscreants had already penetrated to the compound and had taken over the dispensary.

Bruce Clark and I talked that night, and he said he needed ammunition in the worst way, that he could maybe hold out for another day if he had ammo. I set it up to free-fall ammo into his compound the next day from low-flying choppers. This was a hairy and only partially successful operation.

On the second night, January 20–21, Bruce thought he might be overcome on the morrow. So, at my initiative and with the approval of the 1st ARVN Division's BGen Ngo Quang Truong, I organized the reinforcement plan for Huong Hoa. The only force at my disposal at that point was a first-class company of Regional Forces troops belonging to the Province Chief, Col Nguyen Am, and a U.S. Army Huey helicopter unit out of Danang.

The council of war consisted of Col Nguyen Am, myself, LtCol Joseph Seymoe (my deputy province adviser), James Bullington (Department of State), Major Tuyen (chief of the tactical operations center), U.S. Army Major Sanders (tactical operations center adviser), U.S. Army Maj John Oliver (Chief Regional Forces/Popular Forces adviser), U.S. Air Force Capt. Warren Milberg (intelligence adviser), and John Uhler (my USAID special assistant). We decided to call in the Army Hueys to airlift the Regional Forces troops into the area just south of the Huong Hoa District Headquarters defense perimeter. Lieutenant Colonel Seymoe volunteered to lead the expedition. I had some misgivings, but because of the shortage of time to brief the pilots, sending an authority who knew the plan seemed to have some merit.

Seymoe graduated from West Point in 1949. He went into the Air Force and won a Distinguished Flying Cross for his exploits in the Korean War. His hearing became impaired, so he transferred to the infantry. He was new to the province and Vietnam; none of us knew him well.

A good case can be made for bad communications being the root cause for the loss of many a battle: Waterloo and General Grauchy, Gettysburg and Jeb Stuart, and Pearl Harbor and Col Rufus Bratton. At Huong Hoa, it happened this way:

Colonel Seymoe, leading a dozen Hueys loaded with 120 Regional Forces troops, airlifted out of the provincial airstrip at Quang Tri at about 1100 hours on January 21. In the van was the U.S. Air Force forward air controller assigned to my staff, a Captain Cooper. He was to direct and coordinate the four flights of fighter-bombers we had specifically requested for the destruction of the coffee orchard just south of Captain Clarke's perimeter.

Problems began to surface when Captain Cooper arrived in the area with the four flights of heavily armed bombers orbiting above. There was an unexpected Marine forward air controller in the area in a spotter plane—very small, but a hazard to the jets in a precision-bombing run. Captain Cooper tried and tried to get the Marine on the horn, but he got nothing. Meanwhile, the heavily loaded choppers were bearing down on Cooper, and the jets were running out of fuel. Cooper was trying to chase down the errant Marine and, at the same time, telling Seymoe to hold off, that "the planned air strike can't be pulled off yet."

Apparently, Seymoe didn't hear the "yet," so he decided—directly counter to my orders—that he would put the Regional Forces company on the old French fort, then only a grassy piece of high ground about a mile east of the Huong Hoa District Headquarters compound.

Problem was, the old French fort was an NVA stronghold. It was crawling with the bastards. Colonel Seymoe landed his troops out of the first chopper, but as the Huey lifted off, a high-explosive round, either a mortar or a rocket, hit the front and propelled it sideways over the hill and down about seventy-five meters. When the machine came to rest, it was upside down and burning a little. One door gunner was crushed and killed, but the pilot and copilot crawled out through the broken windshield. Colonel Seymoe was alive but unconscious, pinned by an aluminum bar usually used to secure stretchers.

The pilots told me that they and the other gunner tried to free Seymoe, but they could not release him. While they worked, they could see and feel the fire spreading, about to explode on them. At that instant, the NVA soldiers began to descend on them. With pistols, the door gunner got two and the copilot got another. Then the bird went *WHOMPFF.*

The pilots and gunner ran around the chopper and, in the ensuing confusion, escaped into the jungled canyon below the French fort. They eventually made it to the Khe Sanh Combat Base. (In the spring, I recovered Seymoe's body from beneath the burned-out chopper.)

Bruce Clarke knew without being told that the screw-up had occurred. We talked on the radio that night, and it was agreed that he would try to fight his way out to the Khe Sanh Combat Base the next day.

Who should go with Clarke became a hot question. General Truong, of the 1st ARVN Division and thus the strongest Government of Vietnam official in the area with whom I had to deal, was totally opposed to this course of action. His point of view was that this would be the first Government of Vietnam political seat to be lost to the Communists, and that it shouldn't happen without a fight. My point was that the Marines were not prepared to fight for the place, and I was not prepared to lose my team in an unsupported outpost. I sat with General Truong in the Quang Tri Tactical Operations Center for thirty minutes without either of us saying anything while radios chattered in the background. The ball was in Truong's court. Finally, he said, "All right. Try to get them out." Thanks to Bruce Clarke's leadership, we tried and *did*, with almost no help from the Khe Sanh Combat Base. Surprisingly, about seventy-five men from the Regional Forces company made it to KSCB, some with Bruce and some later. They closed ranks, re-formed, and were made a viable force again by the beginning of April. Bruce reported that the bodies of about 250 hostiles were counted on the wire around the perimeter, and many NVA crew-served weapons were temporarily captured.

The Communists were ecstatic about capturing their *first* political headquarters. They went bananas over this, and my Government of Vietnam counterparts could not understand why the American military was so unconcerned. What we should have done was go right back in immediately and retake Huong Hoa District Headquarters. But, by then, our military leaders had embraced the idea of the "set-piece" battle, which they expected to win.

Lt RAY STUBBE
1/26 Battalion Chaplain _____

[DIARY ENTRY] About 1,500 people were at our main gate, including Bru montagnards. About 150 were brought into the base at a time and flown out to Danang, but only the Vietnamese. The I Corps commander, General Lam, forbade the montagnards to leave! It was an example of selfishness to watch the Vietnamese. The older folks would run across the street, leaving their children to run themselves, if they could keep up. The man in charge would ask, for example, for three more, and papa-san and mama-san and another older person would cross, leaving all the baby-sans behind. The children would cry.

26th Marines After Action Report _____

All the Vietnamese who so desired were resettled after the initial hostilities. During this period, the majority of local Bru (approximately 6,000) assembled in the vicinity of Lang Chen, just outside KSCB. However, for their protection, they were advised to relocate to a safe area as they were vulnerable to fire from both sides.

Chapter 9

JANUARY 23

LCpl DAN ANSLINGER
3rd Marine Division Air Section ⎯⎯⎯⎯⎯⎯⎯⎯⎯⎯⎯⎯

I finally got out of Khe Sanh, to rejoin my section at Dong Ha, on January 23. I had to run to scramble up the ramp of a C-123 and hang on while the airplane seemed to take off straight up. I heard a loud metallic bang and, after the plane leveled off, the crew chief pointed out the holes in the deck that the antiaircraft rounds had made. It was horrible, and at the same time, it was wonderful. We were a bunch of kids who knew we were the best in the world and that the NVA was going to find out the hard way.

1stLt PAUL ELKAN
Bravo Battery, 1/13 ⎯⎯⎯⎯⎯⎯⎯⎯⎯⎯⎯⎯⎯⎯⎯⎯⎯

I arrived at Khe Sanh a day after the rest of Bravo Battery. As the battery exec, I had had to stay at Phu Bai to test-fire the 105mm howitzer that had been incorrectly slung beneath a CH-46 helicopter the day before. The howitzer's muzzle had struck the ground and about six inches of hard, compact dirt had been forced into it.

As we landed at Khe Sanh, we were mortared on the strip. I ran from the chopper to the trench beside the airstrip and dived facedown into the trench. There, I found myself face-to-face with my Basic School roommate. The lucky son of a bitch was leaving as I was coming in, and he sure let me know what a picnic the battery had in store for it.

LCpl RAY NICOL
Bravo Battery, 1/13 _____

On the morning of January 23, Bravo Battery moved to our permanent position at the east end of the base. While we were moving, we could see civilians from Khe Sanh village converging on the gate. All of them were trying to be evacuated out of the way of the fight. I felt sorry for them because their village had been blown away by the NVA artillery fire, and then by ours. They had no homes to go home to.

1stLt PAUL ELKAN
Bravo Battery, 1/13 _____

Our battery position was located on the southern end of the perimeter, right next to the ammo dump for the entire base, which was between us and the airstrip. I remember thinking on the way about what a mess it was. The entire area looked like a photo of Berlin after the Russians had shelled it in 1945. There was wreckage thrown everywhere. Vehicles were smashed—windshields shattered, blown tires—tents were shredded, pieces of gear, a shredded airplane, airstrip matting, and torn sandbags were everywhere. The place had been beaten to shit by artillery fire. What had been a combat base looked like rubble.

As we got into the battery area and set the guns up, we noticed that there was a lot of shit lying around—unexpended shells which were steaming as they were being picked up.

There was still a lot of smoke rising from hot metal, burning canvas, and burning wood. One of the problems was that we had COFRAM ammo all over the place. This type of round is shot through artillery; it consists of a "baseball" surrounded by vanes. The thing is led out of the shell by a parachute when it's in the air. It descends to the ground on the vanes, and when it hits the ground it springs up on a spring in the bottom and explodes at about one meter in height. There are thirty little bomblets per shell. Well, these bomblets were all over the area, so we had to be careful not to step on them for fear of blowing ourselves up. EOD came in the next day and started picking them up. They put plaster of paris around each bomblet, let it harden for a half hour, picked them up, and put them in a basket like they were eggs. Pretty neat.

2ndLt DONALD McGUIRE
Explosive Ordnance Disposal _____

When the ASP was hit, my EOD team was operating out of Phu Bai. When the combat-base commander saw the seriousness of the situation, he asked for EOD assistance. My team was dispatched to Khe Sanh and, on arrival, we were briefed on what areas had priority for decontamination. We went to work immediately. The Khe Sanh airstrip, which passed within fifteen meters of the ASP, came first so that the base could be resupplied and the wounded could be evacuated. The ASP was still burning and having secondary detonations. And, as if this wasn't bad enough, the NVA was still harassing the base with mortar, artillery, and rocket fire. That slowed us down some, but not completely.

As we got the airstrip cleared of unexploded ordnance, fragments, and other hazards, we moved to other areas with lesser priorities. During the time this was taking place, we started receiving additional duties in the form of being called to different areas to handle duds. We were constantly on the move. As time passed and things started cooling down, we received working parties to assist in the clearance of non-hazardous items, but they were always under the supervision of an EOD tech. The cleanup of the ASP lasted for several weeks.

1stLt JOHN KAHENY
1/26 Combat Operations Center _____

At about 1600, Dr. Ed Feldman, our acting battalion surgeon, 1stLt Andy Sibley, our battalion intelligence officer, and I were standing outside the battalion command post when we noticed that an A-4 pilot had punched out directly over the base. His parachute was drifting out to the east, past our lines, and on into enemy territory. We immediately jumped into the ambulance. I was so excited that I tried to climb in on the shotgun side, but there's no door on that side of a military ambulance. Also, we had two rifles and all of about four rounds of ammunition.

I was hanging on to the outside of the ambulance as Dr. Feldman drove through the ammo dump and out across the airfield—it was still covered with shrapnel, which I thought was going to burst the tires. Meantime, the A-4 pilot kept drifting closer and closer to the cliff on the east side of the base, but he fell in about fifty yards from the treeline. Fortunately for all of us, a squad from Bravo Company had seen him coming down, and they ran across the field and covered the treeline for us while we went over to see if the pilot was okay.

Capt KEN PIPES
Bravo Company, 1/26 _____

The pilot, Maj William Loftus, was saved from going over into a deep ravine beyond our reach when his parachute shrouds became entangled in our wire. He told the Bravo Company 2nd Platoon commander, 2ndLt John Dillon, "If you weren't so damned ugly, I'd kiss you."[1]

Cpl WILLIAM ROBERTSON
Logistics Support Unit _____

All day long, January 23, the first day planes were able to come into Khe Sanh, we received 155mm rounds, but no primers, no fuses, and no powder kegs. However, the gunners needed four pieces to be able to fire them: a primer, powder bags, the actual round, and the fuse. The gunners had to put the fuse on the round, then the round in the barrel, then the powder behind the round, then the primer behind the powder. Without any one of those four articles, the gunners had nothing to fire, they got no bang. We got planeload after planeload of 155mm rounds. That night, I called Danang and talked to some captain there. Except for the circumstances of what was going on at Khe Sanh, I probably would have been put *under* the jail because I was not too pleased with him. I asked, "What the hell are we supposed to do with these rounds? Bowl? There's nothing else to do with 'em. We don't have any fuses. We don't have any powder. We don't have any primers." In fact, we only had a few 155mm guns, and we had two full batteries of 105s. Everybody up there had a rifle. We had mortars. We had 106mm recoilless rifles. But they didn't send anything except 155mm rounds. I told the captain, "You must have a bloomin' idiot down there, deciding what's going to be sent out to us." Well, apparently he got the message. Starting the next day, we got diversified ammunition loads in. And Colonel Lownds was gracious enough to give us three places to put it. I guess he finally realized what we had been trying to get through to him—that apparently we knew a little something about what we were doing.

Pfc ELWIN BACON
Kilo Company, 3/26 (Hill 861) _____

For four days and nights following the January 21 attack on
Hill 861, Kilo Company was on 100-percent alert. That's a
very long time to be without sleep. If a second attack had
come, we would have been in no shape to ward it off. The
CO must have been terrified of what could have happened,
but I don't think his judgment was correct on that point.

On the second night after the attack—January 23—three
of us were told to go out in front of the lines and act as a
listening post. The senior man was led out by the company
gunny to an old stump which was all charred from fire. We
were told that we should stay there until daybreak. Why the
team leader disobeyed that command and moved us a little
closer to the line and bunkers, I don't know, but we weren't
there but an hour when a machine gun from our lines
opened up on that stump. We would all have been dead for
sure.

Our platoon exchanged positions with that of the one that
had taken the brunt of the attack. The smell from in front of
my new position was enough to make a hog vomit. As far
as I could see into the little valley between our hill and that
next ridge was nothing but bodies. As the days went by, the
odor grew worse and unbearable. Nothing could be done
about the bodies because the sniper activity continued.

Sgt MIKE STAHL
4.2-inch Mortar Battery, 1/13 (Hill 861) _____

Following their attempt to overrun Hill 861 on the night of
January 20–21, the NVA evidently left many of their dead in
the ravine fronting Hill 861. Over a period of days, we
gathered up as many as we could safely reach and burned
them.

We also had our own dead to contend with. The fog was
so thick, and they were so slow getting choppers in, that we

had wounded Marines on the landing zone, waiting for a ride out, for several days. Some of them died waiting on the landing zone. Our dead went out last, after the wounded. During that time we got few if any replacements and very little ammunition or other supplies.

Pfc JIM PAYNE
Charlie Battery, 1/13 (Hill 881S) _____

Incoming again, and choppers were medevacking from the hill. All these guys were getting hit and corpsmen were running all over the hill. When NVA 120mm mortars detonated on the hill, they left an acrid-smelling, soot-like cloud that hung there momentarily before drifting across the landing zone. On this day, Pfc Ronald Pierce and I were flattened out in the gun pit again. Corporal Blucher, who was new in-country, was lying alongside us. Our wires were back in action and Pierce had the gun team headset on.

While taking a quick look-see between incoming rounds, I spotted this big rat about five feet away. The rat was burrowing butt-first in between two sandbags on the parapet wall, leaving its head barely visible. Then I heard a round coming right into the landing zone and ducked back into my helmet. After the round detonated, I took a quick look at the rat. His head had been blown completely off and the headless body was crawling out of the little enclave like nothing was wrong with it. It hesitated, then dropped straight down to the parapet floor right next to me and stiffened in death. I stared at that rat, wondering how I was going to keep my five-foot-eight-inch, 140-pound body alive until noon.

A couple rounds later, Corporal Blucher leaped to his feet, saying, "I'll be right back." I never saw or heard of him again.

Shortly after that, Pierce and I got a fire mission. Pierce was leveling the bubbles and getting on the aiming stakes while I ran to the ready bunker to break out a round. Just as

I turned back toward the gun with a projectile, an incoming round slammed into the landing zone and down went Pierce with an awful hole in his chest. I later heard that Pierce was convalescing back in The World, but I still don't know what happened to Blucher.

□

THE ROCK QUARRY

Cpl BERT MULLINS
H&S Company, 1/9 ⎯⎯⎯⎯⎯⎯⎯⎯⎯⎯⎯⎯⎯

The battalion—less Charlie Company and part of H&S Company, which had been delayed—left the combat base at about 0800, January 23.

HM3 BILL GESSNER
Delta Company, 1/9 ⎯⎯⎯⎯⎯⎯⎯⎯⎯⎯⎯⎯⎯

We left the perimeter and went down into the low ground. The elephant grass was very high. I had never experienced it before. I expected to be hit at any time, and I wondered how the lieutenant could know where he was going. It was hot down in the valley.

Cpl BERT MULLINS
H&S Company, 1/9 ⎯⎯⎯⎯⎯⎯⎯⎯⎯⎯⎯⎯⎯

We had been assigned to one of the hills outside the perimeter from which we could block the western approach route to the base. Our hill was called the Rock Quarry.

The Rock Quarry position consisted of one hill—not high, but large at the top—and a lower area from which the rock had been quarried. From the top of the hill, we could look down into Khe Sanh ville and the combat base. Bravo and Delta companies formed a perimeter at the top of the hill. Outside that perimeter, at the base of the hill, was a stream. The road from the combat base came out toward the hill, hooked back to the left, and went up the hill to the quarry. Alpha Company (and, later, Charlie Company) formed another perimeter along the road, and it met up with the Bravo-Delta perimeter. Hill 64 was north of our position. It was outposted by a platoon of Alpha Company.

LtCol JOHN MITCHELL
1/9 Commanding Officer _____

The first order of the day was to dig in and clear fields of fire. Starting from scratch, a storybook defensive perimeter was gradually, painstakingly molded. Except for the northern sector, no field of fire existed because of three-to-seven-foot grass surrounding the 1/9 positions.[2]

HM3 BILL GESSNER
Delta Company, 1/9 _____

I was walking down toward the 2nd Platoon area when a couple of mortar rounds hit. I hugged the ground, cursing myself for being caught in the open. I waited to see if any more rounds would fall. When they didn't, I headed back toward my position. Just as I got close to my foxhole, I heard more incoming rounds, and I jumped right into the foxhole. I felt something round and soft under my feet. I knew that was wrong so I jumped out while the mortar rounds were still falling, and I hugged the ground until the incoming stopped. My foxhole buddy had seen what I had done, and he ran over to ask me if I was crazy. I said, "There's something in there." We looked in, and there was a cobra in the hole. We called the lieutenant over and then we threw a grenade in the hole to kill it. I must have landed on its head, otherwise I would have been bitten.

Cpl BERT MULLINS
H&S Company, 1/9 _____

We spent the first night at Rock Quarry pretty much in the open. We had no wire or tripflares in front of us because we had gotten organized too late to put them in. Virtually every man along the line was awake.

The three of us in a fighting hole by the stream saw movement during the night, and we elected to throw a grenade out. One of the fellows, excitable and with less time in-country than me, wanted to throw the grenade. I was senior man, so I pointed out exactly where I wanted it thrown—just to the right of a tree in front of our fighting hole. I thought we had all seen the movement, and that he knew which tree I was talking about. It was one of only two trees, and it was the one farthest from the fighting hole. The Marine threw the grenade just to the right of the nearer tree, which was way too close. I knew what was going to happen as soon as he threw it. After the standard three or four seconds, we had shrapnel and dirt all over us. We spent the rest of the night awake. Next morning, we went out in front of our position and found a fiber canister similar to what 105mm rounds came packed in. It had a length of detonating cord attached. We did not touch the canister, and I don't know what was in it.

JANUARY 24

Lt RAY STUBBE
1/26 Battalion Chaplain _____

[DIARY ENTRY] I'm writing this at 2125.

We had another attack today, shorter in duration than the first one, but it was more devastating. One landed right on top of the recon bunker. Painter walked in, in complete shock, shrapnel wounds all over his back and face—little holes all over, with small burn marks and blood dripping out of a few of them. I talked with him, but he couldn't reply. Then more came in—Velardi, Noyes, others. We went into my bunker for safety. Then an Air Force lieutenant colonel who had minor shrapnel wounds in his lower buttocks came in. He took off his flak jacket, and there was a piece of shrapnel just below the collar, in the middle, where it would have hit his spinal cord and probably killed him. Then a shell-shocked postal clerk came in. These seven, in addition to Dr. King, Corpsman Heath, and myself. No one talked; everyone just sat there, silent.

[After the shelling stopped] the Air Force lieutenant colonel left. The rest of us slept in my hooch, in which perhaps two could comfortably live. There were four men sitting on my rack; they couldn't lie down. Wounded but unable to depart because the choppers aren't flying tonight, they just fell asleep in sitting positions, blood all over. I curled up on top of a field desk, about three feet by three feet. The surgeon was lying on the floor, as was Noyes and the shell-shock victim. Incoming kept coming in all night, a few rounds every now and then.

Capt BILL DABNEY
India Company, 3/26 (Hill 881S) _____

We had two NVA run up the nose on the east end of the hill—we had an observation post out there in the daytime—with their hands in the air, wearing nothing but skivvies, and it seems to me one of them was waving a *chieu hoi* letter or some piece of white paper; we couldn't tell what it was. They came to the edge of the wire. As the two of them stood there, one of them got shot from somewhere behind him. The other one started just tearing the wire, coming on through. He was unarmed, not dangerous. A couple of guys from the observation post went out and got him and brought him through the lanes and up on the hill. My exec, 1stLt Rich Foley, spoke Vietnamese. The NVA kid—a big, strapping, muscular, well-fed-looking guy who looked in good physical shape—looked like he wasn't hurt. Just after he came into the trenchline, we had a jet fly very fast over the top of the hill. They used to fly past because they bombed for us so much anyway—kind of saying hello. This NVA guy was standing in the trenchline, and as soon as that jet sound hit his ears, he defecated while standing there. About twenty minutes into our initial interrogation of him, some artillery cut loose from down Khe Sanh on some target near us. As soon as those tubes popped, he fell into the bottom of the hole. The guy was literally psychologically destroyed. You could clap your hands and he'd go spastic.

He said his whole unit was in that kind of shape. "Many, many sick; many, many go away"—that sort of thing.[3]

HM3 DAVID STEINBERG
India Company, 3/26 (Hill 881S) _____

January 24, 1968

My Dearest Darlin',

I am sitting here on top of Hill 881S, sitting in a trenchline where I live 25 hours a day. I am now a corpsman attached to India Company, 3/26, the 3rd Platoon. The NVA would love to have this hill, and we stay on watch all night and sleep in shifts by day. Two days ago, we received heavy mortar fire and lost a few men and had many wounded. I was running in every direction, treating one man and then hearing "Corpsman, up!" and off again. The other corpsman in my platoon was hit and medevacked, but, luckily, today I got a replacement for him.

Today, we had an NVA soldier surrender at the wire, and I had to treat him. I told him, "Me *bac si* (doctor)," and he grabbed my feet and then pointed at his wounds. I gave my .45-caliber pistol to the guard and put some Band-Aids and iodine on his cuts. In exchange, we got information.

The jets have been pounding the hills around this mountain, and we have about 3,000 confirmed kills, but there are many more of them out there. They want Khe Sanh and these mountains bad for a moral victory.

Mail is messed up again. In fact, we get rationed a half-canteen of water a day and three C-ration meals. I haven't showered or shaved in three weeks now and feel kind of scroungy.

JANUARY 25

1stLt JOHN KAHENY
1/26 Combat Operations Center _____

Our battalion commander, LtCol Jim Wilkinson, understood how serious the siege was and realized we were going to be in pretty bad straits for a while. The first thing he did was condemn our entire beer supply, which was staged in the enlisted and officers' clubs. He had it moved to a secured area, put a guard on it, and had it issued out at the rate of one can per man every other day. It lasted at least until mid-February.

This contrasts sharply with what the Air Force contingent had been doing. Just before the siege began, they had been caught by Colonel Lownds selling hard liquor to Marines for $65 per bottle—equal to our combat pay.

One morning, I was making my rounds, checking on the welfare of everyone in the command-post area, when a rocket came in. The nearest place to hide was in one of the Air Force bunkers—which far exceeded in strength anything the Marines had. When I got inside, I found that all the Air Force people were gone. They had left. I went back and reported this to Lieutenant Colonel Wilkinson, and eventually the bunkers were taken over for use as an additional battalion medical facility.

Lt RAY STUBBE
1/26 Battalion Chaplain _____

[DIARY ENTRY] There were six dead bodies, four from the collapsed recon bunker last afternoon. I went from body bag to body bag, looking at the tags, praying my prayers. The first man was Rosa. The second tag—I didn't believe it— was Popowitz. I had just talked with him yesterday. I was with a group and asked, ''Where's Popowitz?'' ''Here,'' he cheerfully said. He was standing right in front of me. I

examined his head after partly unzipping the bag. There was
a small hole in his cheek, about a half-inch in diameter.

Cpl ERNESTO GOMEZ
Marine Medium Helicopter Squadron 262 _____

[NAVY CROSS CITATION] For extraordinary heroism while
serving with Marine Medium Helicopter Squadron 262,
in connection with operations against the enemy in the
Republic of Vietnam. On 25 January 1968, Corporal
Gomez was the Crew Chief aboard a CH-46 transport
helicopter assigned an emergency medical evacuation
mission on Hill 881 near the Khe Sanh Combat Base. The
pilot proceeded to the designated area and landed in the
zone as two Marines began leading a casualty, whose
head and eyes were covered with bandages, toward the
helicopter. When the entire landing zone was subjected to
intense enemy fire, the two men were forced to drop to
the ground. Observing the blindfolded casualty attempting
to reach the aircraft unassisted, Corporal Gomez unhesitatingly left the helicopter and rushed across the 25 meters
of fire-swept terrain to the side of the injured man.
Quickly pulling the Marine to the ground, he selflessly
used his own body to shield his comrade from the hostile
fire impacting around them, and as the enemy fire continued, he took cover with the casualty in a nearby rocket
crater. Corporal Gomez remained in this exposed area
until another crew member rushed to his assistance. Then
the two Marines, protecting their wounded comrade from
further injury, carried him to the helicopter. The pilot was
quickly informed that the injured Marine was aboard, and
the aircraft lifted from the hazardous area for the medical
facility at Khe Sanh. Corporal Gomez's heroic actions
were instrumental in saving his companion's life and
inspired all who observed him. By his courage, selfless
concern for the safety of his fellow Marine, and unswerving
devotion to duty at great personal risk, he upheld the

highest traditions of the Marine Corps and the United States Naval Service.

☐

"NO HEAVY ARTILLERY OUT THERE"
Capt BILL DABNEY
India Company, 3/26 (Hill 881S) _____

During an indirect fire attack [on the combat base], GySgt Robert DeArmond was standing in the trench with me, watching one of the rocket salvos. "Skipper," he said, "I just heard something I haven't heard in a bunch of years." I said, "What do you mean?" He said, "Somebody is firing heavy artillery, and the way my ears are working, it ain't us." I had never had heavy artillery fired at me, so I didn't really know what to keep listening for, but Gunny DeArmond had been at the Chosin Reservoir and in big fights in Korea, so he had some experience with it. I listened more carefully, and after a while, during the rocket salvos—more or less coincidental with them, if I listened closely—I could hear, way, way out west, a kind of *pop*, *boom*, that sort of thing. That's all I ever heard, but if I listened fifteen or twenty seconds later, over the hill I would hear this sound like a squirrel running through dry leaves. The rounds would impact on the base more or less at the same time as the salvo of rockets would impact. But the gunny was telling me those weren't rockets.

We reported it down to Khe Sanh by radio. The response we got back initially was, "Oh, they don't have any heavy artillery out there." We were trying to get somebody to go up with [a spotter plane] and go looking out there, but we got no response at all at first.[4]

Lt RAY STUBBE
1/26 Battalion Chaplain _____

[DIARY ENTRY] Chaplain William Hampton reported in. He was in my bunker for some time, having run in from the incoming. He later stated that I must have been under some shock, for I looked at him blankly and simply said, "Oh, you're here." We walked to the 3/26 command post. On the way, as we approached the 1/26 battalion aid station, on either side of the road, just missing the battalion aid station by no more than ten feet, were two large artillery craters from today's incoming. A man could stand in them and his head would still be below the surface of the ground! We all looked at the ominous holes and, although no one said a word, everyone who saw knew, "What protection is there against something like that?" Not even the regimental combat operations center could take one of these rounds.

Capt BILL DABNEY
India Company, 3/26 (Hill 881S) _____

After a few days, they started firing that kind of fire without coordinating with the rocket fire. They were still thinking in Khe Sanh that this was 122mm rockets. And we were telling them, "No, that was not 122mm rockets. That is artillery, it's coming from a long way out. We don't know what the caliber is, but we can tell you it's artillery." Well, eventually we kept a Marine (without his helmet, so he could hear) in a good tight hole on top of the hill with a radio for the specific purpose of listening for that little *pop* way out west, and the dry-leaf sound. And, as soon as he heard it, he would key his handset and call down to Khe Sanh ("Dunbar County" was the call sign of the battalion with which we had radio contact), and he would say, "Dunbar, this is India. Arty 305!" That is, a 305-degree azimuth from us was where we were getting the sound. And they'd say, "Roger, out." It got to be a joke after a while. He would give them, "Arty, 305, shot, over," and when he saw the stuff impact at Khe Sanh, he'd say, "Dunbar, India. Splash, over." They'd laugh and say, "Roger, splash, out!" Of course, it hit right on top of them. They had some sort of klaxon system down there. From the time those rounds passed over the hill to the time they hit at Khe Sanh was eight, ten seconds or so, which was plenty of time if you had some sort of warning for a guy to jump in a hole.[5]

Sgt MIKE STAHL
4.2-inch Mortar Battery, 1/13 (Hill 861)

My heavy-mortar platoon had an artillery spotting scope and, using it, I could see the NVA rocket trucks displace around the combat base. The trucks would move into covered positions north or northwest of Hill 861, fire off a sheaf of 122mm rockets, and then move back out of artillery range. Usually, we didn't find them until they fired, until we could focus on the smoke from the rockets. By the time we tried to get artillery or our heavy mortars on them, they were gone.

JANUARY 26

SSgt HARVE SAAL, USA
FOB-3 _____

My recon team set up a linear ambush along a "high-speed" trail on January 26. At about 0530, one NVA soldier was observed by my Bru scouts as he approached our kill-zone area. It was noted that his AK-47 was slung across his back and that he wasn't ready for a confrontation with the enemy—us. He was captured instead of being killed. On a quick interrogation, we learned that he was a scout and was looking for routes for *armor* to follow. We secured the man and escorted him to FOB-3 Intelligence for further interrogation. We were told there to take him to the Marine camp and allow their intelligence staff to take the first crack at him.

When I inquired about the NVA prisoner later in the day, I was told, "The Vietnamese person you brought in was waiting in a 'classified and secure' area, so he was asked to leave the bunker." He did. He roamed around the Marine camp for another two days trying to surrender to any Marine who would stop and listen to him. Finally, one Marine got suspicious and took him into custody. That's when FOB-3 was informed that the Marine security people had an unknown Vietnamese in their custody. They wanted to know if

he belonged to us. We got him back under our control and
were able to learn more about the tanks he was scouting for.

JANUARY 27

1stLt NICK ROMANETZ
Charlie Company, 1/26 _____

On January 27, the 37th ARVN Ranger Battalion came
aboard and took over the unoccupied outer eastern sector of
the base, out in front of the ammo dump. About a hundred
yards back were our Marines, in the older fighting positions.

Capt KEN PIPES
Bravo Company, 1/26 _____

The 37th ARVN Ranger Battalion was a good unit—a good,
scrappy bunch. When they came in, they were set in front
of my 2nd Platoon, on the east flank of the perimeter,
covering one of the main routes of advance into the base. If
the NVA could have busted through the line there, they
could have had the base. So, when the ARVNs set in, we
left 2nd Platoon in place to back them up. After we met
with the ARVN battalion commander, Capt Hoang Pho, it
was agreed that my company's artillery forward observer,
1stLt Hank Norman, would go out with the ARVNs when
they needed artillery called.

  We quickly built up a mutual trust with the ARVNs.
They'd come over and steal stuff, but, hell, they didn't have
a hell of a lot to begin with. I wasn't aware of any big
problems.

1stLt NICK ROMANETZ
Charlie Company, 1/26 _____

By the end of the first week of the siege, we had gotten into
our daily routine: take more incoming, dig more foxholes,
put in more covered positions. Eventually, minefields were

put out and barbed wire was improved. On a routine day, we would have reveille around 0500 or 0530, make a head call, shave, stand to, go to meetings, check the wire, set up work parties, improve our fighting positions, clean weapons, brief the troops on what was happening, eat, wait, prepare the positions, just keep going. Once we had it in, we always had to check the barbed wire. There was a fear that the enemy would sneak in at night and cut the wire and put it back together so that, if the ground attacks ever came, they would be able to get through. Besides, the wire was always getting chopped up from the incoming. So, on a daily basis, we had to send a three- or four-man team out to check the wire. This was no big deal until we started to get snipers three or four hundred yards in front of the wire. As it turned out, we had to get up while there was still fog, and shimmy and shake the wire to see what was going on. Then, as the fog started to lift, we had to hope we could get back in. Eventually, a couple Marines did get shot by the snipers.

HM3 DAVID STEINBERG
India Company, 3/26 (Hill 881S) _____

January 27, 1968

My Dearest Darlin',

We are still maintaining our position at the top of this hill. It has been three weeks since receiving mail and two and a half weeks since anybody here on the hill has shaved. We get only a half-canteen of water a day and all our ammo is dropped from helicopters, which don't land here anymore because too many have been shot down.

We have left our sandbag huts on the hilltop and now we live in trenches just off the skyline, like World War I. We each dug a bunnyhole at the bottom of the trench that is big enough to curl up and sleep in. We stand 100-percent watch at night and sleep all day. It is safer because we usually get rockets and mortars during the day. I just stay in my little bunnyhole until dark. I don't come out for anything unless I hear "Corpsman, up," and then I crawl on my hands and knees.

A little while ago, I dove into the trench and buried my head in the dirt and tensed for a mortar barrage, and that's how I fell asleep. I woke up an hour later in the same curled position at the bottom of the trench and realized that I had dreamed I was home. Yes, I was home with you again, which is my every wish. How shocking it is to wake up so far from you, only to brush dust off and grin and bear another day on Hill 881S.

Not having received mail in so long and not knowing when we will, I can only hope that all is well with you and your family. Here it is, almost February, and that much closer to November.

All my clothes are buggy and my full beard and dirty face make me look about like a person I don't know. Strange how being like a caveman can change a person. It must be the hill because I have treated four cases of battle fatigue in the last two days. I had to befriend them and calm them, and everybody reacts different, including pointing a loaded weapon at you. It's like a novel of a strategic hill that must be held and the men who crack up on it for two months.

Chapter 10

1stLt ERNIE SPENCER
Delta Company, 1/26 ⎯⎯⎯⎯⎯⎯⎯⎯⎯⎯⎯⎯⎯⎯⎯

Charlie has moved onto a small plateau near our water point, which lies just outside our wire. This northern part of the base is defended by Charlie Company from my battalion. We pump our water from an undefended pond beyond our wire. I always wait for someone else to drink first.

If I were Charlie, I'd fuck with our water. If I were given a shot at Charlie's water, I'd make every guy who had just been on R&R soak his dick in it. I'd poison the drinks if I had a chance. Give me this morality shit? It's being taken out that's the morality. How doesn't count a rat's-ass worth. I've seen guys die, die so hard, so bad, they would have taken a nuke if given a choice. So fuck the how. You're missing the point if you think that the morality is the how. It's irrelevant how you do it or get it done.

Regiment orders a platoon-sized search-and-destroy mis-

sion on the plateau. They choose Delta Company, and I pick
2nd Platoon. The entire plateau is only 600 meters long. I
wait in my bunker, in radio contact with the lieutenant of
2nd Platoon [2ndLt D. S. McGravey].

Only minutes after starting, the platoon gets it. RPG—a
rocket-propelled grenade—a B-40. The lieutenant's first
report is brief: The hissing of the open mike from the radio
speaker ends, then, "Contact, point!" As usual, the assistant S-3 from battalion requests a report almost instantly. . . . I
sit and say nothing.

The lieutenant of 2nd Platoon is new. A real cocky,
macho, Boston kid. Right from the beginning he calls me
Skip. He's fresh out of Basic School and hotter than a
popcorn fart.

Again the lieutenant speaks. He's freaked. His voice is three
octaves up. He wants a dustoff [medevac helicopter] right now.
Got one guy done real fucking bad. I can hear the shooting.

I ask him, "You still taking?"

"We got something going with the one who hit us," he
says. I hear grenades exploding and rifle fire over the radio
as he speaks. "I need a dustoff, now!" More explosions.
"Right now, goddamn it! You hear me?" He is screaming at
me. "My guy's real, real bad."

As soon as the hiss of the open mikes comes on, I press
the button on the side of the handset. Speaking deliberately
and slowly, I say, "Okay . . . listen to me . . . listen to me. I
don't care what else happens, you hang on. You hang on.
You have got to hold it together. Hear me?"

A brief hiss from his open mike, then, "Roger, 6."

"Okay," I'm saying. "You carry him in. You're right
outside the wire. It's faster than a chopper."

Behind me I hear the battalion radio net telling the
hospital to send an ambulance to the wire at the water point.
A short times passes. The lieutenant calls again. He's got a
couple of others slightly wounded from that one rocket.
They've killed two gooks, and the one who fired the RPG is
critically wounded by a grenade. Pressing the green rubber-
covered button again, I say, "Delta 2, this is 6. They want
anyone who is alive to be brought in, copy?"

"The gook ain't going to make it, 6. He ate most of a grenade."

"If he's alive, you bring him in. You copy?"

"Roger 6." For most of a minute the mike hisses like a tire going flat. Then, "Six, this is 2."

"This is 6, go ahead."

"We're coming in. The gook is a flunk. Over."

"Roger, 2. Six out," I answer softly.[1]

26th Marines Command Chronology

Meanwhile, Charlie Company, 1/26, had observed mortar flashes from their lines. The rounds landed near the patrol and reaction force. 1/26 called fires on the mortar site with excellent target coverage.

The NVA were believed to be a reconnaissance unit from an NVA infantry battalion. They were wearing cloth over their faces and heads which blended with the elephant grass. There were 3 NVA KIA (confirmed). The bodies were stripped of their clothing and documents, and the following weapons were picked up: 1 RPG-2, 1 SKS carbine, 2 Chicom grenades, 2 AK-47s, and assorted documents.

1stLt ERNIE SPENCER
Delta Company, 1/26

After a man's been in a fire fight, his eyes light up, then they slowly darken and sink back into his head. By the time the lieutenant and I meet, he is fast sinking into his sockets. His jowls seem heavy as he speaks, his eyes are almost glazed and sleepy. With minimum details he recounts the ambush. Charlie was dug in and popped him first. His guys moved well, he says. No talking, just dumping. His guys really unloaded, just like in training. "I didn't even have to tell 'em," he said. "They just went at 'em." We stood alone near the entrance to my bunker.

As he is leaving, he says in a hushed tone, "Skip, I did the gook myself. I did him right between the eyes with my pistol. He never would have made it, Skip. I did the gook myself." The lieutenant's eyes are so sad. Good sign, I'm thinking, not the type to lay bad shit off on somebody else. Welcome to the war, macho man.

With that blank look of mine, I pause and say, "You did what you had to do, is all. You did what you had to do. You did real good. Real good."

I can teach guys how to play macho by now; I had become a teacher. If I had tried to comfort him, I would have ruined him, ruined him for war.

As I walk into J.B.'s [LtCol James Wilkinson, the 1/26 commanding officer] quarters, also the [operations] situation room, I can feel the sense of vengeance. Old-fashioned Marine Corps vengeance. J.B. is the first to speak.

"You want them?" His eyes are like those of a coach asking his player. He is looking at me.

"I can take them out, Colonel. I will take them out." We stand for a moment, staring into one another's eyes. "We're up. I'm up, ready."

After the briefing, the air officer walks over and says how great I had been on the radio. How cool, how I calmed the lieutenant right down. With the same blank look on my face, I say, "I was in my bunker. He was taking it. Talking in a bunker ain't shit."

Tomorrow I'll see whether I am just talking.[2]

JANUARY 28

1stLt ERNIE SPENCER
Delta Company, 1/26 _____

There is not much room for creativity. With the plateau my restricted area of operation, it would be like a bird shoot. Ol' boys in Regiment do like to fucking panic. To put an entire company of Marines on that small plateau is redundancy personified. It's a good thing we are understrength, or we would trip over one another. I hope to trick Charlie by having 2nd Platoon leave the base at the water point while 1st and 3rd platoons leave the wire at the other end of the runway. We will sweep outward across the plateau unless it is foggy in the morning. Fog will dictate.

I am ravenous that night. I eat two meals of Cs. I wait and check throughout the evening until the fog comes in, a nice thick fog. I sleep for several hours. Like a child on Christmas Eve, I go to sleep with hopes and dreams dancing in my head—my last remembrance is a wish for fog. I believe it will be close in the fog. I want to do it close. I want to see them. I hope the fog lasts tomorrow.

There is a nice deep, wet, still fog the next morning. After moving the men in small units to avoid arousing suspicion, I'm with 3rd Platoon. Second Platoon moves through the water point and fans out across the top end of the plateau—the place they'd started the day before. Most of the covering on the plateau is chest-to-head-high elephant grass. Numerous artillery and bomb hits scar it, leaving gaping wounds of bare earth like the acned face of one lightly bearded. Hidden from direct view from Khe Sanh, a second plateau lies hidden just below the one we will sweep. Beyond the plateaus a steep, deep valley dives almost straight down to the Rao Quan River. We slip quietly out through the openings in the wire. The fog hangs just beyond the trenchlines like a veil—full and white. There are unexploded artillery shells scattered about like toys tossed by a bored child. The shells are remnants of the ammo dump explosion. Charlie got a direct hit on the ammo dump one day, and the artillery shells started cooking off. Now I look down at them—sterile punches that never were.

With the fog holding and continuing to hide the plateau, I tell 1st Platoon to move out and over the east end of the runway and to move below the edge of the plateau. The plateau opens from that point like the tip of an arrowhead. Second Platoon radios that they are in the assigned blocking position. I stand just beyond the wire at the center of the sickle blade formed by 3rd and 1st Platoons. Sunlight scatters the fog. First in holes, quickly reclosed, and then in large gashes. The fog keeps retreating. It suddenly pulls back across the plateau, over the lip, and back down into the deep canyon.

Lying in front of me is a large cleared area, an area burned by napalm. The clearing is 60 yards across. Marines stand on either side of me, tense and restlessly waiting to go. We are at the edge. Right fucking there—not a doubt in any man's mind. I stand very still trying to show cool, but my heart is redlining like hell. I can hear it stroking in my ears. I feel every little bump and groove in my arterial system. That blood of mine is cascading through my veins like a river out of control.

We must wait for the tip of the sickle blade to show on the plateau to my right. When the lead squad of 1st Platoon shows on the plateau, we will have boxed Charlie in on three sides. The mountains out beyond the canyon jut above the fog. Clouds of fog rest against the mountains, forming a bridge over the canyon to us. The mountains are scarred by B-52 raids and show their earth, like frosting gouged out of a cake.

I see their heads now, the right tip of the blade. The lead squad and the rest of 1st Platoon step silently onto the plateau. I begin walking straight across the opening without saying a word. Marines begin fanning out around me, pointing their rifles from the hip. Some are moving tentatively, in a half crouch, ready to jump in any direction. They are moving too slowly. I want to get through the open space as quickly as possible. Quickening my pace and without a word, I begin waving my left arm, swinging it back to front like a farmer scattering seed in his fields. Walking straight ahead and not looking to either side I move quickly across the opening, waving my men on silently. I know my men will come. They will come with me. Almost rushing now, the men surge abreast of me. Like birds darting forward toward the seeds I've scattered, they now know what I want. I want into the brush as quickly as possible. It is still when we enter the grass, the only sound that of trousers scraping. No words.

This is the first time I'm using rock and roll prior to contact. My rifle is on full automatic and pointing straight out in front of me at hip level. Left hand on the forward handguard, right hand on the grip and just a finger pull

away from making anything in front of the barrel trip the
light fantastic. Each man points to an area in front of him.
Marines on line. I now glance to my left and right as I walk.
My eyes sweep in a wide arc around me. My rifle always in
my arms as I walk and point out my kill zone, rocking left
to right with the motion of my eyes, my rhythms.

I am watching the movement of the line. The lieutenants
are up and slightly ahead of their men. I am tuned in to the
picture, but an inner voice keeps reminding me over and
over again, "If it goes off in front of you, pull the trigger!
Before you move or shit yourself, pull the fucking trigger."
I have no doubt we will hit that day. I have come to that
point with myself: I know it is there, right there.

It goes off to my right, 50 yards away. To the distinctive
pops of an M-16, my head and shoulders jerk to the right. I
plant my left foot, my rifle instinctively rising to my
shoulder. An M-16 sounds so much softer than an AK-47.
We hit first. The line has gone down into firing position.
More M-16 fire, grenades explode. Dropping to my knee, I
yell to my company radio, "Ask 1st Platoon which is the
best way to cover him."

"They're by the edge. Come straight across," he yells
back a moment later.

Up, I'm yelling, "Let's go! Let's go straight across,
come on!" Intermittent fire. Marines moving, grenades
exploding. Everyone goes down when a grenade goes off.
"Don't shoot unless you can see 'em," I'm yelling. "There
are Marines in there. They're all in there. Don't shoot
unless you can see 'em."

I hold my rifle down by my side so I can move quicker. I
move into the site now and see a foxhole with a dead gook
lying in it. A big machine gun sits next to him. A live gook
is lying nearby. A Marine guards him and keeps himself
under the sight lines of the gook's friends by lying next to
him and pointing his rifle right into the gook's face. I move
farther in.

"Grenade!" a Marine screams. I dive straight forward
like I'm doing a starting dive into a pool. As soon as my
elbows hit, I begin pulling in my hands toward my face. I

feel the explosion come across me from behind and to my left. It rocks me, and I instantly feel a sting in the palm of my left hand. A sudden wet runs across my left buttock and hamstring. I'm hit. I can feel the blood. I pump my left leg twice. No pain. I do not want to look down. I rise to my knees and say to my radioman, "Am I hit?"

"You pissed yourself," he says. My canteen on my left hip had taken most of the hit, my flak jacket the rest. I thought the water from my canteen was blood—sure as shit felt that way. A loud ringing is in my left ear as we move on through the enemy position. I move to the edge of the plateau. Foxholes. They lie in a slight natural depression just out of sight of our trenchline at the base. NVA in the foxholes have clear fields of vision and—more important—a clear shot at the air approach to the runway. Shifting sights, I see that Marines to my left are firing down into the lower plateau.

I gaze down at the small treeline that lies hidden in the lower plateau, an ideal shelter. Just as I start to call to the 81mm mortar spotter to fire a mission, a voice behind me gasps, "Oh, shit! Your fucking head!"

My radio operator's eyes are riveted on me. Startled back so suddenly from my study, his words, my turn, his stare are all almost at the same moment of looking behind me over my right shoulder. "Skip, your fucking head!" He motions with one hand darting over his head.

I turn and run to a promontory to my right that gives a better view of the steep hillside. My radio operator runs behind me, chattering at me from a distance of twenty yards. Like a mother hen clucking to her chick, he says, "Went right over your head. Right over you. You didn't even see it. He almost took your head off. You were standing straight up." My radio operators are always giving me lessons that way, punchline at the end.

Reaching the promontory first, I shoulder my rifle. Semi-automatic on, selector straight up. Looking down the barrel at blurred visions, I pick up forms falling downward through the grasses that drop like a slide before me. While my right eye lines the front post in the center of the rear circle, my left follows the target. It's just like a camera mounted on a rifle. Both eyes are open, working independently. The rifle is jumping in its quick-shot jig. My left hand is firm but not fighting as it guides the jumping rifle to the images. My mouth is half open. It is as though I am merely recording this. Ten shots are fired before full realization of what I am doing comes to me. Up until then it felt like just a movie filmed over the barrel of my rifle. Fully in tune now, I finish my clip. The radiomen begin firing off to my right. Marines move over the promontory and down the steep hillside. Everyone is firing. I drop my first clip at my feet and insert another from my right pouch. After several more shots, it is pointless; they are gone from sight. I finish the clip anyway.

As I turn from the cliff, I see Marines at the base standing on top of the bunkers and along the trenchline cheering, screaming. I'm in a fucking game, I think. They're watching it live. They all wish they were down here getting some with us, but I'm just in a fucking game. I walk back to the two gooks.

One is lying down but up on one elbow. "Corpsman!" I call.

"You don't need the corpsman," says the scruffy Marine guarding him. "He's shot clean through his calf, is all."

The corpsman reports no casualties among us and starts bandaging the wounded NVA's leg, while several other Marines search the dead one. As they empty his pockets, the squad leader takes a Buck knife from his own pocket. In almost one motion he opens the blade, tilts the dead man's chin back, and slits his throat.

"Hey!" I yell.

"Just making sure he's dead's all. Don't want him getting some again," wild-eyed and grinning, the squad leader answers.

"Well, you don't take him apart, you hear me!"

Like a scolded dog he turns away and folds his knife. Quickly they unbutton the trousers of the dead man and pull his pants down to reveal his crotch. It's a habit we have, a recent tradition. The rumor is that NVA who are circumcised tend to be officers. Whenever we zap one and get our hands on him, one of our rituals is to drop his trousers and check his pecker. Part of our report is whether he is circumcised or not.

I have the dead man dragged from where he was killed. His buddies will come looking for him. Let 'em look. Let 'em look good. I am a low motherfucker. Charlie can fucking kiss my ass, too. When he's crawling around in the dark looking for his buddies and cussing, it's my payback for all the shit he's been dumping on me.

Even though we are just outside the wire, Regiment wants the wounded NVA flown back into the base. The pilot barely lifts off before he puts down again just outside the wire. I'm sure we impress the hell out of the gook, who gets his own helicopter for a ten-second ride.

As we resume the sweep toward 2nd Platoon, the heat of the day becomes relentless. The fear and exhaustion of the fire fight, its taste and smell are fresh upon me. The grass now seems taller and thicker. My senses are dull and drugged. Too much adrenaline has gone through me; I'm emotionally exhausted. Just before joining with 2nd Platoon, we move over the ambush site of yesterday.

One of the dead gooks is still here, unfound during his buddies' search the night before. In their haste the day before, 2nd Platoon had not searched this one, who was shot while running away. I know everyone up to LBJ will want to know everything they can about Charlie around Khe Sanh. I tell the chief of scouts to search the gook. The soldier had been so well lit up when the Marines shot him that it is like searching in a vat of worms—not too much solidly in place. The scout tosses me the man's personal possessions.

An energy hits me after we get back inside the wire. When I am sure that we have finished the sweep without casualties, new life surges into me. I have an arrogant feeling of power. I feel like a superstar walking down the gangway. Striding down Main Street, I walk oblivious to the possible rocket and artillery barrages. The eyes, the faces, the cheers, the shouts of the people who had fought the battle line my path into the colonel's quarters. Their fight has been watching a map on the wall or listening to radio transmissions from my company while dreaming their own battle. My presence now before them is the confirmation of their dream. The dream that all of us had been dreaming for so long: payback. Charlie has become so arrogant that he fucks with our airplanes, our lifelines, our umbilical cords. But the man who killed the shooters has arrived. I carry the NVA machine gun over my shoulder. It is the reality to those Marines' dreams. They now see that it is true. I stride down the stairs to the battalion headquarters bunker.

J.B.'s eyes hold his smile, his relief, his happiness, his joy. One of his men has done it: got Charlie and walked away. J.B. is very pleased that the men showed enough class to bring in a live prisoner to tell where the others might be. Everyone wants at Charlie.

J.B. pumps my hand while holding it with both of his. He breaks out his bottle of Jack Daniel's. Empty C-ration cookie cans serve as glasses. Toasts are offered to Delta Company by J.B. and the other staff officers. My toast is to my man who was killed the day before.

"What don't you know?" I ask. I know my battalion radio operator always gives an excellent running commentary to battalion during contact. He is as good as any play-by-play announcer. . . .

There are two facts that I omit reporting to Battalion. I don't tell them that the gook's machine gun had misfired. The guy who burned the gook gunner was saved by a misfire. I also don't tell them about thinking I am hit in the leg or about the shrapnel in my left hand. I'll be fucked if the only friendly wounded that day is me.[3]

Chapter 11

HM3 DAVID STEINBERG
India Company, 3/26 (Hill 881S) _____

January 29, 1968

My Dearest Sharon,

This is your favorite caveman in the beautiful resort area on Hill 881S. There are great accommodations if you pick-and-shovel out a little hole to sleep in. The surrounding countryside is in full bloom, with assorted bomb craters and napalm-burnt hills to add to the beauty. Sunbathing while filling sandbags increases one's muscles while at the same time it tends to keep the waistline trim. C-rations are passed out three times a day, and a quarter-canteen per day keeps one's water intake to a minimum. Whenever a helicopter stops in with troops or supplies, the NVA give them a hearty welcome with three or four mortars or rockets. We in turn join the festival by shooting 2,000 rounds into the beautiful countryside from our automatic weapons. Hot during the day, freezing at night, with a fireworks display nightly all add to the great vacationing fun on the mountain called 881S.

Well, dear, I'm still hanging in here despite the fun. I'm about due for R&R, but I'll wait until next month. I think I'll go to Taipei.

Well, Sharon dear, I best get some sleep and maybe dream of you again. Don't worry or be mad if the letters don't come as often, because I don't even know if mail is leaving this damn hill.

I miss you very much and my love is mounting and my impatience to be with you again is slowly coming to a boil. I'm determined to make it home, and even if I have to spend my next two months in a whole mess of mud and trenches, ole Charlie won't keep me.

Gotta cut now and heat up a Meal, Combat, Individual, Beef, Spiced With Sauce, Cookies, Cocoa, White Bread, Canned. Love them C-rations! An assortment of twelve to choose from for a whole year.

Sgt JESUS VASQUEZ
Explosive Ordnance Disposal _____

[NAVY CROSS CITATION] For extraordinary heroism while serving as an Explosive Ordnance Disposal Technician with the Ammunition Company, Supply Battalion, First Force Service Regiment/Force Logistic Command in connection with operations against the enemy in the Republic of Vietnam on 30 January 1968. During a mortar and rocket attack at the Khe Sanh Combat Base, several rounds landed in the ammunition supply point, igniting a stack of ammunition. Sergeant Vasquez unhesitatingly rushed to the burning munitions and assisted in fighting the fire. Observing an 81mm mortar round burning and aware of the proximity of his comrades and the possibility of detonation, he lifted the round in an attempt to throw it into a deep crater where its lethal effects would be absorbed should it detonate. In his attempt to throw the round, it exploded, mortally wounding him. By his bold initiative, gallant fighting spirit and loyal devotion to duty, he was instrumental in saving his comrades from further injury or possible death by absorbing most of the impact with his own body. His great personal valor reflected great credit upon himself and enhanced the finest traditions of the Marine Corps and the United States Naval Service. He gallantly gave his life for his country.

Maj TOM COOK
26th Marines Assistant Logistics Officer _____

I departed for Vietnam from Okinawa on January 23, my thirty-seventh birthday. Upon my arrival at Danang, I thought the first thing to do was go over and tell them I wanted a flight into Khe Sanh. It didn't work that way. After sitting around there for a day, I still didn't have a flight to Khe Sanh. I asked about it, and the man at the counter suggested I try flying to Dong Ha. So I hopped a flight to Dong Ha and sat around there for a day. Next morning, I inquired about how in the world I was supposed to get to Khe Sanh. The man suggested I try Quang Tri. So I got a hop to Quang Tri and sat around there for a day. Finally, I asked if they ever had anything going to Khe Sanh. They told me it wasn't likely, that I should try Danang. So I went back to Danang and sat there for days, until I finally found a C-130 that was going to Khe Sanh. I asked how to get on it and the man told me to just throw my duffel bag into a shovel on a front-end loader because it was going to Khe Sanh, that if I stayed with it I would get to Khe Sanh too. It worked. Me and the driver of the front-end loader took off for Khe Sanh on the morning of January 30.

When we landed at Khe Sanh, the crew chief started throwing stuff out the back of the C-130. Then the front-end loader started driving down the ramp. The plane hadn't even stopped yet! The crew chief yelled at me, "Get off!" So I ran down the ramp and got off. The plane just kept rolling. Before I could get off the runway, that C-130 was back up in the air.

Maj JIM STANTON
26th Marines Fire Support Coordination Center _____

Everybody wanted to try something out. For example, we got to test Controlled Fragmentation Munitions—COFRAM—which was just being introduced. This was artillery-delivered bomblets that were scattered when the air-burst artillery shell opened. A little vane stabilized each bomblet and caused it to flutter down to the ground, where a fuse extending out from the bottom caused it to bounce three feet into the air and detonate at the right level to take a man down. It arrived with new firing tables and fuse settings, different from the tables we used for standard-type rounds. The Army's Artillery Center at Fort Sill sent us a team led by a brigadier general to show us how to shoot this stuff! These guys—in clean, starched utilities—came down into the regimental Fire Support Coordination Center on January 30 with a movie projector and film—a film!—and we all crowded into the bunker to watch it. I cannot think of anything that could have been more incongruous.

On February 7, 1/13 fired the first COFRAM—or "firecracker" —rounds used operationally in the Vietnam War.

JANUARY 31

Cpl DENNIS MANNION
Charlie Battery, 1/13 (Hill 861) _____

January 31, 1968

Joe—

I guess we're in a pretty hot situation over here.
The gooks are hellbent on trying to take over this
area—and it isn't over by a long "shot" (pun!) yet.
Sometimes it gets pretty hairy on this motherfucker—
and I've come close a few times. Not close enough,
though. Anyway, I want to say that I'm not afraid
of dying. I'll just feel sorry for my folks, brothers,
and sister. And you. There's no way I can describe
what good friends we two are and how much your
ugly presence means to me. I'll feel sorry about
pulling out so early, Joe. Kinda like I let you down.
Without being too, too clichéd, I'll say there's so
much to say and do and no time or place to attempt
it. If—if I should go, I'll have to say it's been a
fantastic life, full of the best of everything. No
regrets, a barrel of laughs, good times and bad,
happy and sad, etc., etc. I wouldn't have wished it
any other way. And I'll feel most shitty for you,
man. So much we got planned. So much we're
gonna do. Hell, I'm only taking it one day at a time
now, leaving it up to the Big Referee in the Sky.
He's the one who makes the rules and takes out
players and sends in subs. Nothing else really counts.

I feel shitty just writing this mess, but it's been
on my mind *constantly* in the last twelve days and
I had to let you know the score. Just in case. I
think you know what I mean. Now that's over and
done with. Come October '68 I'm gonna stand in

your driveway and watch you put a match to this
piece of crap. And that's no lie.

   I gotta hustle. Sun's almost gone. Another month
shot to shit.

                               See ya pronto,
                               Dennis

   P.S. What's this I hear about Anderson (#44) being
offside (but not detected) on the Dallas six-inch
line? Why? Why? Why? Why!

DIGGING IN

Pfc JOE GIBNEY
Charlie Company, 1/26 _____

When Charlie Company first occupied the Blue Sector
trench, there was only one strand of concertina wire in front
of us. We put out concertina wire, a new type [German
tape] with razor blades attached. There were three rows: two
on the ground, next to each other, and a third row on top of
the other two. Tall metal engineer stakes were driven into
the ground so we could secure the wire. Right in front of the
triple concertina we had 55-gallon drums cut in half and
filled with fourgasse—a sort of napalm mixture. Coming
from the cans were claymore mine igniters. Next, in front of
the fougasse drums, was a wire apron—eightfoot engineer
stakes with three rows of wire barrier pitched at an angle. A
side view looked like the side of a tent or half of a house
roof. Outside of the apron we had tanglefoot—wire stretched
across two-foot-high spikes in one-foot squares—crisscross,
up and down, across and over. In front of the tanglefoot
was another wire apron. And, in front of that, was a wide
minefield. There were also mines between the various rows
of wire.

   We dug night and day; twenty-four hours a day, we were
digging. The NVA could hear us, and we could hear them
digging. All that time, many of the black Marines were
playing cassette tape players—Supremes, Temptations, all

the soul music. We all loved the music, and I guess the gooks did, too. At night, the music was just blasting all over the place; there was no need to keep down the noise.

As we got heavier incoming, we dug the trenchline to shoulder height and moved underground. We stole aluminum matting blown up out on the runway and put it over our hooches. Eventually, they told us to dig down so the edge of the trenchline was over our heads. We had to build a step up to our fighting positions, which were in the wall of the trench. We built our living bunkers into the interior of the trenchline.

One day, just after I got off watch in the trenchline, a 152mm artillery round hit the fighting position I had just turned over to my relief. I was sure my relief had been killed—it was a direct hit—but I found him buried up to his neck. He was in shock and out of it. After we got him out, we squared off the shell crater, which was huge, and built a hooch bunker walled up with dirt-filled ammo boxes.

We had this constant battle between the Northerners and the Southerners in my platoon. It was constant trouble. One day, I had to tell a big Southern guy to stop leaving his trash in our living bunker because it was attracting rats. We got into an argument and then, after a while, into a fight. He was a real big guy and I was just a little shit, but I fought him. We were going at it head-to-head on top of the bunker, and incoming was coming in. Everybody—the officers, the sergeants—was screaming at us to stop. We couldn't hear them; we weren't paying any attention. We wanted to kill. I fought the big guy to a draw until, finally, other Marines came over and dragged us down into the bunker. The stress factor was really high.

All the heavy weapons that could be moved around were in Blue Sector, covered by Charlie Company. There weren't many tanks or Ontos in the combat base, so, during the day, they put them with us. At night, they moved to Gray Sector, on the south side of the base. Apparently, the commanders thought the NVA were going to attack from the south, over the flat ground in front of Gray Sector. To help fool the NVA, we built mock guns and vehicles from the canisters from the 81mm mortar rounds. We replaced the vehicles which were with us during the day with the dummies as soon as they left at night. The NVA observing the southern sector during the day saw no tanks or Ontos, so, if they had attacked Gray Sector at night, they would have run into them without realizing they were there.

I heard that the entire 101st Airborne Division was on constant alert, ready to come to our rescue if we were overrun. If that happened, we were to set off the fougasse drums in front of our position and call air and artillery strikes right in on our position. The 101st was supposed to parachute in a circle around our perimeter and attack toward the base, into the rear of the NVA.

One of the really weird aspects of the siege was the loudspeakers our people had set up to try to talk the North Vietnamese into surrendering. There we were, surrounded by two divisions of NVA, telling *them* to surrender. I thought that was a good example of reverse psychology.

When it all sank in, everybody was trying to get medevacked out. Some guys tried to put their butts in the air so they would get hit. Everyone was panicked. Communications were terrible. We never really knew what was going on. As far as I was concerned, the people running the show had their heads up their butts. They made a lot of bad decisions.

LCpl PHIL MINEER
Bravo Battery, 1/13 _____

When we first got into Khe Sanh, one of my buddies and I dug a hole with an entrenching tool. We got very deep very quick, but it still wasn't enough. We were exposed, we had no overhead cover. We got hit all night that night. Didn't get much sleep until daybreak, when it let up.

Next morning, an engineer came in with a tractor to dig holes for everybody. When he got to us, where we left off with the entrenching tools, the hose on the side of the bucket broke and pink hydraulic oil splattered all over the place. So my buddy and I wound up digging our sleeping bunker by hand. I guess it was about eight feet by eight feet. We filled 105mm ammo boxes with dirt and stacked them on the inner wall like bricks. We looked for some kind of support to put up to hold all the sandbags we were going to put over the top. We went over to see the Seabees, who had stacks of big timber. We only wanted three timbers. Until then, the Seabees had always been cooperative when we needed stuff. This time, they told us, "You guys, we been telling you to dig in, telling you to dig in, offering to do it. But you been putting it off 'cause you macho Marines want to live aboveground. You need us now, but we don't need to give you this stuff." I couldn't believe it. I had just gotten there! I didn't give a shit about the sins of the guys before me. All I wanted to do was get some cover up. Anyway, we stole some runway matting and then snuck back over to the Seabees and stole one or two of their timbers. We got the top on our bunker, laid on sandbags about six deep, and built a baffled entrance to keep anything that blew up in front of the door from blowing in. We even built racks in there, and got a camouflaged parachute to drape from the ceiling and down the walls. We had a battery-operated record player, but the only record we had was "Sergeant Pepper's Lonely Hearts Club Band."

Word got around the battery about the trouble the Seabees had given us over use of "their" timbers. The feeling was that they deserved some payback. At the very end of January, we saw a chopper coming in with a 50,000-watt generator hanging off it. When they set it down on the runway, we saw it had a Seabee insignia on the side. When the skipper, 1stLt George Wood, heard, he allowed one of us to wear his cover with the silver bar on it and get a six-by truck. One guy even had a clipboard in his hand, to make us look official. We drove over to the runway and hooked the generator to the trailer hitch. As we were working, a guy on the runway asked us what we were doing, and the guy with the clipboard said, "If you get the manifest for this, we'll sign it. See the lieutenant." We were on the verge of bullshitting our way out when the NVA mortars started firing on the runway. There was a lot of confusion, and the kid checking us off the runway told us to "just get the hell outta here!" So we did. From the time I drove the truck into the battery area until that generator was in place was less than an hour. In that time, it was painted Marine green and marked in red with Marine insignia. We hooked it up and every hole and bunker in the Bravo and Charlie battery area had electricity. Even better, the Seabees went nuts trying to figure out what happened to their 50,000-watt generator. Believe it or not, in the middle of all the stuff going down at Khe Sanh, they started an official investigation, but it ended as abruptly as it started and we kept the generator.

1stLt JOHN KAHENY
1/26 Combat Operations Center _____

The Seabees were mad at the Marines because we used to rip them off all the time. If they weren't looking, we stole it. That was because we were at the end of the supply line, and the grunts were not getting the kind of support one would think they would be entitled to. For example, if they left a pallet of plywood out, it would be gone in the proverbial sixty seconds. Meantime, they lived in a very nice, secure bunker with all the amenities, such as a rather generous supply of Johnny Walker Black. There were thus some pretty hard feelings between the Marines and the Seabees.

When David Douglas Duncan interviewed the Seabees for his book *War Without Heroes*, they told him horror stories about how the Marines had not built the base up well enough during the summer and fall of 1967. I found this interesting because the Seabees weren't there during the summer; we had only the battalion of Marines—1/26—there, and the local timber was not useful for building bunkers or other structures. Other units, which arrived as the siege was getting under way, certainly could not be blamed for not digging in soon enough. And, in fact, 1/26 lost only one Marine killed during the bombardment on January 21, and not many altogether during any bombardments.

WEATHER REPORT

LCpl PHIL MINEER
Bravo Battery, 1/13 _____

They told me how hot Vietnam was going to be, but when there was cloud cover over Khe Sanh, the cold was bone-chilling. The temperature did not get to where it should have *seemed* cold, but it got me all the way to the marrow. It was a constant chill.

Cpl TERRY STEWART
Mike Company, 3/26 (Hill 881S) _____

A lot of folks believe that Vietnam is tropical and hot. That just isn't the case in the hill country in winter. The monsoons were wet, cold, and miserable. On many nights, we had to pry our nearly frozen hands from the pistol grips of our rifles after we came off watch. And when we were awakened to take our watch, it was necessary to have our partners help to get our fingers around the grip to hold our rifles and be instantly ready. We slept curled up in balls, leaning against the walls of our bunkers. It was wet, and the rain just washed right over us. It was as miserable a place and time as I have ever been or experienced. The damp chill seemed to knife directly to the very center of the body, then radiate out. Of course, the bones and joints were the places that we really felt it. Thank God we were young.

Cpl BERT MULLINS
H&S Company, 1/9 _____

I had to wear my rain suit as a windbreaker because we had brought no field jackets. When they did get us field jackets, there weren't enough, so the radio operators didn't get any. They all went to the riflemen because they had to stay outside.

The fog was really scary. Some days it didn't burn off at all, and visibility was only a hundred feet at the most. The NVA could have sneaked up on us very easily.

☐

MORTALITY

1stLt PAUL ELKAN
Bravo Battery, 1/13 _____

I was laying the battery from a platform we had in the middle of the battery area, using an aiming circle. Some motherfucking sniper was actually trying to personally kill me. Bullets were zinging all around my ears. It was the last time we laid in the whole battery from the platform. After that, we did nothing but reciprocal lay—one gun would lay off another. Christ, there was nothing but gooks around us anyway, so it didn't make any difference where we shot.

We were surrounded. We knew we were cut off. We knew we were at what people said was another Dienbienphu. I wasn't really worried about it. The way I figured it, well, if I don't get hurt, that's good. If I get wounded, they'll ship me home. If I get killed, I won't care because I won't be here to think about it.

LCpl PHIL MINEER
Bravo Battery, 1/13 _____

Most of the missions that came down were shifting-zone missions. An order like "one round, shifting zone" worked out to nine rounds actually fired as we elevated and traversed the tube through a fixed routine. Of necessity, we had to keep a lot of rounds near each gun. We knew what that meant. If the ammo bunker on the gun took a direct hit, we'd get blown to hell.

In ten months in-country, I had never seen rounds come in like they did at Khe Sanh. It was relentless, constant. I used to lie in my rack with my face right up in the ceiling of the bunker, looking at our camouflage parachute. I thought, if I get a direct hit here, I'm already in the coffin.

Cpl WILLIAM ROBERTSON
Logistics Support Unit _____

On many occasions, when the incoming rounds started to
come in, and they were getting close, and they just vibrated
me in the bottom of a ditch, I thought, Go on, give me a
direct hit and get it over with; it'll be a whole lot better. I
was tired of putting up with it. Quite a few others felt the
same way sometimes. It's one thing, I guess, when you can
fight somebody, but this was coming from miles and miles
away, and I had no defense against it.

Capt JIM LESLIE
26th Marines Assistant Communicator _____

During the first week or so at Khe Sanh, after seeing so
many Marines killed or wounded near me, I gave up the
hope of going back home alive. At that point, the war
became tolerable. It was like back on the farm in Pennsylva-
nia when it first started to rain. I would try to keep dry, but
the harder it rained, the wetter I became until I got soaked.
At the point when I could get no wetter, the rain became
somewhat pleasant. So it was with the war. When I couldn't
be more miserable, more hungry, more bored, more scared,
or more lonely, then I got situated and the war became
somewhat pleasant.

Chapter 12

THE SET-PIECE STRATEGY

26th Marines After Action Report _____

With the commencement of active hostilities on January 21, the enemy was generally disposed with the 95th Regiment [325C Division] to the north and west, occupying the high ground opposite the 881S/861 complex. The 4th Battalion was located with the regimental headquarters, the 6th Battalion was in the vicinity of Hill 881N, and the 5th Battalion was east of that position to, and south, along the Rao Quan River Valley. The 101st Regiment was believed to be headquartered with a battalion in the vicinity of Lang Hoan Tap. A second battalion was along the Dong Dang ridgeline. A third battalion was in the vicinity of Co Put and along Route 9 north of Lang Vei. One battalion from the 304th Division may have alternately held this site.

Following the Battle of Khe Sanh Village [January 20], the 66th Regiment, 304th Division, was identified from documents. Except for the position on Hill 471, which may have been alternately occupied with elements of the 101D Regiment, 325C Division, elements of [the 304th] Division generally remained south of Route 9....

MGen TOMMY TOMPKINS
3rd Marine Division Commanding General _____

My whole plan for the defense of Khe Sanh was to make the enemy come to us.[1]

I was confident that, so long as our Marines held the key hill positions and we could keep them supplied by helicopter, the NVA would have a difficult time in attacking the base. It was clear to me that we could not allow ourselves to be bled to death by indulging in fruitless adventures that did not contribute to our assigned mission—"Hold on to Khe Sanh Combat Base; it must not fall into enemy hands."

The four infantry battalions at Khe Sanh averaged about 950 men each. The NVA infantry battalions—some eighteen in the two divisions opposing us—averaged about 550 men each. On the basis of infantrymen, the NVA had almost 10,000 against our 3,800. Or, to put it another way, the total ration strength at Khe Sanh was some 6,000 men against two NVA divisions totalling about 20,000 men.

In view of the manpower imbalance, we developed a "set-piece" type of defense against which the enemy would have to come to us.

The daily papers in the United States, I am glad to say, made much of the fact that we were "locked into our positions and did not engage in patrolling." I hoped that the enemy high command believed this rubbish because such was not the case. Patrolling outside the KSCB perimeter was constant, but I put a limit of 500 meters on them. This was to prevent a patrol from being "mousetrapped," with rescue forces, in turn, becoming entrapped.

Maj JIM STANTON
26th Marines Fire Support Coordination Center _____

General Tompkins, the division commander, and Colonel Lownds, the regimental commander, decreed that we would just defend the perimeter and not go out after them, that there were just too many of them. Effectively, we traded the offense for a defense in depth, which really meant that we expanded our perimeter through the use of fire. We ringed ourselves with fire. It became a battle of attrition. We couldn't patrol and they couldn't get close to us. On the strategic level, it became a hide-and-seek game. In this game, we tried to find them and shoot at them while we were trying to dodge the incoming.

Maj JIM STANTON
26th Marines Fire Support Coordination Center _____

We had a massive grid that we applied to the entire Khe Sanh area. Every square kilometer was numbered with a discrete number so that if we wanted an Arclight in any three particular kilometer squares, we simply sent the Air Force a series of four-digit numbers. Sometimes we sent requests for double, triple, or quadruple Arclights. The typical Arclight was composed of three B-52s deployed in echelon, one behind and off the wing of the one ahead. We murdered them with the Arclights; if there was somebody there, he wasn't there when it was over, but each mission really only covered a very small portion of the combat area; 1,000 by 3,000 meters is not very much ground.

Capt HARRY BAIG
26th Marines Target Information Officer _____

A B-52 aircraft is an extremely accurate weapons system and is capable of being used with great finesse. I targeted these planes in the same manner as tactical aircraft or conventional artillery; and they were extremely responsive to all our requirements. Arclight missions were submitted to the Division Air Officer fifteen hours before drop time at the rate of eight strikes every twenty-four hours, each strike being made by six aircraft. At three hours' notice, I could divert a strike to a new, unscheduled target. This diversion capability enabled us to respond quickly to enemy buildup. On high-threat nights, indicated by the sensors or concluded by intelligence, these heavy bombers were diverted from their scheduled targets to a new target block, corresponding to the threat, which may be as close as 2,000 meters from the original target area. Close or far, it made no difference to the Air Force.

Our entire defense philosophy was to allow the enemy to surround us closely, to mass about us, to reveal his troop and logistic routes, to establish his dumps and assembly areas, his truck park and artillery positions, and to prepare his siege works as energetically as he desired. The result was an enormous quantity of targets, located in dispersed but common areas. Such complexes were ideal for heavy bombers. . . . Once the enemy had firmly embraced us, we had him fixed. His siege doctrine and battle plan (prepared at a headquarters other than Khe Sanh) forced him to stay; and the facts of military circumstances and logic bound him to perform foreseeable and determinable functions. He had to do certain things and to be in certain places because, given the situation, there was little choice open to him. Arclights were dropped on all the places where the enemy was known or estimated to be. Bombs were not cast into the jungle just for the sake of doing so. The vast number of secondary explosions and the considerable quantity of casualties reported by the Bru, which friendly forces discovered later, clearly indicated that our concepts were correct and the targeting accurate. The point to emphasize here is that the principles applied were those of normal Marine supporting-arms doctrine, which has guided us for three years. Ninety-five percent of all Arclight strikes were targeted and requested from Khe Sanh— *not* Saigon, as certain authorities would have us believe.[2]

Maj JIM STANTON
26th Marines Fire Support Coordination Center _____

When we began to get infrared photography of the combat zone, we could see little rings of fire. The NVA bivouac areas would always be characterized by small smudge fires— for boiling water—that would always be laid out in rings. The photos came to us the next day, so we only knew where they had been on the night before. But it was a tool we could use to help us target the enemy.

Pfc ROBERT HARRISON
Alpha Company, 1/26 (Hill 950) _____

A B-52 strike was truly awesome. There would be no hint of a strike arriving until the bombs exploded. The bombs fell in a staggered pattern. First one bomb, then another to the right and front of the first explosion, then another to the left and front of the second explosion, and so forth. The bombs created a long pattern of craters, churned up earth, and blasted trees. After the bombs had exploded, I would be able to hear the planes. They produced a weird, low moaning that lasted until they were out of range. I never saw the planes since they bombed from a great height.

Pfc MIKE DeLANEY
Echo Company, 2/26 (Hill 861A) _____

One day they told us, "Take cover! They're going to bomb the valley." My first reaction was, Run for your life! I thought fighters were going to do the bombing, but I couldn't see any in the sky. I was with my friend, one of the forward air controllers, and asked him what was going on. He just pointed to the sky and I saw several B-52s. They were just little dots in the sky. Little! They looked smaller than birds flying around. They started at the far north of the valley and walked their bombs toward the runway. I couldn't tell how close they got to the combat base from where I was, but it looked very close.

The bombs exploded in parallel lines. It started at one end and rippled like a chain reaction. Someone told me that the name "Arclight" was from the electricity the explosions threw in the air, a charge. It was a white light, bouncing back and forth across the valley in waves. The hill—861 meters up—was rumbling. The ground was shaking. Looking down into the valley, I could see that the explosions were devastating.

1stLt NICK ROMANETZ
Charlie Company, 1/26 _____

One day, at about 1630, we were told to get into the trenches and put our helmets and flak jackets on. There was going to be a B-52 Arclight on the ridgeline about a thousand meters in front of us. Everybody ran and got their cameras and stood up in the trenches to watch. It was still overcast at the appointed time, 1700, and we all looked up into the sky. Nothing. But three or four minutes later, we heard this eerie sound—a *bubba-bubba-bubba* sound, like when you put a balloon on your bicycle wheel so the spokes hit it. Suddenly, the whole ridgeline exploded from one end to the other. There was a dark gray flash from dirt that started blowing up. Unfortunately, the wind was blowing right at the base, so this dark cloud of dirt and chemicals from the explosives drifted over the base. It was a sight to behold, a mountain blowing up right in front of us.

Sgt FRANK JONES
26th Marines Scout-Sniper Platoon _____

We had a prisoner, an NVA first sergeant, who had been moving south to join the siege when it seemed like the ground opened up and swallowed his entire battalion. He didn't even hear the bombs.

LCpl CHARLIE THORNTON
Lima Company, 3/26 _____

The air power displayed was incredible. There were constant bombing runs by all kinds of fixed-wing aircraft. By far the most impressive were the B-52 bombing runs. The ground would actually rumble under our bodies as we lay in a bunker while the bombs erupted around our perimeter. I often wondered how the NVA withstood the constant pounding, but I guess their gear and determination was no different than ours. I am convinced that the bombing prevented a major troop confrontation at Khe Sanh and perhaps a major battle loss by the U.S.

1stLt ERNIE SPENCER
Delta Company, 1/26 _____

If war is life, then bombs are religion. Bombs are religion because they can bring you right to the essence of existence. Any guy who gets caught in the depth or radius of an exploding bomb gets religion immediately. War religion.

I see what the bomb ceremony does to Charlie. I laugh my ass off when I hear about NVA officials mocking the effectiveness of American bombing. If our bombs aren't effective on Charlie, then there are a whole lot of dead motherfuckers from someplace else out there. I see them and smell them rotting. I am a witness for those big fucking Kahunas, the B-52s. Saturation religion. Baby, I believe![3]

Capt HARRY BAIG
26th Marines Target Information Center _____

Without the Arclights, we would have been hard-pressed.[4]

Pfc MICHAEL LEE
Helicopter Support Team (Hill 881S) _____

We actually felt sorry for some of the NVA.

Sgt MIKE STAHL
4.2-inch Mortar Battery, 1/13 (Hill 861) _____

The tenacity of the North Vietnamese was awesome. If they had dropped an Arclight on me, I'd have *chieu hoi*-ed the next day.

FIRE SUPPORT

Maj JIM STANTON
26th Marines Fire Support Coordination Center _____

The best intelligence came from the guys who could see what was going on while it was going on, and who could assess the battle damage after we shot our missions. These were the aerial observers and forward observers, primarily, but also anyone else who could see the target and adjust fires real-time.

Capt HARRY BAIG
26th Marines Target Information Officer _____

The daylight hours were passed in a vulgar free-for-all, wherein air and artillery, under the local control of forward observers and tactical air controllers who attacked anything and everything that looked peculiar. Targets were taken under fire as they appeared. Repeated checkfires, caused by the presence of resupply aircraft and helicopters, prevented a systematic approach to target reduction. Arclights continued unabated in accordance with the regular schedule.

But the night was a different matter. As the siege progressed, more and more targets made themselves apparent. What is more, because of the enemy's rigid adherence to doctrine, it became possible, upon finding part of a target complex, to estimate the location of the remaining and unfound portions of that complex. Consequently, we had far more known and confirmed targets than we could possibly use. Eventually, we began to attack them en masse instead of individually. Radar-controlled artillery and radar-directed aircraft, as well as B-52s, were assigned overlapping portions of target complexes in a concentrated effort to destroy, damage, and slow down the construction of the enemy's siege works. Mortar and artillery positions, of which the former were not worth counting and the latter exceeded 160 separate sites, were bombed and shelled nightly in patterns of fire, corresponding to NVA doctrinal position-area engineering, to destroy the unseen battery ammunition dumps. Success was remarkable in pursuit of the latter intent.

In summary, at night Arclights, radar-guided aircraft, and artillery were employed together to obtain a single result. In the daytime, each type of supporting arms was employed separately to obtain multiple results.[5]

Maj JIM STANTON
26th Marines Fire Support Coordination Center _____

We were outgunned, totally outgunned. Their 130mm guns could sit out beyond our range and shoot us up something awful. We had nothing that could reach them, not even our two towed 155s. Their 130mm guns had a 27,000-meter maximum range and our 155mm guns had a 14,000-meter maximum range. Even their 100mm guns and 122mm rockets outshot us. They parked everything 1,000 meters outside of our artillery fan. We knew where they were, but we couldn't reach them from inside the combat base with our guns and howitzers. We needed Arclights and air strikes to get them.

When you're the target in an artillery barrage, it feels good to hear your own artillery shooting back. Artillery must never be silent during a rocket attack or artillery barrage. The artillerymen *must* get out of the bunkers and shoot back, even when they know they are outgunned. We had hip-pocket targets we could always reach out against, so we fired on them while their unreachable artillery and rockets were firing on us.

Capt HARRY BAIG
26th Marines Target Information Officer _____

Artillery response [was] . . . the least that [was] expected of artillery. We thought in terms of artillery attacks and bombardments—in the manner of the First World War. Separate or combined ''time on targets'' by massed batteries of Marine and Army guns; battery zones, shifts, or both;

harassment-and-interdiction [H&I] fires by battery volley instead of single pieces; artillery boxes and rolling barrages: these and other types were the forms of fire adopted by the Fire Support Coordination Center. Our motto was "Be generous."[6]

Maj JIM STANTON
26th Marines Fire Support Coordination Center _____

The artillery time-on-target [TOT] mission was designed to bring rounds from all the guns involved to a particular piece of ground at precisely the same instant. Since there was no warning for the people being targeted, TOT shoots usually caught them in the open and did them serious damage.

Capt HARRY BAIG
26th Marines Target Information Officer _____

[At night] the artillery initiative was ours. . . . An average night's pattern of preplanned fires is as follows: combined TOTs from night batteries (4–6); separate battalion TOTs (Army 4–6, Marine 10–15); battery multiple-volley individual missions (40–50); battery H&Is (20–30). Normal, one-gun, one-round H&Is were not used; this type of fire is of little value. Marine and Army artillery were employed in target areas and at ranges to reduce to a minimum checkfires caused by the arrival of radar-guided and reconnaissance aircraft. Later, as we learned finesse, air was given the targets south of the base and west of the maximum range of the 175mm guns; one-third was given any target whose range required a maximum ordinate of less than 14,000 feet (altitude of a radar-guided aircraft run); and the 175mm guns were assigned targets to the north, northwest, and east of the base. Such were the preplanned fires.

There were targets of opportunity and missions created by the constantly updated intelligence picture. Sensors accounted for at least twenty battery missions a night. Indications of high threat or imminent attack required the execution of area-clearance fires. For this, target blocks 500 meters by 500 meters were designed for multiple-volley, nine-battery

TOTs; and when completed, the adjoining blocks would receive the same treatment. Intelligence later confirmed the correctness of this approach to disrupting enemy formations (prisoners, body count, surveillance, sensors, agent reports, etc.). In addition to these nonscheduled missions, there were the Mini- and Micro-Arclights, the artillery portion of which required multiple-volley TOTs also. Three or four Minis to six to eight Micros were executed on most nights. Frequently, TOTs were fired into a recent Arclight area ten to fifteen minutes after the bombers had passed to catch the survivors with a further issue of unpleasantness. Thus the scheduled and unscheduled missions accounted for a considerable volume of fire throughout the area of operations.[7]

Maj JIM STANTON
26th Marines Fire Support Coordination Center _____

The Mini-Arclight was a fire-support exercise par excellence. It consisted of a flight of two A-6s carrying a total of 56 500-pound bombs combined with every available artillery tube at the combat base plus the 175mm guns at Camp Carroll and the Rock Pile. We had an ASRT—Air Support Radar Team—manning an AN/TPQ-10, a relatively simple radar set with a computer. The ground controller would set the aircraft up on a heading and an airspeed and the computer would fly the *bombs* to the target. The A-6's were extremely flexible in that they could each drop their twenty-eight bombs one at a time or in pairs or in ripples or strings of almost any size, interval, or frequency. The results were almost always awesome.

Capt HARRY BAIG
26th Marines Target Information Officer _____

The Mini-Arclights and Micro-Arclights were developed by Capt Kenneth Steen and myself. Captain Steen, the assistant fire-support coordinator, contributed the methodology and the mathematics; I contributed the initial concept and the subsequent targets. The regimental air liaison officer, Captain Fitzsimmons, contributed the names and the aircraft—

and convinced the ASRT and Marine Air Support Squadron that this system of bombardment did not violate aircraft-safety procedures. Minis and Micros were employed nightly against close enemy siege works within a range, generally, of 500 to 1,500 meters. Often, secondary explosions were observed as [petroleum, oil, and lubricants] and ammunition dumps were hit. The troops on the line loved them because they could see this physical manifestation of the enemy's discomfiture. Successful strikes of this nature were often exploited further with nine-battery, multiple-volley TOTs.

The best and most intense Mini-Arclight was directed against a major headquarters shortly after the assault against Hill 861A. In the second week of February, Maj Jerry Hudson and Maj Robert Coolidge positively learned that a force-wide meeting of staffs and commanders would occur at a certain time in a schoolhouse located in a village near the Laos border. A special Mini was prepared to welcome the delegates. The target block was 500 meters by 300 meters—normally Minis are 1,000 meters by 500 meters—about the schoolhouse to take in the hangers-on and other idlers who usually congregate around large staffs. Twenty minutes after the meeting was scheduled to start, the Mini struck. Two A-6s and four F-4Bs dropped 152 500-pound bombs into the box in concert with the opening volleys from eight batteries firing a total of 350 rounds.

[Subsequent events tend] to lend credence to our hope that we did catch the senior commanders and their staffs in the schoolhouse with the special Mini; for, if anyone could have changed their attack master plan, in view of our determined opposition, these officers could. Since the plan was never changed, perhaps they died in that building.[8]

LtCol JOHNNY GREGERSON
Marine Air Support Squadron 3 _____

A particular problem that was never solved to my satisfaction was caused by space limitations. The Direct Air Support Center could not be co-located with the Fire Support Coordination Center because of lack of space in the command bunker. This problem should not have existed and was caused by a lack of understanding and foresight on the part of personnel involved in the early layout of the Combat Operations Center complex. I pointed out the need for co-location of the Direct Air Support Center and the Fire Support Coordination Center to Colonel Lownds and LtCol Edward Castagna [26th Marines Operations Officer], but by the time they agreed to increase the size of the bunker, it was too late. Enemy incoming was zeroed in on the Combat Operations Center/Fire Support Coordination Center bunker, and it was impossible for working parties to function outside in that particular area. The Direct Air Support Center was set up in an Air Force bunker about seventy-five meters from the Combat Operation Center and remained there for the remainder of the operation. Problems occurred on coordination of the air effort in the overall fire-support plan because of lack of instantaneous communications and joint understanding of problems involved.[9]

Chapter 13

1stLt ERNIE SPENCER
Delta Company, 1/26 ⎯⎯⎯⎯⎯⎯⎯⎯⎯⎯⎯⎯⎯

In the first few weeks of the siege, company commanders and the battalion commander continue standing in the command bunker during a barrage. We are cool. Charles wasn't going to interrupt our morning briefing.

Nobody plays more macho than Marine Corps officers. Only cool, ice macho counts with us. Expressionless eyes. Passion is not a desirable trait in a Marine officer. Emotions kill.

But Khe Sanh is a bitch who does things her way with you. We go from meeting like that, standing, to where it is perfectly appropriate to sit your ass down any fucking place you want to. You can go down or under anything when a barrage starts.

After more time passes, we don't even bother with meetings.[1]

1stLt PAUL ELKAN
Bravo Battery, 1/13 _____

We walked around with our helmets off and our ears pointed
to the north so we could hear their rounds going off. If it
was 100mm, you could hear the *pop* about a second before
it hit; about four seconds for a 152mm. You couldn't hear
the mortars. I used a lot of Q-tips to keep my ears clean, so
I could hear better. One time I heard a round popping off; I
could tell by the sound it was a 152. Somehow, from the
sound, I could tell whether a round was coming at me or
not. I could tell with this one that I had about four seconds
to find cover, that it was coming right for my ass. I dived
down this chute stairway into the corpsman's bunker, and as
I was diving, the plywood that formed the wall above the
bunker was riddled with shrapnel.

Maj TOM COOK
26th Marines Assistant Logistics Officer _____

A young lady reporter from *The Christian Science Monitor*
was at Khe Sanh for about a week. She was a brave girl, but
she became a little shaken by the experience. When she was
getting ready to get out of there, I told her I would walk her
up to the airstrip in case something happened. We took off
down the street, walking along, when I heard a distant
thump, thump, thump—rockets leaving their tubes. My ear
was tuned to the sound, but hers was not. I grabbed her and
threw her into a ditch, and then I jumped on top of her. This
kind of frightened her—why is this Marine throwing me
down and jumping on me? She was squirming, fighting,
trying to get out from under me. But then we heard large
explosions. Suddenly she decided to lie there quietly until
after the explosions stopped. I apologized to her for the
rough treatment and she seemed to understand.

2ndLt SKIP WELLS
Charlie Company, 1/26 _____

We had to run some air right in front of our lines, and I
talked with the aerial observer in the spotter plane. We
signed off and I watched the plane fly away to the east. I
wanted to be in that plane so bad I had tears in my eyes. I
was supposed to be one of the gung-ho ones. I still have this
picture in my mind of that plane in the sky with the hooches
and mountains in the background. I felt sad, lonely, and
scared.

1stLt FRED McGRATH
Bravo Battery, 1/13 _____

During January 1968, I was a member of Headquarters
Battery, 4/12. We were at "Artillery Hill," north and west
of Dong Ha. The battalion commander told me to pack my
seabag and catch a hop to Khe Sanh. It seems that word
came down that all units there were to beef up to 110
percent of authorized strength. Since I had been a forward
observer with Bravo Battery, 1/13, for six months, I was the
logical choice to go.

I flew from Dong Ha to Danang on a Marine helicopter.
In Danang I boarded an Air Force C-123 for the flight to
Khe Sanh. Prior to boarding, we were briefed that, since the
plane was only delivering and not picking up, it would
continue to taxi while on the strip and would not stop. We
would debark from the rear, on the run. (Even though I
knew Khe Sanh was heating up, this bizarre debarking
procedure made the seriousness of the assignment sink in.)

It happened just the way we were briefed. On the strip,
we were waved to a trenchline paralleling the runway as
soon as we put our boots on the runway matting. After
several rounds of incoming landed, we were given an

all-clear. I asked for directions to Bravo Battery's position, thinking it could not be too far. The Marine at the terminal said he would call for transportation as it was quicker—and therefore safer.

I arrived at Bravo's position and checked in with 1stLt George Wood, the CO. I was greeted by the rest of the officers, whom I had not seen for two months. Fresh meat! They filled me in on life in the fast lane. They emphasized that bunkers and trenches were the way of life here, and movement in the open tempted fate. Each howitzer was dug in, and the crew of each had its own solidly constructed bunker. Very little interplay among gun crews was the order of the day. No troops were allowed to wander about. No business to conduct, no movement allowed. Simple.

I took a tour of the position, to get a feel for the relative placement of the guns. We ran from gun to gun—I'm a quick learner—and I talked with the men, who, if not physically on the gun, were either in their bunkers or hunkered down close by. I found them to be in good spirits. Most of them wished they could move about more freely, but all understood the jeopardy in doing so.

Pfc ROBERT HARRISON
Alpha Company, 1/26 (Hill 950) _____

Our normal conversation usually centered on getting back to The World and what we would do when we got back. Food was the central topic of a lot of conversations. Sex was not discussed as often as one would think, and I cannot ever recall discussing the politics of the war with anyone. All we cared about was doing our thirteen months and getting home in one piece. This is not to say that the people in the platoon did not care for one another, because we did. I believe one of the best things about the war was the camaraderie that existed among the people doing the actual fighting.

The 3rd Platoon, alone on Hill 950, consisted mainly of what you would call blue-collar kids. There was no racial tension within the platoon at all. I would say that the median age of the platoon was nineteen. Our day-to-day life on Hill 950 consisted of digging deeper trenches, improving existing bunkers, laying concertina and tanglefoot barbed wire, and playing a card game called Back Alley.

Action would usually pick up when we were being resupplied by helicopter. The NVA would open up with heavy-caliber machine-gun fire and mortar fire. We would usually be able to call in some close air support to suppress the enemy fire.

Each night we would be required to stand line watch on the perimeter or go out on the listening post. For me, the listening posts were the worst type of duty. They usually consisted of a four-man fire team. We would take a radio and leave the perimeter after nightfall. We were to listen for enemy movement and warn of an impending attack. The NVA would send in sappers at night to probe the perimeter and sometimes try to draw fire. If ever an attack occurred, the listening post would never make it back inside the perimeter. It seemed that when I was on listening post, all sounds were magnified. When leaving the perimeter, I would always get caught on the barbed wire and make a lot of noise getting untangled. Once we left the barbed wire, we tried to find a place to set in which offered some concealment and cover. Once we were set in, we informed the platoon command post by radio. The listening post checked in with the command post at least once each hour. Nighttime in the jungle has to be the darkest of dark; you cannot see your hand in front of your face.

My fire team was on a listening post one night in early February when, suddenly, we had movement in the wire. The sound was behind and to the left of our position. My hair literally stood up on the back of my neck. The barbed wire shook a little bit, as if someone was crawling through it. The next thing we knew, someone stood right next to us. We could have shot him, but we didn't want to give away our position. So we threw two or three frags (grenades) and hoped for the best. I don't know how he kept from getting hit, but he did. I could hear him running through the undergrowth toward the NVA position. The next morning, there was no blood or anything. It was like it never even happened.

1stLt NICK ROMANETZ
Charlie Company, 1/26 _____

One day in February, a rocket hit dead center in the helo pad area. It buried itself and exploded several feet underground. Lo and behold, some yingyang up in intelligence decided we should send some Marines to dig up the fragments so they could find out what kind of round it was. Since it was in my sector, I had to take some guys out with picks and shovels and dig down several feet to try to find the fragments. This was the most asinine thing I was ever asked to do. There we were, exposing four or five Marines to possible harm, just so we could dig up that damn thing. We knew it was a rocket from the size of the entry hole. Who gave a damn if the thing was made in Czechoslovakia, Hungary, or Russia? Picking the unlucky guys to go out there was one of the hardest things I had to do during the siege. It would have been silly to lose someone if incoming got us or if a sniper shot one of us. I went out with them, and we dug the damn things up as quickly as we could, and got the hell out of there. The intelligence people got what they wanted and we were lucky, we didn't take any incoming or get sniped at.

Capt JIM LESLIE
26th Marines Assistant Communicator _____

After a day of running wire, patching antennas, and kicking the teletype machine, we would try to get our pinochle group together in the evenings, about dusk. I looked forward to that game with increasing anticipation every day. We would drink coffee, deal the cards, and discuss the day's events.

Sometimes the NVA would let us play cards in peace and sometimes they wouldn't. We had the routine pretty well analyzed by February. The NVA would start dropping in artillery rounds about dusk, but they would start at the far end of the runway and drop about twenty-five meters with each of their five-gun volleys in an attempt to cover our entire camp, volley after volley, day after day, night after night.

One evening the NVA started walking the artillery in on us. We knew from where they started—at the far end of the runway—that we had three or four minutes before they would start hitting around our bunkers. This was more than enough time to finish the cards we held in our hand before we dived into little rat holes that we had dug inside the bunker. Well, one of the NVA had his dope screwed up and dropped a round in our bunker about two and a half minutes early. Dust flew, our card table collapsed, and cards flew as all four of us lay on the floor waiting for the explosion to take us to the great card game in the sky.

We waited and waited, but the round didn't go off. We squirmed into our rat holes. The round still didn't go off. We waited twenty or thirty minutes. Still nothing. 1stLt Jack Blyze said, "It must be a dud. That was it, men. That was the one with our number on it, and the fucker didn't go off." After more than half an hour, we decided to see what had happened.

The artillery round had gone through the side of our bunker and into the ground. It left a hole about six inches in diameter just under our card table. Jack probed the hole with an eight-foot fence post to see how deep the round went. He could not touch it. We came back inside the bunker, set up our card table, picked up the cards, and just roared with laughter until the tears rolled down our faces.

"That was it," Jack said, "that was the one meant for us, and the little fucking gooks forgot how to make it go off." Just as he said that, the round went off. It blew our card table over, knocked sandbags down on us, and filled the bunker with dust, but no one was injured. I said a thank-you prayer as Jack and I made our way through the dark to our bunker, twenty meters away.

LCpl PHIL MINEER
Bravo Battery, 1/13 _____

There were times, when the cloud cover was real heavy, that we would take a few H&I rounds here and there. But when it was clear, they really laid it in on us. We didn't do too bad. Probably, for every round that came in, we gave them ten back. Every time it got bad, we'd be out on the guns, shooting back. A guy from 1/26 who was right in front of us, on the perimeter, told us, "You guys are crazy, out there in all that stuff." I reminded him that that was the artillery's job. There was always a little friction between the grunts and the artillery. They thought we rode everywhere we went. But the grunts who came into the base couldn't wait to get the hell out of there. A few grunts in from the hills came by and said, "Bet you wish you were out there with us. It sure is something in here!"

1stLt NICK ROMANETZ
Charlie Company, 1/26 _____

Life didn't stop because of the siege. We still had guys getting promoted when they deserved it. One day, during a lull, we had a promotion ceremony in our trench. There were seven Marines who were being promoted standing *in* the trenchline while the company commander and I were reading their promotion warrants while we stood *outside* the trench. I thought it would have been smarter if we had *all* stood in the trenchline. Apparently our NVA sniper was on a vacation that particular day, so nothing bad happened.

2ndLt SKIP WELLS
Charlie Company, 1/26 _____

Patrolling was difficult at first, because of the elephant
grass. It was tough to move and impossible to see anything.
On the first patrol, we made contact with a few NVA and
never even saw them. We heard them firing at the perimeter
off to our right (east) about a hundred yards away. We
moved over that way, they heard us, and after an exchange
of fire, they either left or stopped firing. We then moved
through the area but didn't find anything.

Later, as the artillery and air strikes thinned the vegetation, we had another problem. Now we did not have any
cover at all. We would leave the perimeter prior to daylight
or under the cover of the fog, move to our objective, and
then hold until we either got a reaction or had good support
for our move back to the perimeter.

The north side of the perimeter was not good for the
NVA. We never made contact with more than a platoon, and
they never prepared any real positions—only separated bunkers and spiderholes. On the bad side, because of the low
ridge opposite our perimeter and about 400 yards out, there
were constant fire fights between our trenchline and their
positions. We had quite a few wounded by small-arms fire
during the first couple of weeks, before we learned that any
movement outside the trenches in good visibility had to be
rapid and covered by fire.

1stLt JOHN KAHENY
1/26 Combat Operations Center _____

One of my duties was to go out to Bravo Company or
Charlie Company lines with Capt Neil Galloway, our battalion forward air controller. I would direct our artillery or
81mm mortars to mark the target for air strikes. The worst
part of the assignment, of course, was when we would get
spotted by the NVA. On one occasion we were spotted

primarily because a CBS camera crew came out to ask us what we were doing. We kept telling them to get down in the trenches because the enemy could see us, but they kept asking us questions. The cameras were rolling, so I said some foul things—just before the snipers opened up and the mortars started coming in.

□

1stLt ERNIE SPENCER
Delta Company, 1/26 _____

There were always rats at Khe Sanh. Not your stereotypical Asian variety of chopstick-using rats. Khe Sanh rats are snarling gray suckers with big heads. Having evolved in a jungle environment, those rats are capable of fighting anything.

The garbage dump set off their population explosion. The dump is in a narrow gully just outside the south side of the base. Before the siege the rats had to stand in line to take their shot; a garbage dump in Vietnam is the trendiest restaurant around as far as the natives are concerned. How disgusting to watch the montagnards—a beautiful, gentle people—slogging around in our slop. With empty sandbags over their shoulders, they would diligently pick through the dump every day. They would swarm around and over any vehicle taking out a fresh load. Our garbage is the best we had to offer to those whom we are there to save.

The rats began exerting themselves several breeding cycles into the siege. A rat jumps on my chest one night. On my back on my cot, I slap the shit out of him with my left hand while I try to shield my face with my right. The fucker is grinning at me, I swear.

Rats love the sandbag walls. Since the walls are several layers thick, the rats have a lot of room for their quarters. You can hear them in there screaming, eating, fucking, and kicking each others' asses. Rats are nasty fuckers—they are always fighting.

Rats behave more logically during the siege than we do. They let their feelings out. You can hear them squeaking and going bullshit during a barrage. Us macho men just sit quietly and take it.[2]

1stLt PAUL ELKAN
Bravo Battery, 1/13 _____

I used to sleep with my pistol under my pillow. There were seven rounds: six for the gooks and one for me. The only thing I ever got close to shooting was a rat, a big motherfucking rat. I dreamed my hand was in a jet exhaust; I could feel the hot air on my hand. I woke up and a rat the size of a cat was breathing on my hand. By the time I got my pistol out, the rat had gotten out of there.

We had a big problem with rats. We used to feed them peanut butter mixed with C4, a plastique explosive. They were supposed to eat that shit and explode. Actually, they didn't explode. But they got really thirsty and drank themselves to death.

Pfc ROBERT HARRISON
Alpha Company, 1/26 (Hill 950) _____

Large jungle rats used to provide a form of entertainment. They lived in our bunkers and would come out at night to look for food. Each evening we would set out traps baited with peanut butter, then compare body counts the next morning. We could always hear them moving around when we were trying to sleep. No one was ever bitten, probably due to the fact that we were not able to bathe for about five months.

Cpl DENNIS MANNION
Charlie Battery, 1/13 (Hill 861) _____

We never went outside the trenchline to do anything about the North Vietnamese who had been killed on the night of January 20–21 within our three concentric rows of wire. Using heavy ship's binoculars that were flown in shortly after the attack, I was able to see clearly that the bodies turned to skeletons within three weeks. There was no flesh left on them, just skeletons wearing North Vietnamese uniforms, packs, and helmets.

1stLt PAUL ELKAN
Bravo Battery, 1/13 —————————————————

I was walking around one of the guns to see if there was any trash lying around the back of the bunker. If there was, I would tell the guys to police it up. I had just turned the corner of the bunker when three mortar rounds landed in the gun pit. A couple of the guys were wounded. One of them, a lance corporal, was only lightly wounded and he was confined to his bunker to recuperate. He soon went batshit. He had an M-16 rifle, which he put on semiautomatic and started shooting at the rats inside his bunker. Unfortunately, his bunker mates were also inside with the rats. The shooting really pissed them off. We had the lance corporal flown out as a "head case" the next day.

Cpl DENNIS MANNION
Charlie Battery, 1/13 (Hill 861) —————————————

February 4, 1968

Joe—

Yep. So today's the day. One year ago at this time I was doing 900 side-straddle hops because of the extra amount of mail I received. A whole mother year ago.

I had a quiet day—only eight incoming mortar rounds hit the hill (1 WIA) and two rockets *missed*— not by much, but they missed. I spent the better part of the day digging a new hole and bunker. I had the feeling that our present one was getting to be too well known. Besides, a change is always good.

Had my birthday dinner about ten minutes ago—

beans and franks, bread with peanut butter and apricot jelly, and pound cake. All courtesy of Uncle Sam's Combat Meal, Individual. Not like some of the other birthday meals I've had—but I've had worse.

Well, the USMC is fucking with us again (not unusual). Word has it that we (881S, 861, and Khe Sanh) are "bait" for a trap the generals hope to pull on the NVA. Plan is to let those bastards hit into us (supposed to be three divisions plus two regiments) and then, during the height of the attack, drop the entire 101st Airborne Division behind the NVA and close in. All well and good. I just don't fancy the idea of holding off so many NVA until the fucking doggies show up. I almost feel like Davy Crockett at the Alamo. This hill is tough, but it won't hold forever. And these NVA are run by some brass who kicked the fucking French to shit in 1954, mainly at the battle of Dienbienphu, the fight where they lugged 105s into the hills—and the French didn't think they could do it.

Anyway, that's the situation, and I don't really like it. Still, I'm confident, and no matter what happens we'll have their ass in a sling in the final quarter.

To be honest, I don't rate my chances of coming out unmarked too good. Sorry, man, that's the way I feel. However, I'm psyched for the best—and the worst—and I'm leaving it all up to the Good Lord. It's in his hands, just like it was on February 4, 1946. Somebody's got to come out of this mess A-OK—right?

Chapter 14

FEBRUARY 5
ATTACK ON HILL 861A

2/26 Command Chronology _____

On January 23, Echo Company, 2/26, was chopped to 3/26 and subsequently deployed on [Hill 861A], to the west of Hill 558, based on agreement between COs of 2/26 and 3/26. 3/26 assumed operational control because of the proximity of their forces on Hill 861.

Capt EARLE BREEDING
Echo Company, 2/26 _____

The NVA couldn't take Khe Sanh Combat Base without first taking Hill 861 and, once we go there, Hill 861A. If the NVA had owned those two hills, they would have been looking down on the combat base and on 2/26, which was on Hill 558. It was very important to hold 861 and 861A.

Pfc MIKE DeLANEY
Echo Company, 2/26 _____

After landing at Khe Sanh, Echo Company kept moving around. I don't know if they couldn't make up their minds or if we were supposed to be moving, but we kept going during the day and spent each night on high ground, then we moved again. It didn't feel like we had a purpose. We stopped moving around when we went up on Hill 861A.

There was nothing but double- and triple-canopy jungle on the hill when we got there. It was heavy, heavy growth, and we saw a lot of wildlife on the way up the hill. It was very pretty, very picturesque.

It was super hot. It was like a smothering heat. Very little wind. The vegetation held the heat close to the ground. It was also humid, constantly humid. The fog would roll up from the valley. Sometimes it was like looking down on the clouds. That was scary because we couldn't see anything below us.

Nobody had any idea what to expect. Until we got to Hill 861A, our unit had been running daytime patrols and night-time ambushes, working out of villages and through rice paddies and small jungle areas. Then, all of a sudden, we're working in the middle of a huge jungle. There were no people, just other Marines.

We had very little communication about what was going on. The only events we knew about were those we could see—fighting on Hill 881S, for example. We knew something was going on around us. It didn't seem to be super heavy, but it was going on.

Tension was rising, the mood was changing, the people in charge of the company were getting very serious. When we first got to the hill, we just laid around. Then we started getting organized, digging in. The captain walked around, talked with the lieutenants, said, "I don't want a gun here, I want it there," getting ready for something. It was typical of the military; none of us seemed to know what we were doing. Captain Breeding seemed to know what he was doing. He was very squared away.

Pfc MIKE DeLANEY
Echo Company, 2/26 _____

January 28, 1968

Hi Mom & Dad,

Well, I got your box of socks, magazines, and long johns. Boy, that stuff is great, but the radio doesn't play up here on the hill. I might send it back to you. Tell Uncle Gene he can send some canned fruit and juice.

Mom, it is bad here, but I don't want you to worry. If you want to know, I'll tell you a little about how I've been living. For the last two days, we went without water and food. Then a chopper came in and we got a couple of meals and about a glass of water for two days. We don't wash or shave. I've got a full beard and no change of clothes. I sleep on the ground, and we get some of our water from the bamboo plants, and eat the roots. We try to catch rainwater and the dew with our ponchos. They try to make it better, but the NVA shoot down the choppers. We get bombarded every day, and at night we get sniper fire. The company on the hill next to us [Kilo, on Hill 861] loses a man or more a day. Our company has not lost anyone yet. I have lost about fifteen pounds. We work all day in the hot sun and get so little to eat and drink. But I'm in real good health. I'm fine and I watch everything I do, so don't worry.

We had been catching some hell by then. It wasn't a lot, but it was enough to catch our interest.

I wrote home again on January 30, which happened to be my nineteenth birthday:

January 30, 1968

Dear Mom and Dad,

Well, what's new in The World this morning? I don't feel any different today. Just hungry, and I need some water. Some ice-cold water would be fine.

Well, it's been a good day so far. I'm still alive, and I think that's enough to be happy about. People back in the States don't know how lucky they've got it. People take too much stuff for granted. A little letter to me makes me so happy. I can't wait to get back to the States.

Send me some V8 juice, orange juice, or canned pop. I want a bottle of pop or Pepsi so bad that I think I'm going to go crazy. I can't live on a glass of water a day, so please send a lot. Please. I just lie in the hole at night thinking of kinds of stuff to drink. I think I will go nuts if I don't get something to drink. Send me some Wash-'N-Drys and some cough drops. Mom, can you get a little mirror like the one you have that opens and closes? That way it won't break.

I will pay for all the liquid stuff you can send. Just tell me what it costs you.

I'm in good health. I need a bath and a shave, and I probably do smell. I sure would like to be home. There's no place like home. Take my word for it.

Thanks for everything you guys do. I couldn't ask for better parents.

February 1, 1968

Hello Mom and Dad,

What is my wonderful family doing?

Well, it's about 4:30 in the morning, and I've got gun watch (60mm mortars), and so I thought I would try to write a couple lines. I'm down in my hole in the ground. It's about six foot by six foot by five foot deep. That's my home over here. I've got a little candle, so I thought I would write. I can hardly see.

I just wrote Uncle Gene. I just got a box of goodies from him today. Boy, was I happy.

How is everyone at home? Great, I hope. Me? I guess I'm okay. I just want some water and food. Boy, I stink. I need a bath. No water to wash with—not much even to drink. People in the States don't know how lucky they are. At least a bum can drink all the water he wants and doesn't have to live in the ground like a rat. It's hot during the day and it's cool at night. We dig holes all day and build bunkers. They are really pushing us to dig more trenches. We're always working. No time to do anything, like writing. That's why I'm writing at night.

Did you get my letter about sending some pop and juice? I pray every night that you will send some, and hurry up. I must sound crazy to you, but I can't stop thinking about water and stuff to drink. I'm so dry.

Mom, you and Dad better not be worried about me. I'm watching myself pretty good over here. You take care of each other. I don't want anyone to worry about me.

On my birthday, I tried to hide, but they found me and put me to work. I told them I wanted a day off. They asked me, "Why, do you have a date?" How stupid!

My candle is just about gone, so I will be saying goodbye for now.

Capt EARLE BREEDING
Echo Company, 2/26 _____

I was not a commander who believed the troops should not shoot, so it was policy in Echo Company that anyone could fire his weapon anytime he wanted to unless he was on an ambush. But the troops knew that if a gun went bang, there had better be something dead at the other end of its trajectory. Some battalions had a policy that permission to *return* fire had to be granted by the operations officer.

One night, shortly after we got to Hill 861A, the troops on the west side of the company perimeter called the command post to tell me they had movement in the saddle between us and Hill 861. When I went out there, they told me they had heard movement and shouted a challenge. When the response came back in English, they assumed that Kilo Company was running a patrol down there. I knew that Kilo wouldn't run a patrol without telling us, but I called Kilo anyway. Sure enough, they didn't have any patrols out. As soon as I heard that, I got every weapon that could bear firing into that draw. I don't know if we got anyone, but I made sure I told my troops to shoot anything that moved outside our wire. They sure as hell weren't running a patrol of English-speakers for the hell of it. We were being targeted.

Pfc MIKE DeLANEY
Echo Company, 2/26 ⎯⎯⎯⎯⎯⎯⎯⎯⎯⎯⎯⎯⎯⎯⎯⎯

February 4, 1968

Dear Mom and Dad,
   What's happening back home? Well, things here are getting a lot better. We've been getting more food and water. I'm just fine. Nothing is wrong with me. Sometimes I feel like saying to hell with all this. But I think of coming home and I get to feeling better.
   So many guys go nuts over here. There is so much stuff on your mind. I never thought stuff could be the way it is over here, and the Marines

get the worst—but do the best of all of them. The
Marines are the best and the hardest. To be a
Marine is to be something else I can't put into
words. You go through living hell, but when you're
done you know you've really done something no
one else could have done. You walk with your head
up high and say, "I was a Marine and never had it
easy. I did my part and am proud." They give the
Marines the hardest and the roughest jobs over
here because they know we can do it.

How is my family? Great, I hope. Mom, I wish
and pray that you don't worry about me. I'm fine
and I don't take any chances. My hair is getting
longer now, and I can just about comb it. I think
about being home all the time, watching TV, just
you and me and Dad, and eating all the stuff in the
house. It would be great to go on a vacation, just
you and me and Dad, at least for two months or so
when I get home.

I want Philip [brother] to go in the Air Force,
like Dad told me to do. Philip could be a Marine, but
I don't want him to go through what I go through.
I want him to have it easy. No sense him being in
this situation.

I'm writing this letter with a flashlight while I'm
on gun watch. I've got to fire a round in a few
minutes, so I better say good-bye for now.

After I wrote my letter and got off gun watch, I was lying
in my sleeping hole, on my back. It was completely dark,
pitch black. I couldn't see my hand in front of my face. As I
was falling off to sleep, I had the sensation that my heart
and lungs had stopped. It woke me up. I couldn't breathe. I
thought, What the hell is happening? It was teargas!

MGen TOMMY TOMPKINS
3rd Marine Division Commanding General _____

Sometime around mid-January we received a message at 3rd
Marine Division Headquarters, in Dong Ha, that set forth
the format for "Spotlight" reports. We had no idea what
this was all about, but within the next few days we were
told that the sensor acoustical devices would be dropped by
planes in the areas to the northwest of the Khe Sanh Combat
Base and west along Route 9.[1]

Maj JERRY HUDSON
26th Marines Intelligence Officer _____

Approximately January 18, a team from MACV Headquarters, in Saigon, visited Khe Sanh and offered the use of
some electric [sic] devices which would give indications of
enemy presence. [These were later] called sensors. Within
48 hours we began receiving reports that the devices were
being implanted in likely avenues of approach to the combat
base. Approximately the same time, we also began receiving reports that the devices were indicating enemy activity.
(Everything in the area was considered enemy.) These
reports increased in volume to over 100 per day.[2]

Lt BARNEY WALSH, USN
Observation Squadron 67 _____

We were stationed at Nakhon Phanom in northeast Thailand,
a Navy outfit on an Air Force Air Commando base. We
were committed to support the "electronic barrier" that
Secretary of Defense Robert McNamara thought would keep
the North Vietnamese from infiltrating down the Ho Chi
Minh Trail. Our particular job was to use our old Navy
antisubmarine warfare patrol planes, flying at 180 knots, to
lay a string of sonobuoys along the trails to listen to troop
and truck noises. Once the enemy was identified, air strikes

would be called in on the trail adjacent to the listening devices.

We laid numerous strings of sonobuoys north and north-west of Khe Sanh. We dropped sonobuoys that hung in the trees and others that dug into the ground and transmitted seismic information. After we dropped, EC-121 aircraft were in constant orbit at altitude, relaying information back to Nakhon Phanom. Each sonobuoy had a unique frequency so the noise could be pinpointed and enemy progress through the area could be followed.

Around Khe Sanh, there weren't any trails that I could see, so I figured they just wanted a wall of buoys to give warning of infiltration. We had a sister Air Force squadron flying A-1 Skyraiders. They dropped "gravel" around the sonobuoys to protect them. The gravel was an explosive shaped like a Vietnamese leaf that was carried in a container along with a Freon solution. When released, it scattered over the ground like tree leaves, and when it warmed up, it could blow the tire off a jeep or the leg off a man. The A-1 squadron was trained to fly with us and drop the gravel around the buoys to discourage the enemy from picking them up. However, we didn't fly too many missions together because we were quite a gaggle, flying in big, slow aircraft at 180 or so knots with three or four A-1s on either wing—sitting ducks for antiaircraft.

Maj JERRY HUDSON
26th Marines Intelligence Officer _____

The information from the Infiltration Service Center (ISC) at Nakhon Phanom was passed direct to the intelligence officer of the 26th Marines over a dedicated clear-voice-radio circuit. A covered teletype circuit also existed. We talked to Nakhon Phanom many times a night attempting to "learn to swim."[3]

For the first days, the reports were received with some anxiety as their meaning was not clear. However, after exchange of numerous messages with various commands involved in implanting, read-out, and interpretation of the information, definite patterns could be detected and were targeted.

Prior to the advent of sensors, it was command doctrine to shoot numerous H&I artillery missions each night. These missions were usually based on map inspection, suspect areas, and yesterday's intelligence. The sensor provided [nearly] real-time information, and the words [harassment and interdiction] were virtually removed from the 3rd Marine Division vocabulary in favor of "Moving-Target Fire."[4]

MGen TOMMY TOMPKINS
3rd Marine Division Commanding General _____

For the first few weeks, we used the sensors as a targeting method, which was in accordance with instructions we were given by the MACV briefing officers. The results were better than H&I fires, but that is saying very little. We then began using the sensors as an intelligence-gathering medium. The trouble with using sensors as a targeting device was that we didn't know exactly where the sensors were located. The reports from [Nakhon Phanom] took some time to get to Khe Sanh Combat Base, and the sensors frequently reported our own fires.

Sensors as an intelligence-gathering medium were highly successful. At night and at times of low visibility, they were our only means of obtaining information on enemy movement and activity. When sensor reports could be checked by aerial observation, following an air/artillery strike, the system came into its highest development.[5]

Maj JERRY HUDSON
26th Marines Intelligence Officer _____

I believe that sensors played an important role in the defense of Khe Sanh. I know that they were relied upon heavily in determining my estimates of the enemy situation to Colonel Lownds.[6]

Capt HARRY BAIG
26th Marines Target Information Officer _____

During the nights of February 3–4 and 4–5, "Mussel Shoals" sensors had reported numerous heavy movements from the northwest of Hill 881S. At a distance of 4,000 meters, the movements turned south and later turned east. The intruders were last reported south of [Hill 881S]. Sensors to the southeast of the hill did not sound an alarm. The total count of enemy troops, reported by the sensors, added to a possible 1,500 to 2,000 men in the course of those two nights. During the first night [February 3–4], my interpretation lay in the direction of resupply convoys, and the Fire Support Coordination Center reacted by attacking each sensor target as it appeared. During the second night, I veered toward the thought of an enemy regiment and a probable attack. Majors Coolidge [Division Intelligence representative] and Hudson tended to agree.

We concluded that an attack in the thick mist was imminent. Enemy doctrine calls for an attacking force to move to its assault position in echelons, make a last-minute reconnaissance, and attack in waves. If this was indeed a regiment, then the force would probably be disposed in a regimental column, battalions in line one behind the other. As time passed without activation of the easterly sensors, we three became convinced. A target block, 1,000 by 3,000 meters, was described on the map south of Hill 881S at about a point where a large force, moving at two kilometers per hour (NVA rate of march in darkness and mist—more doctrine) would have reached in the time interval since the activation of the last sensor. At each end of the block, a gently curving 1,000-meter line was drawn, extending toward and about the southwestern and southeastern slope of Hill 881S.[7]

Maj JERRY HUDSON
26th Marines Intelligence Officer _____

[The enemy was getting ready to assault Hill 881S or Hill 861A, or both together.] A decision had to be made which

one to interdict. The choice was in favor of 881S as the
artillery there could be employed in support of 861A if
required.[8]

Capt HARRY BAIG
26th Marines Target Information Officer ⎯⎯⎯⎯⎯⎯⎯

Colonel Lownds, having accepted the reasoning . . . gave
permission to fire. For about thirty minutes, commencing
approximately 0300, February 5, five batteries of 1/13
within KSCB and four batteries of [U.S. Army] 175mm
guns from outside the base poured continuous fire into
various places of the block and along the two circumscrib-
ing lines at each end. Later, [sensor monitors at] Nakhon
Phanom Center told me that acoustic sensors in the area to
the south of Hill 881S recorded the voices of hundreds of
men running in panic, through the darkness and heavy fog,
in a southerly direction. The seismic sensors went wild.[9]

Maj JERRY HUDSON
26th Marines Target Information Officer ⎯⎯⎯⎯⎯⎯⎯

We felt we had preempted the attack on 881S.[10]

Capt HARRY BAIG
26th Marines Intelligence Officer ⎯⎯⎯⎯⎯⎯⎯⎯⎯

It never occurred to me that night that the enemy's intent
was, and always had been, to attack Hills 881S and 861
simultaneously. I had forgotten the NVA battle plan. There
were no sensors near Hills 861 and 861A. So, when the latter
was attacked two hours later, I, the Target Information Officer
and alleged expert on NVA doctrine, was caught flatfooted.[11]

Capt EARLE BREEDING
Echo Company, 2/26 ⎯⎯⎯⎯⎯⎯⎯⎯⎯⎯⎯⎯⎯⎯⎯

Marines on the point of the 1st Platoon sector passed the
word, ''They're coming through the wire.'' That news

spread up the trenchline to the right and left. All the way along the trenchline and up the chain of command, Echo Company was hearing, "They're coming through the wire." Nobody said which part of the wire, and nobody could see anything. The average Marine thought the NVA were coming through the wire in front of him because he had heard it from the guy next to him. So, all of a sudden, within seconds of one another, I got the word from all three of my platoon commanders. It sounded to me like they were coming through the wire all around the hill. I thought I was getting hit from all sides at once. I had the troops throw gas grenades and I called for all the artillery support the combat base could give me.

The gas probably did us more harm than it did the NVA. It started filtering into the low-lying areas—our fighting holes and trenches.

Pfc MIKE DeLANEY
Echo Company, 2/26 _____

The gas—it must have been theirs—got everyone up and moving in the open, disoriented. When you're running around grabbing your chest and having the sensation that you can't breathe, you're not thinking about manning a weapon.

Then I started to hear gunfire. I could hear guns popping. It sounded like a little pop, followed by small-arms fire, and then another little pop. As I bolted out of my hole, it finally dawned on me that I was breathing gas. I got back down in my hole and ran my hand over everything, looking for my gas mask. I found it, climbed out of my hole, and started running around while I put it on and adjusted it.

Capt EARLE BREEDING
Echo Company, 2/26 _____

They had zeroed their mortars in on us the night before, but I hadn't realized what they had done. They had fired one round, not the normal group of three at maximum range. If it was us, we'd have fired round after round after round and adjusted the fire. They fired just one mortar round from fairly close in. They made their adjustment on that one round and held their fire until the attack started. When their 82mm mortars hit us, I believe they expected to catch our people fleeing toward and off the south side of the hill.

Pfc MIKE DeLANEY
Echo Company, 2/26 _____

The whole skyline to my left—the 1st Platoon area—was starting to light up. There was yellow and orange color coming off the horizon. There were things going off—the 60mm mortar over there, the Chicom grenades, machine guns—and I could hear people talking and yelling. People were screaming. People were running, scrambling. People were looking for their gas masks. All kinds of shit was hitting the fan. We were very disorganized at that point. Whatever the NVA had in mind, it worked. They definitely caught us by surprise.

Capt EARLE BREEDING
Echo Company, 2/26 _____

They came up the northern slope, the only approach they had. I knew they would; they weren't going to come around the other side of the hill in the face of direct artillery fire from the combat base and 106s from the 2/26 position on Hill 558. As it was, they had all the cover in the world between the dark of night and all that high elephant grass.

The company perimeter was much longer than it was wide, and there was a salient in the west side. We tried to round it off the best way we could on the northern point, which was held by 1stLt Don Shanley's 1st Platoon. That was a slight disadvantage for us because we could bring less fire to bear, but it was also a disadvantage to the NVA because they could not see how many troops I had set in on the rest of the hill. It is possible—reasonable—that they thought we were a platoon outpost from Kilo Company, which was on the adjacent hill. Without illumination, no one on the hill could see a white handkerchief in front of his face. It was absolutely pitch black.

Pfc MIKE DeLANEY
Echo Company, 2/26 _____

They hit the 1st Platoon because it was stretched across a finger that was lower than the rest of the hilltop, easier to get to. The 60mm mortar and M-60 machine gun with 1st Platoon got it right off the bat. The best anyone could figure out was that the NVA had watched us shoot H&I fire for days and had marked the gun positions. Since the crew-served weapons were dug in, we never moved them. The positions were permanent from the time the company lines were established. The NVA knew where all the crew-served weapons were before they started to attack.

Capt EARLE BREEDING
Echo Company, 2/26 _____

When the NVA broke through Shanley's 1st Platoon, they had nowhere to go. They were faced with a steep climb to the top of the hill. In fact, they didn't break through Shanley as much as they *absorbed* through him. There were 1st Platoon Marines down there manning their positions right through the fight.

Pfc MIKE DeLANEY
Echo Company, 2/26 _____

I had a stinging sensation down my nose and throat, but there was so much going on, so much adrenaline, that I overcame it. But my eyes were watering. It was night and I was trying to see through the gas-mask lenses with my eyes watering. It was a mess.

It was the first time ground forces had tried to enter our wire. We had been mortared before, but now they were in our wire. This was it! Everything I ever thought war could be was happening, right now. I wasn't scared like I had been when the mortars hit. There was so much going on that my mind couldn't comprehend it. We had the gas, there were people running, people screaming, stuff exploding. I knew I had a job to do, I had to go look for my 60mm mortar. It was only yards away from me—the whole squad was in bunkers we had built right around the gun pit.

The only members of my 60mm mortar squad in the pit were the gunner and the assistant gunner. Four of us, ammo humpers, were on the outside, opening crates of ammo and passing rounds in like a nurse would pass a scalpel for a doctor. When the round went out, *boomp*, one of us slapped another round into the assistant gunner's hand, whatever he called for—illume, high explosive, whatever. We tore off powder increments as we handed each round over, whatever charge the gunner called for.

When we started firing, the mortar was tilted slightly toward the north, toward the 1st Platoon sector. People were calling fire to us—"Bring it up the hill," or "Bring it down the point." They were calling the fire by screaming; no calls came in by radio. We were alternating illume and high explosives as fast as we could get rounds down the tube. It was obvious that the rounds were going too high, so we started firing the rounds with the base charge. When we got to the point where the NVA had crossed the 1st Platoon wire, most of our rounds were fired almost straight up because we really didn't want any distance on them. When the NVA penetrated the 1st Platoon bunkers and broke through, we fired straight up. We knew the consequence, but we had no choice. The only way to keep them off of us was to throw around as much shrapnel as possible. We had flak gear on, and we were laying in among the sandbags, passing rounds into the gun pit, so we thought we would be okay. The NVA were all in the open, running past us.

Capt EARL BREEDING
Echo Company, 2/26 _____

I kept thinking, What am I going to do if they shoot off my radio antennas? When it was all over, I had no radio antennas up. They were all down. The only reason I was able to communicate with outside headquarters was because of our elevation.

My command post was about halfway back along the hill from the 1st Platoon area and a little to the east of the military crest. There was a big tree right at the top of the hill, and since I wanted to leave as much of the natural vegetation in place as possible, I tucked the command post in under its branches, mainly to protect the radiomen. Also, my company sickbay was in a huge bomb crater left over from the Hill Fights in mid-1967—also protected by the tree.

I had to keep the NVA away from the sickbay bomb crater, which was filled with men who couldn't fight back. Also, my command post was filling up with Marines who had been temporarily blinded by gas, flash burns, or grenades and mortar rounds going off at close range. So, as soon as things settled down enough for me to make sense of what was going on, I began feeding fire teams forward from the rear platoons in order to build up a line across the top of the hill. I truncated the company position with anybody I could get, more or less cutting off the 1st Platoon's nose and sealing off most of the NVA who had filtered through the 1st Platoon. The new line was made up mostly of 1st Platoon people, but anyone else who wanted to be part of it was welcome.

It sounds more organized in the telling than it really was. There was too much loud noise for me to shout direct orders; my desire seeped through the company, and individual Marines reacted on their own. I had to rely on training and instinct. But, from the time we got the new line built up, I wasn't concerned. I knew we were going to hold. Nevertheless, there was a moment in which I would have liked to get out of there, but I knew there was really no way. I wasn't about to retreat, and besides, there was no way to leave the hill. That was scary. There was no way to leave that hill at night, and certainly there was no way to do it without leaving our dead and wounded behind.

Pfc MIKE DeLANEY
Echo Company, 2/26 _____

People were shooting with handguns. We were shooting at
each other with handguns. We were throwing fragmentation
grenades at point-blank range; I'd throw a frag, turn my
back to it, and hunch up my neck and shoulders, hoping I
wouldn't catch chunks large enough to take me out. We did
whatever we thought would work.

While the 1st Platoon guys were fighting hand-to-hand—
using entrenching tools, whatever—the NVA were running
through the perimeter, doing as much damage as they could.
They were throwing satchel charges and grenades at the
crew-manned weapons. They were everywhere. They blew
up the 60mm mortar near 1st Platoon, killing four of the
Marines in and around the pit. It was such chaos from that
point on that, whenever I brought up my M-16, I had to
glance at whoever was going by to make sure he was an
NVA, and not a Marine. We had illume, but it moved
around overhead and made shifting shadows. They made it
seem like *everything* was moving. It was just very scary.

Capt EARLE BREEDING
Echo Company, 2/26 _____

It was uncontrolled pandemonium. I'd like to say that I was
about to win this one fight, and the Marine I was fighting
would like to say he was about to win, too. Luckily, a flare
went off before we killed one another.

Capt HARRY BAIG
26th Marines Target Information Officer _____

The artillery and air response to the enemy's assault may be
divided into three phases, all of which occurred simultaneously.
1/13 loosed the protective fires on the slopes of Hill 861A
with three batteries. A fourth battery concentrated in the
area where the enemy movement was the thickest and then

rolled down the slope to prevent the enemy from retiring or from being reinforced. This was the first phase.

The second phase began with the four batteries of [U.S. Army] 175mm guns from Camp Carroll and the Rock Pile delivering their ordnance along two arms of a broad **V**, which embraced the base of the hill from the northeast. The objective of the guns was to saturate the area wherein the enemy reserve battalion was estimated to be. Slowly, the **V** crept up the slopes until it reached a point 200 meters from the wire. Within this space, the fourth battery from KSCB rolled to and fro, covering the area from which the attackers had come and into which Captain Breeding was energetically heaving them. Meanwhile, the remaining batteries continued their protective missions or were adjusted in accordance with the garrison's desires.

The third phase involved the rapidly assembling aircraft. AN/TPQ-10 radar-directed air strikes, in the form of 200- and 300-meter ripples, were dropped outboard of, and parallel to, the **V** to avoid checkfires. Bombs fell on known mortar clusters, possible assembly areas, and throughout the area to the far rear of the assault battalion.[12]

Capt EARLE BREEDING
Echo Company, 2/26 _____

We were drawing fire support from five separate locations: our own 60mm mortars; the 81mm mortars and 105mm howitzers on Hill 881S; the 2/26 106mm recoilless rifles on Hill 558; the 105mm howitzers from the combat base, and the 175mm howitzers at the Rock Pile and Camp Carroll. But I couldn't adjust anyone's fire because I didn't know friendly from hostile incoming. Not only were our surviving mortars firing on the hill, we were under a constant NVA mortar barrage. In addition, I was later told, the friendly howitzers were dumping variable-time rounds on us—airbursts. Getting hit or not getting hit was a matter of luck, for us and the NVA.

Hill 881S was farther from Hill 861A than the maximum range of the 81mm mortar rounds they were firing. Firing the maximum charge at maximum range was barely enough, but the rounds reached us because we were 20 meters lower. They were barely accurate, but they did enough. The Marines on Hill 881S used up just about all their 81mm ammo to help us.

Capt EARLE BREEDING
Echo Company, 2/26 _____

The way the teargas didn't affect the NVA at all leads me to believe they were hopped up on drugs. The gas was an irritant, and they should have been bothered. *We* were bothered. During the first lull, I found one of them with his AK-47 slung over his shoulder. He and others were going through our living hooches, more interested in reading *Playboy* magazines than in fighting the war. That's when we counterattacked.

It would be nice to say that everybody stood there, did a dress right dress, and fixed bayonets while I shouted, "Port arms, forward march!" But it just didn't work out that way. It was a matter of individual Marines saying to their buddies, "Hey, come on. Let's go kick 'em outta here." All the troop leaders could do was lead the way or kick ass.

Capt HARRY BAIG
26th Marines Intelligence Officer _____

Enemy attack doctrine frequently positions the reserve battalion directly behind the assault unit. At all costs, the Fire Support Coordination Center was determined to prevent their juncture. Hence the multiple bands of fire. The reserve battalion never materialized. The second attack, at 0610, was made by the survivors of the first assault. These unfortunate remnants could neither retire through the rolling barrage nor be reinforced by the reserve, which in turn had been caught between the 175mm artillery and the air strikes.[13]

Capt EARLE BREEDING
Echo Company, 2/26 _____

I'm sure they were only out there to drag away the bodies of
the NVA who were killed in front of our wire.

Pfc MIKE DeLANEY
Echo Company, 2/26 _____

Finally it slowed up and they backed off. I looked around at
all the powder increments I had ripped off 60mm rounds, at
all the grenade canisters, LAAW rocket tubes, and piles of
empty brass. Stuck in a sandbag only a foot or so from
where I was handing rounds into the gun pit was an NVA
rifle grenade that never went off.

When they first started to pull away, there was very heavy
fog. It was clear when we started, but it was very thickly
overcast when it petered off. I have no idea when the fog
rolled in. It was just there.

There were bodies everywhere. Their bodies were in full
uniform. That scared me. Until then, I thought we were
fighting Viet Cong guerrillas. We had been fighting VC
before we got to Khe Sanh; I didn't know they had NVA
soldiers up there until I saw them dead on the ground inside
our perimeter. It scared me; it really drove it home that we
were fighting a uniformed army, not a bunch of people who
were farmers by day and who ran around at night being VC.
These people were well armed.

Captain Breeding grabbed me in the morning and ordered
me to help get a body count. I went around to each position
on the hill, asking Marines if they knew where any NVA
bodies were, counting them up. After the count was completed, they were stacked up.

I had never seen young dead people. The only dead
people I had ever seen were old. In my mind, old people are
supposed to die, but not young people. I had sat around the
day before smoking cigarettes and sharing C-rations with
some of the dead young people on that hill. Their skin was

gray and rubbery; they didn't look human anymore. Picking
them up gave me a funny feeling. It never stopped bothering
me, the feel of the bodies. I had never felt a dead body
before. And now I was being asked to carry them around—
and pick up body *parts*. That upset me, picking up an arm
or a leg—from people I knew, from my own squad, from
the 60mm mortar crew and the M-60 machine-gun crew that
had been with the 1st Platoon.

Quite a few of the NVA we killed inside our wire were
bandaged—that night. It was obvious that they had sent
their wounded back up to fight the battle. That scared me to
the point that I could not believe that people who had
already been wounded and messed up still wanted to fight. I
figured they had a lot more drive than I had. Those people
were scary, like they were almost superhuman. We found
drugs—syringes and chemicals.

Capt EARLE BREEDING
Echo Company, 2/26 _____

I don't think they would have gotten through us if we had
had the gear we needed. We had been up there only a short
while, and we had not had an opportunity to build our
position up. We didn't have enough wire. We didn't even
have sledgehammers to pound in the engineering stakes to
secure the wire. It really came down to saving money over
saving people's lives. It was just dollars.

After it was over, my top priorities were getting the
wounded out and getting replacement people and crew-
served weapons in. We were given top priority in all of I
Corps. They gave us everything we needed—had needed
before the attack.

LCpl WILLIAM MAVES
2/26 Tactical Air Control Party _____

After the second NVA effort toward morning failed to take
Hill 861A, I started to take a count of casualties and move
them into position near the landing zone for medevac.

At dawn, we were fogged in solid, which was common

up there. It usually didn't burn off until 1000 or 1100. This forced upon me the biggest decision of my life. If Danang sent the fleet of choppers I had requested for thirty-five wounded and they couldn't get through the fog, it would be hours before they could come back again after refueling. What to do? I had emergency medevacs waiting in the landing zone who would not live another hour if I waited. If they couldn't get in, more would die with the longer wait.

I looked at the men lying there and told Danang to send the birds. When they got there, I stood in the middle of the landing zone with a red star cluster in my hand, staring up through the fog, listening to the rotors circling overhead. One pilot said he would circle lower and lower until I could get a visual. It seemed like forever until I finally saw the bottom of that bird go over in the fog. I shot the red star cluster up at him, and down he came through the fog, onto the landing zone.

The rest was easy. He left straight up and another bird was circling, ready to drop down in the spot the first one came out of. As it turned out, the fog didn't lift that day until about noon. Sunshine filled the valley and everything looked scenic again. I could only wonder if last night had been a bad dream.

Pfc MIKE DeLANEY
Echo Company, 2/26 _____

February 6, 1968—0230

Dear Mom and Dad,

Just in case you heard on the TV news or radio, last night they tried to overrun our hill, 861A, in mass-wave attacks.

0430—Well, I had to stop writing this letter for a couple hours. We just got hit again.

In two days we have lost eight men dead and about sixteen hurt, and about thirty-five WIAs, some in real bad shape. Four of my real good friends got killed on the night of February 5, Monday. No one died tonight, just three wounded. We had to use gas on them. We all had to wear our gas masks. Boy, is it hard to run around and work with one on.

I'm fine and only tired. I wanted you to know that I'm still alive and okay because I know this will be in the papers. I don't want you to worry about me, so I thought I would let you know how it was. We won the fight. Everyone comes and thanks us for doing such a good job because, without our gun, I don't think we would have kept this hill. They call us the Dirty Half-Dozen because there are six of us and our gun is the best one they've got. There's only two. The other one was blown up the first night. That's when my buddies got killed. That morning, after the battle, I carried the dead and wounded to the choppers and counted the dead enemy.

Boy, Mom, it hurts to see people you know in little pieces. We just threw their arms and legs into rubber bags. It's really getting bad around here. We should be here for many months, on the hill.

I haven't got any mail for over a week now. If you send me any boxes or stuff, don't insure them because they won't get up here on the hill.

When they probed us on the morning of February 6, we threw a few grenades at them and they threw a few chicoms at us. It was just enough contact to keep everybody up. It didn't last for more than an hour, and it wasn't continuous.

Chapter 15

FEBRUARY 7
LANG VEI

SSgt HARVE SAAL, USA

FOB-3 _____

Just after midnight—February 7—the Special Forces camp at Lang Vei came under heavy attack from the west. Upon hearing heavy gunfire to the FOB's southwest, I turned on and monitored my recon team's radio, which was a radio frequency shared by the FOB and the Special Forces A Team in Lang Vei. At various times, I heard the following:

"They've got tanks out there." Moments later, I heard the FOB-3 [Khe Sanh] radio operator say, "We'll be down [off the air] for a short time." Then, within the next five minutes, the Lang Vei radio operator called the FOB, but got no answer. The Lang Vei operator called the FOB again and shouted, "There's tanks on our [radio bunker] roof." Then there was a rushing sound and the Lang Vei radio went silent.

1stLt FRED McGRATH
Bravo Battery, 1/13 —————————————————————————

I had the battery exec pit the night Lang Vei was overrun. We had Lang Vei on the radio and were providing fire support, based upon the Special Forces personnel adjusting the rounds. The last transmission was to the effect, "Oh, hell, they have tanks. They're right on top of us." We didn't hear anything else. We tried several other frequencies, but could not contact Lang Vei.

SSgt HARVE SAAL, USA
FOB-3 ———————————————————————————————————

Since I felt that no one from the FOB radio team had monitored this last message, I notified the FOB sergeant major as to what I had heard. All attempts at communicating with the Special Forces camp at Lang Vei went unanswered. I told the FOB sergeant major that something had to be done for the Special Forces team in Lang Vei. He agreed.

The commander of the 26th Marines, Colonel Lownds, was notified and briefed on the Lang Vei situation. Since Lang Vei fell within his designated operational area of responsibility, nothing could take place in this area without his approval or knowledge. Colonel Lownds was asked to mount an immediate operation into Lang Vei in order to find and rescue all possible survivors. He refused the request and said that he would not sacrifice any *American* lives. He was reminded that the Special Forces survivors were, in fact, *Americans*, too! He just glared through us like an X-ray machine and dismissed our thoughts as so much bravado. He restated his refusal to mount a rescue attempt.

Maj JIM STANTON
26th Marines Fire Support Coordination Center ———————

It is true that we had an agreement to go to the aid of Lang Vei in the event it was threatened with being overrun, but the situation at the combat base deteriorated so quickly and so completely that it should have been obvious to anyone that we could no longer guarantee their security. It was too long a march, particularly at night. Nevertheless, the night of the attack, there was serious talk about mounting a relief force. At the same time, the Special Forces headquarters in Saigon was saying that they would rescue their Special Forces people at Lang Vei. In the end, no one was sent. It was the right decision. If we had sent a company or even a battalion out there, they would have been murdered. We were sure that the attack on Lang Vei was a ploy to get the Marine relief force outside the combat base wire, that they had set an ambush for the relief column before they even began attacking the Special Forces camp. Our intelligence people were going crazy. We had no idea what they had out there, and Lang Vei was telling us they had "tanks in the wire."

LCpl ARMANDO GONZALES
Bravo Company, 1/9 _____

I heard the sounds of tanks over our radio, and some Marines in the battalion claimed they could hear the tanks' engines themselves. Many of us wanted to go out to help the Lang Vei defenders, but there was no way that any unit large enough to help could have gone out at night through that terrain, with all those NVA out there, without getting ambushed. We knew it, we didn't like it, we felt bad and angry, but, realistically, we would have been wiped out easier than the base that was getting hit.

LtCol JIM WILKINSON
1/26 Commanding Officer _____

In November 1967, Colonel Lownds directed that I determine an overland route between KSCB and Lang Vei, with the time/space factor for moving a rifle company to Lang Vei on a tactical mission. Alpha Company, 1/26, moved through the jungle between KSCB and Lang Vei to determine possible routes to be used in the event Lang Vei was to be reinforced. It was determined that a rifle company, avoiding well-used trails to preclude ambush, could move by foot from KSCB to Lang Vei in approximately nineteen hours.[1]

1stLt JOHN KAHENY
1/26 Combat Operations Center _____

On the night Lang Vei was attacked, I heard their call sign, Spunky Hanson, on the regimental tactical net, asking that we go down there and rescue them. But we knew by then that it was impossible to get down Highway 9 without being ambushed.

The Army was really seriously upset because we did not send a convoy down to relieve the camp when it was under that armored attack. We did not know at the time that they were just PT-76s, but, even given that, the chances of a successful breakthrough that night down Highway 9 were nonexistent.

SSgt HARVE SAAL, USA
FOB-3 _____

We notified the pilots of several Marine Huey helicopters of our impending intentions to mount a rescue operation into Lang Vei. Then we rallied FOB Special Forces volunteers and Bru montagnards for the impending operation. Meanwhile, there was a degree of confusion concerning the basic rescue plan. I told the FOB sergeant major that all we needed was a search-and-security team, and he agreed.

The FOB Special Forces volunteers and montagnards were formed into search and security elements. I was placed in a search element because of my prior social visits to and knowledge of the Lang Vei Special Forces camp. I knew the layout at Lang Vei.

We were flying at a jerking-type pace to ensure that the NVA gunners weren't presented with good targets. As we bounced over the last treetops in choppers, we were able to see too-many-to-count smoldering embers on both sides of Highway 9 and basically concentrated inside the perimeter wire of the camp. Dense smoke, both gray and blackish, obscured the ground, so few details could be made out at a distance of approximately a half-mile.

I could see that some men from the lead chopper were jumping out into the camp at a height of about twenty feet. The forward speed of their chopper ranged from almost still to up to at least ten knots. At first I thought the chopper had been disabled by ground fire and that they were "unassing" the crashing chopper, but, as we came closer, it became obvious that there was a semblance of security. As they spread out toward the camp perimeter wire, it was evident that they were *not* firing their rifles. It therefore seemed that the NVA presence, so far, was not menacing. I hoped that they had not remained to secure and use the camp.

After I disembarked from the helicopter, and soon after it lifted off, I could smell burnt grass and burnt flesh. It was certain that the NVA had used flamethrowers in conquering this camp. I moved past a trenchline where burnt bodies were still smoldering. This was my first opportunity to see what effect flamethrowers had in the outcome of a pitched battle, and it was a devastating awakening for me.

A cursory look about the camp revealed some Russian tanks, which were disabled and motionless. I then recalled the radio message that morning in which the radio operator had reported, "There's a tank on the roof." I ran to the general area in which the A Team's underground bunkers were located. There it was. The tank was dead still, destroyed, over what I knew was the location of a bunker.

I paused briefly near the entrance of the bunker. A quick glance revealed a U.S. jeep with the body of a lifeless Special Forces soldier. He was slumped against the firing tube of a 106mm recoilless rifle. That tube was pointed directly at a destroyed Russian tank. It didn't take a genius to figure out that he had wiped out the tank at the same moment the tank gunner had shot and mortally wounded him. He was SFC Eugene Ashley, and he received a posthumous Medal of Honor.

I went to the bunker door and tried to open it from the

outside. It was sealed tightly. I pounded on the metal door and yelled, "Is anybody in there?" Silence; no answer.

I tried again. This time, there was a faint reply from inside the bunker, a faint "Fuck you, asshole." I yelled, "Hey, motherfucker, open that fuckin' door so we can take you back to the FOB with us." The team sergeant, SFC Thomas Craig, reluctantly opened the door. Not much time was spent on thanks. I later learned that the NVA were yelling down the air shafts in English, trying to prod someone inside to open the bunker door so they, the NVA, could take the occupants prisoner. The NVA also used hand grenades, satchel charges, and CS teargas canisters against the defenders in the bunker. Fortunately, the survivors didn't give in so easily and still held hope that they would be rescued.

After we ate lunch at the main bunker, the surviving Special Forces soldiers were guided to and loaded on the Marine choppers. They were eventually flown out of Khe Sanh to Danang. Our original intentions were only to rescue the American survivors at Lang Vei, but, as it turned out, we managed to rescue a large portion of the CIDG force as well. Also, Laotian civilian refugees who were in the protection of the camp defensive perimeter began moving out of camp, east along Highway 9.

After the rescue, we could see that some of the Asian survivors were different in a peculiar sort of way. They didn't seem to fit in well with the others. They had short haircuts and appeared to be in better health than some of the other survivors. It developed, through interrogation, that a few of them were infiltrators. Their orders were to go to a refugee camp and gather intelligence. Some others were given the task of causing general havoc and distrust among the refugees.

I did not encounter any NVA troops while I searched through the camp for survivors. I really did not know until later, after the rescue, if there was any resistance from NVA troops still within the camp. To our delight, after we compared notes, it was thought by all involved that the NVA did not purposely leave any combat forces in the camp.

After-operation intelligence estimates of enemy intentions during our rescue operation assumed that the North Vietnamese thought we were retaking the Lang Vei camp and that we would then prepare to hold it. With that in mind, they pulled back to regroup for another attack on Lang Vei.

We rescued sixteen out of twenty-three Americans that day and lost *no* lives as a result of our ''lunacy.'' We were reported by Colonel Lownds to General William Westmoreland as being uncooperative and unprofessional. The general called our commander to Saigon for a tongue-lashing. He told him to be more responsive to the Marine commander. Then Westy congratulated him on a rescue job well done.

□

"TANKS IN THE WIRE"

Lt RAY STUBBE
1/26 Battalion Chaplain _____

[DIARY ENTRY] I saw casualties from Lang Vei, who began arriving. Captain Willoughby, their CO, told me the NVA pounded the camp with 152mm artillery and then brought in tanks. One tank stood directly on top of the command-post bunker. We, ourselves, are now more vulnerable—from Russian tanks! Everybody knows it!

26th Marines After Action Report _____

The use of PT-76 amphibious tanks in the attack on Lang Vei Special Forces Camp made real the little-known NVA armor threat. The large, relatively safe area of Laos, the very thick vegetation common to much of that area of operations and neighboring portions of the country, and the flat or gently rolling terrain near the KSCB made the use of tanks against the base quite possible. The strong-point defenses being used in the area of operations and the success at Lang Vei made the use of tanks likely because of their shock effect and their wire-breaching and bunker-busting capabilities.

Although the use of tanks against KSCB was quite possible, certain factors tended to reduce the likely effectiveness of such an enemy course of action. First, the abundance of antitank minefields and organic and attached antitank weapons would substantially reduce an attacking armor force. Second, the shock effect of the tanks had already been partially diminished by their initial use at Lang Vei. Also, it was believed unlikely that the shock effect would be as effective against American forces once [they were] alerted as it was on indigenous forces caught by surprise.

Maj JIM STANTON
26th Marines Fire Support Coordination Center _____

Our aerial observers found the camouflaged PT-76s that had attacked Lang Vei tied up to the bank of the Xe Pone River, in Laos. They apparently had run out of gas. We called in Marine A-4s. After a couple of strikes, we heard the aircraft had blown the camouflage away to reveal damaged and destroyed vehicles. As more bombs were dropped farther afield around the PT-76s, we got reports of secondary explosions, which indicated ammo dumps dug in along the river. This led to more strikes, more destruction, more serendipitous discoveries, and so forth.

26th Marines After Action Report _____

Within ten days after the battle of Lang Vei on February 7, air reconnaissance showed that eight tanks and armored personnel carriers had been destroyed near Lang Vei and to the south along the Laotian border. Since only seven tanks had been used against Lang Vei and ten to twelve were [believed] to be the maximum likely enemy capability, it was felt that the most immediate threat had been substantially reduced. Reports of tank sightings in the DMZ and Laos continued to be received, and agent reports frequently made reference to major armor attacks in the northern Quang Tri area.

1stLt JOHN KAHENY
1/26 Combat Operations Center _____

We were as vulnerable to enemy armor as the Special Forces camp was. I had drafted the rough counter-mechanized plan for 1/26, and I knew that if the NVA ever deployed any armor against us, we would have a difficult time defending ourselves against it. This was mainly because we had only five M-48 tanks and ten Ontos in the area. Also, we didn't have an area in which we could operate our armor effectively. It would have been a very nasty scene if tanks had broken through. We basically said that, once we ran out of LAAWs, we could always tape thermite grenades onto the engine hoods. This was, on the face of it, a facetious way to allay our fears.

LCpl CHARLIE THORNTON
Lima Company, 3/26 _____

Our commanders began to prepare for tank attacks by the NVA. Our weapons platoon was chosen as a "tank killer" group. We were trained how to stop a tank, crack it open with explosives, and finish it off with a flamethrower. It seemed like such a ridiculous idea during the days of modern weapon systems and explosives. I was chosen as the one to carry the flamethrower. As usual, the equipment was of World War II vintage. We prepared every day to defend against tanks.

LCpl ARMANDO GONZALES
Bravo Company, 1/9 _____

After Lang Vei, we dug what we called "suicide holes" out in front of our lines. These were about six or seven feet deep and large enough for a good-sized Marine to jump into standing up. The idea was that volunteers carrying explosives would be in the holes, ready to attach the explosives to the bottom of a tank going by overhead. We knew that tanks never operated without infantry, so there was no guarantee that a Marine manning one of those holes wouldn't be found by the infantry.

Chapter 16

FEBRUARY 8
ALPHA-I

Pfc LAWRENCE SEAVY-CIOFFI
Alpha Company, 1/9 _____

I was a forward artillery scout observer assigned from Delta Battery, 2/12, to Alpha Company, 1/9.

The 1st Platoon of Alpha Company, 1/9 (Alpha-1), manned a forward outpost slightly over a quarter-mile due west of 1/9's position [at the Rock Quarry]. Essentially, the platoon's observation post was a small, cleared hilltop [Hill 64], our farthest westward position in the valley. The perimeter was oval-shaped, with an area approximately 40 meters long by 20 meters wide. My artillery observation bunker was on the northernmost end of the hill, ten feet in from the hill's perimeter trenchline. I shared my bunker with my radio operator, LCpl D. A. Smith.

In the predawn hours of February 8, 2ndLt Terence Roach came to my bunker. He requested to borrow the penlight I used for night map reading; he said he needed it in order to check our lines. At the time, I did not think too much about loaning my penlight to him because late in the afternoon the day before I had been cleared for a registered on-call for close fire support directly onto our position.

My on-call artillery plan was given a target number by the Fire Support Coordination Center and personally cleared by Lieutenant Roach. I had discussed this option with the lieutenant for several days. Numerous outposts were being assaulted along the rim of the valley, including Hills 881S and 861. These NVA attacks seemed to occur primarily at night, and the NVA were often in the barbed wire before artillery support calls were finally radioed out. Lieutenant Roach and I had discussed the option of a surprise attack at night, where the enemy might suddenly penetrate our perimeter by surprise. The low visibility, especially at night—low highland cloud ceiling of winter, patches of condensation, and wisps of fog that at times even prevented a full view of our hilltop from one end to the other at night and early morning—severely limited the use of artillery observation. Further, the slopes of our hill were too steep to predictably place artillery rounds at the exact bottom of our slopes. A shell may have been placed on the more gradual northern slope, but what if an attack was directed from another side? Therefore, Lieutenant Roach and I agreed, as a last resort, in the event of our being overrun and outnumbered, that I would call in the grid of our position for a fire mission of only one gun, one round at a time. In terms of howitzer ballistics and our outpost's topography, this translated into critically close artillery fire support but not necessarily a direct hit on top of our hill, because our position was less than one adjustment—forty meters by twenty meters. So my first shot would probably be a near miss, landing at the hill's base or on one of its slopes.

As a further safety precaution, Lieutenant Roach passed the word to all his staff noncommissioned officers that, in the event we were suddenly overrun, everyone was to remain in place, either in the trenches or preferably in their bunkers, with helmets and flak jackets on.

The attack against our outpost was launched in the absolute dark, at approximately 0415 on the morning of February 8.

The North Vietnamese laid down an accurate mortar barrage that hit within our perimeter and awakened me, Lance Corporal Smith, and everyone else, I'm sure. For a moment I fumbled in the darkness for my penlight. Then I remembered that Lieutenant Roach had needed it an hour earlier. We couldn't go outside, so we both listened to what developed into an all-out ground attack. After the three- or four-minute mortar barrage, there followed small-arms fire, screaming, and grenade bursts. Immediately after that, we could hear Vietnamese commands being shouted in the north trenchline, ten feet behind us. It happened incredibly fast. I quickly concluded that we were overrun, and then and there I decided to call in the registered artillery targeted directly onto our position.

Grenades were exploding outside our bunker, and I detected movement on our roof. Not only was I without my penlight, but my radio operator, in the dark, was unable to locate his pistol. We had only my rifle. Enemy grenades now were going off right outside our bunker. We could literally hear a conversation in Vietnamese being conducted just in front of our hole.

The on-call had been registered the afternoon before, but given the state of affairs and in total darkness, I was unable to remember its registration number. That was no problem, as I had it written down on my map. There was no penlight, so I had Smith hold my map while I struck a match. He blew it out and said not to light a match again. I can't blame him, as the poncho covering our entrance was partly open. No sooner had my match been blown out than several grenades were thrown down into our doorway. They were stopped by the poncho. We were blown back against the wall of our hole, hit in the legs. I struck another match and got the registration number, but Smith blew the match out and said they were right outside, not to light any more matches. We called in the registration number and gave the order to fire as more grenades were thrown. The reply from the Fire Support Coordination Center was "Checkfire."

Two more grenades rolled right inside with us. I kicked one of them into the doorway and Smith did something to the second one, or tried to, because both detonated in the doorway, which absorbed most of the shrapnel. At this point, nearly all I could hear was ringing. I was speaking at a very high volume and my radio operator was concerned about the enemy outside.

The reply on the radio said my fire mission had to be cleared by our commanding officer. I kept insisting that we had previous clearance, but to no avail. Then our outside radio was blown up and more grenades came in. We kicked them into the doorway. We had another radio inside. Smith was unable to reach Lieutenant Roach, there was a battle raging outside, and the checkfire by the Fire Support Coordination Center had us stymied. I told Smith that we had to locate Lieutenant Roach and confirm his clearance again for my close artillery fire support. The position of the Fire Support Coordination Center was that my fire mission had only been cleared to be registered and needed a second clearance to be fired. That was news to us.

Smith advised me against going outside because there was an NVA right outside. I told him we had to get out and find Lieutenant Roach, but he disagreed. I told him I was going out. He told me it was useless to go outside because there was an NVA right outside, less than three feet away. Smith took my rifle, went to the doorway, and commenced firing, killing the NVA.

I had no helmet, flak jacket, or weapon, and I was wounded in the thigh, but I was set upon finding Lieutenant Roach. This was my first time in close combat, things were not working as planned, and the confusion was the worst part of it. I thought, If only I can get to Lieutenant Roach, then he will know the solution. As Lance Corporal Smith fired, I attempted to run out across the top of the hill to Lieutenant Roach's command-post bunker. Except for my night vision and occasional explosions, visibility was close to nil. I sprinted painfully about five yards, but my leg slowed me up and I tripped on a prone body, stumbled, and fell right into the laps of three NVA. Before I could get up, I was being clubbed by their weapons. I spun around, still on the ground, so that their blows were falling on my legs. I thought they were breaking my knees, so I began kicking wildly. I was expecting to be shot at any moment. They didn't shoot, so I got to my feet. Two of the NVA literally jumped onto my back and weighted me down to my hands and knees. One of them pulled my right arm up behind my back. I was flailing my left arm wildly around so they couldn't get to it and pin it. At this point, I started thinking they weren't going to shoot me but were holding me as prisoner. At arm's reach, I could feel a metal object with a grip on it. Heavy, like a radio, I think it was an overturned jerrycan of water. When I got my grip on its handle, I suddenly dropped to my stomach so that the NVA straddling me and holding my right arm lost his balance. Still holding the jerrycan, I jumped up onto my feet and started spinning around like a top, holding the metal can straight out, whipping it horizontally like a propeller in the dark. It worked. I struck one of them squarely in the head, and, on the fourth or fifth spin, I also hit some steel and heard a weapon hitting the deck. I was becoming dizzy from spinning around and reckoned that one man was down and one weapon was down and that it was a good opportunity to try for Lieutenant Roach's bunker again. The only problem was, after wrestling in the dark, being clubbed, and spinning around like a helicopter's propeller, I had absolutely no idea which direction was toward the south end of our hill.

I stumbled and rolled down a depression that I assumed was angling toward the south side, but actually it was along the west side. In the dark, I was then running along this depression until I hit a sandbag and realized I was still on the northwest side of our hill. Right below me in the trench were two silhouettes talking in my direction, possibly to me, in Vietnamese. I picked up a trenchline sandbag and hit one of them over his helmet. Figuring I was now on the northwest side of the hill, I turned and tried running at an oblique angle toward the southeast or south. This time, I duck-walked because I still couldn't see well and didn't want to trip again. I heard objects clunking and rolling behind me. The NVA in the trench had thrown grenades after me. Oddly enough, at this point, almost all the fear had left me and I guess the adrenaline pumped me up so much that I was operating unconsciously or mechanically.

This time I crossed the hill, and as grenades were going off behind and around me, I was hit again in my lower left calf. More grenades were landing everywhere and suddenly I dropped safely below ground. I'd fallen into the east trenchline. A grenade detonated a second later, right over and behind my head, only inches from the trenchline's edge, just above the ground. I correctly assumed I was now somewhere on the east trenchline and, crouching, I started to slowly feel my way down the trench toward the south end.

There was a flash of illumination and small-arms fire up ahead, so I stopped. This was minor illumination, like a hand flare, so I assumed we must have had people up ahead who were still holding out. There was a little light to see by now, and I moved ten or fifteen feet at a time. After each staggered section of the zigzag trenchline, I looked around before proceeding. The trenchline was not in a straight line but slightly zigzag. There was still occasional shooting, explosions, and screaming, so I knew we were still holding out.

I worked my way down two or three sections of trenchline and noticed weapons and ammo scattered about. I spotted several rifles that were damaged and some others that seemed okay. I collected three rifles and I was proceeding down the next section of trench when I glimpsed two NVA advancing up the trench in my direction. I didn't know if they saw me. I knew there were still NVA behind me, as I could hear them calling out to each other from time to time, so I didn't want to go back to the north end. Now the passage to the south end was also blocked. I instantly stepped away around a zigzag, but now I had to completely check out at least one weapon to make sure it worked before

trying to jump out and fire it. The NVA were walking and I
had to move silently and slowly, so I crept up into a bunker
to work. There were some Marine bodies, but no one was
alive.

The first rifle's magazine was jammed. I put it down
quietly and was trying to feel if the second one worked and
if it had a round in its chamber when the two NVA stopped
right outside the bunker I was in and talked to each other in
low tones. I thought for sure they knew I was in there. I put
the rifle down quietly and just listened. One of them walked
away, but I knew there was one still outside.

I waited for what seemed like half an hour but probably
was no more than a minute or two. I felt around for one of
the rifles in the dark. My hand touched an entrenching tool.
The spike on it was extended at a 90-degree angle, so I
decided it was as good a defense as anything and a better
club than a light, fiberglass M-16. I didn't want to shoot
unless it was necessary. I still could hear him shuffling
around outside the bunker. I was crouched with the entrenching
tool inside the darkness of the bunker. With night vision, I
could see his form squatting just outside my doorway. I had
room laterally for a considerable stroke against the side of
his head, like the swinging of a baseball bat, but I wanted to
be absolutely sure he wasn't a Marine, though his form was
small. I cocked my arms, studying him. There was a
glimmer of light from a grenade explosion and I caught
sight of his uniform and rifle silhouette. He was North
Vietnamese. I swung furiously and with all my might.

I was about two feet away from his bare head. He jerked
back and my sweaty grip slipped from the handle. He went
falling back against the opposite trench wall, with the
entrenching tool's spike embedded in his head. I looked up
and down the trench and saw no one else. He rolled over
and lay on the floor of the trench with the spike buried just
above his ear. I didn't like looking, but he was making the
most bizarre hissing sound that I ever heard another human
being make. It sounded like an air hose, and it was nearly as
loud. I hoped he was at least unconscious. I pulled the spike
out and drove it in again, higher into the side of his head.

He quieted, but in a few seconds he was gasping—not moving, just gasping for air. I didn't necessarily want to kill him; I really only wanted to quiet him. I wondered why he wasn't dead after two blows like that into his head. I had never killed a man before, and I couldn't pull out the spike to hit him again with that entrenching tool. It was an overwhelming thing for me to do for the third time. So I left it there, after the second blow, still implanted in the side of his head. I don't think I realized what I had just done.

He was still gasping, but not as much as before. Somehow, I had to quiet him. There was a Marine bayonet a few feet away and I picked it up quickly, trying to decide where to stab him. I was worried about stabbing him in the heart because I didn't know if he could still cry out. After deliberation, I decided on cutting his throat. I asked God to forgive me for what I was about to do to another human being, but then I figured, what the hell, and tried telling myself he was probably going to die anyway and that this was an act of mercy. Besides, he hadn't come onto my hill to discuss peace terms. So I tried cutting his throat. It was impossible. The damn bayonet was as dull as a butter knife. Weren't all bayonets sharp? Next, I tried stabbing and slashing at his throat to open it up. Blood was everywhere. I felt numb. At this point I was a wild man. I was somebody else and yet me. I clicked bone with the blade tip and realized I had torn down into his spinal column. Now he was no longer gasping, but he was gurgling. When was this man going to die? His chest was making wild, frantic heaves, and a haunting, gurgling rattle was desperately respirating out of the gap I had torn open in his throat. Oh God, I thought, please just quiet him down, let him die, for his sake as well as mine. I kept asking myself, Why isn't he dead yet? His gurgling was almost as loud as his gasping had been. It was too much. I had to get away from him. I started down the trench toward the south end of our hill again. Then, as an afterthought, I went back to the unconscious and dying NVA and covered his head with three sandbags, muffling his death rattle. I wondered, Why didn't I think of that sooner?

* * *

Private First Class Seavy-Cioffi found the Alpha-1 survivors holding the southern end of the hill and learned that Lieutenant Roach was missing and presumed dead. Seavy-Cioffi located the 1st Platoon co-commander, a newly arrived second lieutenant who, owing to his wounds, was restricted to a southern bunker and was thus unable to assume effective command. Taking command of the platoon, Seavy-Cioffi rallied the survivors, retrieved most of the immobile wounded, and began building up the outpost's interior defensive line.

Pfc LAWRENCE SEAVY-CIOFFI
Alpha Company, 1/9 _____

We held a small crescent of trench on the southeast end of the hill with about a dozen able-bodied Marines, three or four rifles, maybe a dozen magazines, and half a dozen grenades. We had another dozen Marines on the southwest trenchline. The men reported to me that our northwest machine-gun bunker and its machine gun had been destroyed. Many bunkers had been blown up with men inside, and they represented the survivors who had pulled back. Altogether, there was less than one functional rifle for every three Marines. If the NVA had pressed their attack then, they might have wiped us out. But fortunately they paused and eventually several other live Marines were located.

At this point we had a total of about thirty Marines accounted for, and about ten of them were wounded, four of them seriously.

The NVA were now starting to lob grenades over to our south end of the hill, so I first ordered all our trenches on the south end cleared of wounded.

Had the NVA battalion realized our vulnerability at that time, when I first took command, they might have swept over and annihilated my platoon. But they hesitated. A lull now came after the first thirty to thirty-five minutes. I decided to take advantage of this lull in the action.

We were holding the south quarter of our hill, and I had the rifles, men, and ammo evenly distributed. I kept one extra rifle on our southeast end, and had Pfc Wayne Welchel and LCpl Arnold Alderete looking over the sides and out across the top of the hill. There was sporadic visibility now, as Khe Sanh was firing illumination.

I searched out the first three or four bunkers on the southeast trenchline. I made three or four trips with no complications. However, there was more ammo lying around than there were operable rifles.

In the first three or four trips, I brought back four or five bandoliers holding varying numbers of M-16 rifle magazines from the bunkers. I also brought back seven or eight rifles, but two or three of them were damaged beyond operation. We had about five good, additional M-16s and an improving supply of ammo. I had also passed up another five or six M-16s—pieces of M-16s—that I didn't even bother trying to salvage. Every now and then I might get a surprise and find things such as hand flares, some grenades, a first-aid kit, a canteen of water, etc. Generally, though, I first concentrated on ammo and weapons, and then finally on whatever else I could find that would be useful. The bunkers had no living occupants. Finally, I had picked the bunkers clean halfway up to the east side. We were much better off on ammo, but still every man was yet to be armed.

Desperate to obtain ammunition for the survivors' single M-60 machine gun, Seavy-Cioffi advanced northward to locate some that the gunner had been forced to leave behind. In a series of heart-stopping trips into overrun positions, Seavy-Cioffi retrieved the machine-gun ammunition and additional M-16s and M-16 magazines. In so doing, he armed most of the Marines still capable of putting up a fight. Despite Seavy-Cioffi's many absences, command of the defense fell into his lap, though he was outranked by many of the survivors and had only rudimentary training as an infantryman. In extreme combat situations, attitude and command presence often take precedence over rank.

Plagued by unexpected resistance and uncertain as to

what they were facing, the NVA occupying the northern one-third of the outpost were reticent to press home an assault. The NVA had an ample supply of hand grenades, and these they used in ongoing efforts to dislodge the surviving defenders.

Pfc LAWRENCE SEAVY-CIOFFI
Alpha Company, 1/9 _____

Grenades were still raining down, and people were taking cover in the bunkers. I told them not to do that or we'd lose ground. I told them to keep sandbags ready, and, if any grenades landed behind our walled-off barricades, to quickly cover the grenades with the sandbags, move back, let them explode, then move back up to the wall again and keep firing down the trench if anything moved—or we'd get pushed back into a tight bunch again and they would wipe us all out with their grenades.

Finally there was another lull on our east side and then the NVA started hitting our Marines on the other side, on the southwest side of our hill. I went over to them with my rifle and an extra rifle. It was a good thing, because two of their rifles were jammed up with dirt from grenade explosions and couldn't fire. I gave them two working rifles and took the jammed ones for Cpl Edward O'Connor to fix later. I went all the way up to the southwest trench wall, where the trench had also been barricaded with sandbags, checked to see if anyone was wounded, encouraged our men, and told them we were not only holding our position but also actually were gaining ground and that now everyone was armed and that we had just recovered the machine-gun ammo. Everyone's morale picked up with this news, and I gave our Marines on the southwest trenchline the same directions as those on the southeast side: that no matter how intense the hails of grenades or gunfire were, to keep firing from behind the sandbagged wall, down the trench, when they saw movement, and to keep a lookout not only down the side of the hill but also out across the top of the hill, because we had no people we knew of in our hilltop's interior, so the enemy could be anywhere. Also, I directed, if grenades landed in the sections of trench behind their sandbagged barricade, not to panic, but to calmly throw a sandbag or two over the grenade, temporarily pull back and let the grenade explode, then immediately push back up to the wall and commence firing up the trenchline so that no more ground would be lost.

I started back around again for the southeast side, where O'Connor, Alderete [the M-60 gunner], and Welchel were. I brought along the two jammed rifles for O'Connor. He was especially fast at unplugging jammed M-16s. He was something of an expert at it. Though he had been wounded several times, O'Connor provided the only ongoing maintenance for our M-16s and was thus instrumental in saving Marine lives on Alpha-1.

I went on around with the two jammed rifles to the southeast side, because now they were starting to get hit again over there. By the time I got over there, all hell was breaking loose. The NVA had advanced down to the bunker just outside our southeast barricade wall, about twenty feet away, and had showered the barricade with about thirty grenades, killing one Marine and wounding just about everyone else. Then they were storming our wall. The Marines had already thrown the last few grenades they had and fired their M-16s until their magazines were empty or jammed. When the NVA rushed, they had no other choice but to pull back. These were all men who were now wounded for the second or third time in this attack, ears ringing, some of them unable to hear, dazed, disoriented, and outnumbered. I stopped their withdrawal at the second bunker behind our wall, brought up some borrowed, unjammed rifles and magazines, and told them we had to rush the wall. We retook the wall, and then some more grenades hit, but I flung sandbags over them.

O'Connor came up—wounded again, but not too seriously—and I told him to go into the bunker behind us and unplug the two other jammed rifles. The trench wall had been kicked, knocked, or blown over. Welchel, Alderete, and I were starting to build it back up when the NVA rained another twenty or thirty grenades down on us once again, but they didn't follow it up with a charge. The grenades were bad enough. The NVA grenades were slowly thinning us out, but the fact that there were fewer of us made the grenade attacks less efficient.

The twenty-five survivors, many of them wounded, who were still able to fight, rebuilt and continued holding the perimeter trenchlines in the eerie light of virtually continuous overhead illumination within shifting eddies of fog.

Pfc LAWRENCE SEAVY-CIOFFI
Alpha Company, 1/9

Now that we were established in the southern third of our hilltop's trenchlines, I became increasingly concerned about our hilltop's interior. What if the enemy was crawling toward us over the interior? They might crawl up to a section of our southern third of trench and throw in grenades or try to launch a troop assault from within our hill's interior.

Because we could not see all the way across due to darkness, the shifting threads of fog, and the topographical rise in the center of our hilltop, I next decided we had to form a 350-degree defense and link up the two opposite barricades by positioning our Marines prone, out across the interior of the southern third of our hill. I went all along the trenchline, from east to west, and told our Marines that there would be someone checking out the interior, crawling about, so not to fire indiscriminately. I went back to the southeast barricade and had people keep an eye out across the top of the hill. I decided not to take a rifle along for this, but rather to concentrate on crawling quietly and trying to spot the enemy first. Shooting would only draw grenades anyway. I started out flat on my belly in a dead man's crawl. I would go ten or fifteen feet and then play dead. I observed only when the illumination was dimming. In full light, I lay still, as if I was dead. I maneuvered to different locations so that I could observe every square foot carefully and check

out the one or two bunkers in our hill's southern interior.
There were some bodies and debris in the interior, but, at
the time, no living NVA.

I returned to the east barricade and positioned three of us
in the hill's interior—myself in the center, one Marine
between me and the southwest barricade, and Alderete, with
his M-60 machine gun, on my right, between me and the
southeast barricade, where Welchel and O'Connor were
positioned with two other Marines. We now had a 360-degree
defense line. It was just in time.

The NVA began probing our southern interior. We were
always just one step ahead of them. They probed us first
with hails of grenades. They began throwing twenty-five or
thirty grenades at a time into our hill's interior. Fortunately,
we only had the three of us out there or it would have been
disastrous. Grenades were landing all around us. They often
landed inches from us; one actually bounced off me. We
would wildly flip back and roll away, yelling "Chicom!" to
warn the others. That was good because the NVA knew the
interior was occupied.

You had to be careful where you rolled. As one grenade
blew up, I rolled right onto another one. I felt something
like a brick under my chest, put my hand beneath me, and
felt the grenade. I flipped my body away again. It blew up
about three feet away, but a full C-ration case partially
between me and the grenade saved me. The Marine to my
left was not so lucky and was soon killed. We put another
man out. For the next fifteen or twenty minutes, all the NVA
did was throw twenty-five or thirty grenades every two or
three minutes. It was unbelievable how many Chicom grenades they had.

At one point during this sustained hand-grenade barrage,
just after we beat back an NVA charge on our east-side
barricade, I brought to the east-side-trench some sandbags I
had collected from our hill's southern interior. At that time,
O'Connor was coming forward from the trenchline bunker
we were using to stage ammo and gear and in which he had
been servicing malfunctioning M-16s. Alderete was chucking
sandbags to Welchel, making repairs on the trenchline

barricade. I was in the trench with them just as more
grenades hit all around us, all but one on our side of the
barricade. Our having so many extra sandbags on hand was
a blessing. As ten or so grenades landed in the trenchline,
Welchel, O'Connor, Alderete, two other Marines, and I
instantly covered seven or eight of them with sandbags and
instantly pulled back. Other grenades that had missed the
trenchline began blowing up aboveground all around us, and
the concussion was deafening. After the NVA grenades stopped
exploding, I had to dash to turn O'Connor around; he was
calmly walking up the trenchline, through the partially blown
barricade, right toward the NVA. I had become disoriented
early in the fighting, so I understood his predicament.

Somebody reported to me that he had found an unopened
box of our own grenades in a corner of one of our south-end
bunkers. I had them move it up near to our southeast
barricade, and then had Welchel and O'Connor pass grenades out to Alderete and then on out to me. Keeping count
(fifty in a box), I decided to immediately throw twenty-five
to make the enemy think we were better off than we really
were. It was a gamble of sorts, but we had to answer these
new grenade attacks or they might think they were weakening
us. I wanted to make the enemy think it was more than just
one man in one location, throwing the grenades—to appear
stronger than we actually were. I threw the 25 grenades in
every possible direction, most toward the north end, but a
few over the east, west, and south slopes for good measure,
one right after another. I really gave them a taste of their
own medicine. I threw some with all my might, briefly
standing up, so they detonated way out over the north side,
at our hill's base. Others I threw way up into the air, letting
the spoons spring first, so some fuse burned, so that they
exploded just about when they hit the ground. Otherwise,
they would all have rolled down the sides and exploded
beyond our hill's base. I heard three screams—two of them
from the north end, the other one from somewhere down the
north slope or in the valley beyond. The NVA on the north
slope only knew that the grenades were coming down on
them from the hilltop.

I passed the remaining 25 grenades out among our men. I instructed them only to throw our remaining grenades at specific targets with extremely careful aim.

After observing NVA on the north slope throwing their hand grenades into areas he knew were held by other NVA, Seavy-Cioffi concluded that the attackers were still confused as to the number and location of the American defenders.

Pfc LAWRENCE SEAVY-CIOFFI
Alpha Company, 1/9 _____

I concluded three things: (1) the enemy apparently did not yet fully realize we were restricted to the southern end of the hill; (2) the enemy did not realize how great our losses had been in the first twenty to twenty-five minutes; (3) the enemy did not have coordinated, if any, communication between their men in our north trenchlines and their men spread out on our north slope.

I began to think of ways I could use this to our advantage and further confuse the enemy.

The NVA were still pelting us with grenades now and again, though not as intensely as earlier. However, every casualty we took, whether dead or wounded, was very serious as we were now down to fewer than twenty-five functioning Marines, not counting all the seriously wounded, who were unable to participate. So it was now less the question of our weapons and ammunition supply than the question of our troop strength. We had to get the NVA grenades off us. I began thinking again about the NVA on the north slope who had mistakenly thrown their grenades up onto the north end, killing their own men. If we could make the enemy think we were not where we actually were, we could get them to waste their own grenades. I called Alderete over and told him my plan, a decoy tactic.

There was an abandoned bunker in the north center of our hill, the highest point on our outpost. It was about ten or fifteen meters ahead of where I had lain out in the center of the southern third of our hill's interior. I told Alderete that if we waited until the illumination burned out, we could then crawl forward on our stomachs to the south side of this bunker, wait until the next illumination burst overhead, stand straight up, throw a grenade each, and shoot if we saw some NVA. During the last few seconds of illumination, we would lower our heads straight down and move back to the southern third of our hill's interior, attempting to draw their grenades onto the bunker.

Alderete and I crawled up. We decided I should throw only one grenade, as we were down to our last two dozen grenades. Besides, he had to handle his machine gun and its ammo can. The idea was that firing the machine gun would make them think we were in a permanent position. We got up to the bunker and, when the next overhead illumination burst, stood up. I could see a dozen or so NVA heads sticking up in our north-end trench. After Alderete commenced firing short bursts, I tossed my grenade in their direction. After it exploded, I sprayed about one-half of my rifle magazine at a few heads that popped back up again. No one fired back; they seemed surprised. Then the illumination dimmed and we lowered our heads straight down. We were beginning to crawl back when the NVA completely covered the decoy bunker with grenades. Of course, we were back on our hill's southern third by the time they exploded.

Each time we did this, the NVA threw at least fifteen to twenty grenades, all wasted because, by the time they exploded, we had pulled back. The first few times we stood up we let out fierce growls and guttural howls to make sure that they knew we were positioned by the bunker. After a while, the NVA would call back to us: "Hey, Marine, tonight you die!" or "You die, you die, Mr. Custer, you die!" or "Give up, Marine, or you all die tonight!" Once, Welchel, yelled back, "It may be plastic, but it will kick your ass!" A reference to our M-16s.

We did this two or three more times, and then Alderete and I decided that that was enough use of his machine-gun ammo because he had used up about one-third of his can. Alderete also suggested doing the decoy tactic without his

machine gun because crawling back quickly was difficult
with his M-60. I crawled over and asked Welchel and
O'Connor how their side of the hill was doing. They said
okay, so I decided to position Alderete's machine gun on the
opposite side, on our left hand, at the southwest trenchline's
barricade, with an extra man and rifle to guard it. I gave
directions not to fire unless there were specific targets. The
machine gun now had about two-thirds of its ammo remaining,
which I told them to use in short bursts and make it count.

In a separate incident concluding at 0625, Private First
Class Welchel stopped an enemy squad advancing down our
east-side trenchline by himself after the other Marines with
him were killed or wounded too seriously to continue
fighting. This was the final NVA charge against our east-
side barricade.

Alderete and I continued to crawl up to the decoy bunker
every ten minutes or so, in between illumination, and fired
at the NVA in the north-end trenches. We didn't use any
more grenades. We brought just one rifle and one magazine
each. After a while, when we stopped throwing grenades
and stopped using the machine gun, the NVA got bolder, no
longer ducked their heads, and tried shooting it out with us.
Sometimes we appeared around the sides of the bunker so
they would not know where to expect us. However, that
dangerously exposed our flanks and Alderete said he thought
he was taking sniper fire from across the hill, from the
northwest trenchline. He suggested that we take a break
because his rifle barrel had been hit by gunfire. But we were
still successfully drawing the NVA grenades onto the decoy
bunker, so I told Alderete to take a break and had someone
switch places with him.

The NVA must have wasted over 200 grenades on our
decoy bunker. I am sure we saved many casualties and lives
by deceiving the enemy into thinking our lines were farther
forward than they really were and our surviving troop
strength was greater than it actually was. If anything, this
one tactic focused the enemy's attention away from our
southern trenches and toward the northern hilltop interior,
where we had no men except when we crawled up to the

bunker. After the NVAs' second major attack down the trenchline failed and during my continuing decoy tactics, their momentum was nearing its demise.

The NVA rushed our trenchline only one more time. They tried all out to take the southwest barricade. Fortunately for us, that was about five or ten minutes after I set up the machine gun there. The machine gun stopped the charge. I heard it firing away, a volley of enemy grenades going off, then M-16 rifle fire, some feeble AK-47 reply bursts, screaming, then two or three of our own grenades going off, and then silence. My Marines had stopped the charge, but we had taken one killed and three more good Marines wounded.

That was the last enemy charge down our trenchlines. The enemy was now almost exclusively pinned down in our north-end trenchline, along with many others on the north slope. I kept up my decoy tactic, using rocks to rout them from our north trenches onto the slopes so that their own men on the slopes threw more grenades onto the north end, once again killing and wounding their own. After a while, though, they caught on to my rock tactic. But throughout the morning, at least until dawn, they never seemed to perceive that we actually had no men permanently positioned at the decoy bunker. They always tossed some grenades after I pulled back, but the number of grenades steadily declined until they were only throwing six or seven and then, finally, only two or three at a time. By dawn's first light, I think they began to realize that it was a decoy, but by then their numbers were thinned out and they must have been low on grenades and ammo, because their return fire steadily diminished each time. By daylight, 0715, it was too late for them to take our hill. I still kept up the decoy tactic, figuring that, as long as they had grenades to throw and bullets to shoot, it was better to get them to hit our decoy bunker than have them charging the barricades or throwing the grenades onto our outpost's southern end.

At about 0715, our company commander radioed that reinforcements would move out after some Vietnamese Air Force propeller-driven fighter-bombers bombed and strafed the surrounding area. I kept engaging the enemy at the decoy bunker so they couldn't pull back, keeping them thinking that someone was always at the bunker. However, the NVA set up a sniper on the west side. The last time I had someone with me, it was light enough to see, and when I pulled back, I realized I was alone. The sniper had shot the Marine who had gone along with me. He had killed him with a single shot in the temple.

I went out alone to get the sniper. I spotted him, pinned him down about three-fourths of the way up the northwest trench, and shot it out with him. We ducked down, but I didn't pull back. I changed magazines, and he must have done the same. We looked up and began shooting at each other again. We were both adjusting our bursts, which kicked up dust around the sandbags protecting us. I adjusted my last burst a split second faster than he did. His bullets hit the sandbag in front of me, about two inches too low. I stepped aside so when he adjusted and raised, he was just off to my left. He hardly grazed my elbow. I elevated my barrel and saw the last of my rounds walking right up from the dirt and sandbags into his chest, and he was flung back. One of his bullets, or a fragment of some sort, had grazed me through my shirt sleeve, but it had not drawn blood.[1]

Private First Class Seavy-Cioffi never received official recognition for his leadership of the outpost's defenses, but he was recently recommended by Wayne Welchel and Edward O'Connor for the Medal of Honor. A decision is still pending.

LtCol JOHN MITCHELL
1/9 Commanding Officer _____

At 0730, a relief platoon led by the Alpha Company commander, Capt Henry Radcliffe, made its way to the beleaguered platoon, and by 0900 had assaulted the eastern slope of the hill and established contact with the remnants of the trapped platoon. The southern position of the 1/9 sector, with its high ground and cleared fields of fire, lent itself well for supporting fires to Captain Radcliffe's assault. Delta and Bravo companies, supported by one section of tanks, delivered murderous fires to the flanks and front of Alpha Company, blunting enemy attempts at reinforcement. Captain Radcliffe led his combined Marines on a frontal assault across the tiny hill, and within fifteen minutes the Alpha Company outpost had been completely cleared of the enemy and positions [had been] reestablished. The grim policing of the battleground was then begun; many NVA dead and equipment littered the tiny hill outpost.[2]

1/9 Command Chronology

At 0825, the relief column reached the crest of the hill. Fighting continued until approximately 1100, when the outpost was retaken. At the same time, Delta Company observed a large number of enemy withdrawing from the Alpha-1 outpost. Delta Company opened fire with all available arms.

The results after the day's fight were 24 friendly KIA, 29 friendly WIA, and over 150 enemy bodies found by Alpha and Delta companies.

As the gunfire and grenade detonations died over Hill 64, the ordeal of Khe Sanh was set to enter its second, grimmer phase. The NVA divisions had given their all to dominate the Khe Sanh Combat Base by seizing the dominant high ground, but they had been rebuffed at every turn, had suffered insupportable casualties, had gained nothing.

As the sun rose over Khe Sanh, as the 1st Battalion, 9th Marines, resecured Hill 64, the Communist forces arrayed on the Khe Sanh Plateau backed off from the assault and set themselves the task of squeezing what nectar they could from the bitter fruits of a grim attritional battle. The Siege of Khe Sanh—what everyone had been calling the struggle for nearly three weeks—truly began after the failed attempt to overrun Hill 64.

On February 8, 1968, the defenders of the Khe Sanh Combat Base and its outlying hill positions still faced their gravest ordeal and their greatest casualties. The worst of the random maiming and killing lay before them.

Be sure to read the second volume
of this oral history:
THE SIEGE OF KHE SANH,
a June 1990 paperback from Warner Books.

NOTES

CHAPTER 3

1. Col William H. Dabney, Marine Corps Historical Division [MCHD] Oral History Interview. Hereafter, *Dabney MCHD Interview.*
2. MGen Rathvon Tompkins, MCHD Interview. Hereafter, *Tompkins MCHD Interview.*
3. *Dabney MCHD Interview.*
4. Maj Mirza M. Baig, comments on Marine Corps Khe Sanh Monograph, December 23, 1968. Hereafter, *Baig Comments.*

CHAPTER 4

1. *Dabney MCHD Interview.*
2. Dabney, Col William H., "Under Siege," *The Elite*, Orbis Publications (Vol. 2, No. 13).
3. Excerpts from an endorsement for a Bronze Star award recommendation for LCpl James Schemelia, a member of the 2nd Platoon's 2nd Squad.
4. Dabney, "Under Siege."

5. Ibid.
6. Ibid.
7. *Dabney MCHD Interview.*
8. Ibid.

CHAPTER 5

1. *Baig Comments.*
2. *Dabney MCHD Interview.*

CHAPTER 6

1. LtCol James B. Wilkinson, comments on Marine Corps Khe Sanh Monograph, December 19, 1968. Hereafter, *Wilkinson Comments.*

CHAPTER 7

1. Spencer, Ernest, *Welcome to Vietnam, Macho Man* (Walnut Creek, Calif.: Corps Press, 1987).
2. *Tompkins MCHD Interview.*
3. Col John F. Mitchell, comments on Marine Corps Khe Sanh Monograph, January 31, 1969. Hereafter, *Mitchell Comments.*
4. *Dabney MCHD Interview.*
5. Ibid.

CHAPTER 8

1. Maj Jerry E. Hudson, comments on Marine Corps Khe Sanh Monograph, January 2, 1969. Hereafter, *Hudson Comments.*

CHAPTER 9

1. Maj Kenneth Pipes, comments on Marine Corps Khe Sanh Monograph, undated.
2. *Mitchell Comments.*
3. *Dabney MCHD Interview.*
4. Ibid.

5. Ibid.

CHAPTER 10

1. Spencer, *Welcome to Vietnam*.
2. Ibid.
3. Ibid.

CHAPTER 12

1. *Tompkins MCHD Interview*.
2. *Baig Comments*.
3. Spencer, *Welcome to Vietnam*.
4. *Baig Comments*.
5. Ibid.
6. Ibid.
7. Ibid.
8. Ibid.
9. LtCol Johnny O. Gregerson, comments on Marine Corps Khe Sanh Monograph, January 3, 1969. Hereafter, *Gregerson Comments*.

CHAPTER 13

1. Spencer, *Welcome to Vietnam*.
2. Ibid.

CHAPTER 14

1. Statement of MGen R. McC. Tompkins, USMC, November 13, 1970. Hereafter, *Tompkins Statement*.
2. Statement of Maj Jerry E. Hudson, USMC, date unknown, 1970. Hereafter, *Hudson Statement*.
3. *Hudson Comments*.
4. *Hudson Statement*.
5. *Tompkins Statement*.
6. *Hudson Statement*.
7. *Baig Comments*.
8. *Hudson Comments*.
9. *Baig Comments*.

10. *Hudson Comments*.
11. *Baig Comments*.
12. Ibid.
13. Ibid.

CHAPTER 15

1. *Wilkinson Comments*.

CHAPTER 16

1. Adapted from "Our Victory for Alpha One," by Lawrence J. Seavy-Cioffi. (Unpublished manuscript, used with permission.)
2. *Mitchell Comments*.

BIBLIOGRAPHY

BOOKS

Camp, Richard D. Jr., with Eric Hammel. *Lima-6: A Marine Company Commander in Vietnam*. New York: Atheneum Publishers, 1989.

Nalty, Bernard C. *Air Power and the Fight for Khe Sanh*. Washington, D.C.: U.S. Air Force, 1973.

Pisor, Robert. *The End of the Line: The Siege of Khe Sanh*. New York: W. W. Norton & Company, Inc., 1982.

Shore, Capt Moyers S., II, USMC. *The Battle for Khe Sanh*. Washington, D.C.: U.S. Marine Corps, 1969.

Spencer, Ernest. *Welcome to Vietnam, Macho Man*. Walnut Creek, Calif.: Corps Press, 1987.

PERIODICALS

Dabney, Col William H. "Under Siege." *The Elite*, Orbis Publications (Vol. 2, No. 13).

Kashiwahara, Capt Ken, "Lifeline To Khe Sanh." *The Airman*, July 1968.

Pipes, Maj K. W. "Men to Match Their Mountains."
Marine Corps Gazette, April 1974.

Studt, LtCol John C. "Battalion in the Attack." *Marine
Corps Gazette*, July 1970.

Tolson, LtGen John J., 3rd. "Pegasus." *Army*, December
1971.

Watts, Maj Claudius E., III. "Aerial Resupply for Khe
Sanh." *Military Review*, December 1972.

UNPUBLISHED MANUSCRIPT

Seavy-Cioffi, L. J. *Our Victory for Alpha One*.

OFFICIAL SOURCES

Various and voluminous official documents were used in
piecing this story together. Among them were the Command
Chronologies and After Action Reports submitted for the
siege and breakout periods by the 26th Marine Regiment;
the 1st, 2nd, and 3rd Battalions, 26th Marines; the 1st
Battalion, 9th Marines; and the 1st Battalion, 13th Marines. Also, many of the letters by participants commenting
on draft copies of Capt Moyers Shore's official Marine
Corps Khe Sanh monograph are quoted, as cited, throughout the text. All of the documentary materials are archived
at the Marine Corps Historical Center, located at the
Washington Navy Yard in Washington, DC.

PRIVATE SOURCES

The bulk of this book is composed of excerpts from taped
accounts and interviews and letters collected by the author
from siege participants. It is safe to assume that any
undocumented entry was obtained from the person cited at
the head of the quote. The author has donated this collection to the Marine Corps Historical Center.

EDITORIAL NOTE

For purposes of clarity, style, and consistency, many—perhaps most—of the passages appearing in this book have been edited or corrected by the author. However, the substance of the edited quotes has not been altered except in the case of errors of fact corrected by the author.

Index